9/95

ROBERT FROST: THE AIM WAS SONG

Other books by Jean Gould

WINSLOW HOMER

A GOOD FIGHT

THAT DUNBAR BOY

YOUNG MARINER MELVILLE

Robert Frost

THE AIM WAS SONG

JEAN GOULD

DODD, MEAD & COMPANY

NEW YORK

Library of Congress Catalog Card Number: 64-16193

Third Printing

Printed in the United States of America
by The Cornwall Press, Inc., Cornwall, N. Y.

ACKNOWLEDGMENTS

The author wishes to offer acknowledgment to the following publishing houses and individuals for their kind permission to quote passages from various books and periodicals:

Dodd, Mead & Company, for permission to quote three lines from *The Soldier* from THE COLLECTED POEMS OF RUPERT BROOKE. Copyright 1915 by Dodd, Mead & Company, Inc. Copyright 1943 by Edward Marsh. Willard E. Fraser and Robin Fraser Hudnut, for permission to quote six lines from *I Always Knew* by Marjorie Frost Fraser (1936). Horace Gregory, for a passage from his biography, AMY LOWELL, published by Thomas Nelson & Sons, New York (1958). Mrs. Alfred Harcourt, for a quotation from SOME EXPERIENCES by Alfred Harcourt. Copyright 1951 by Ellen Knowles Harcourt, New York (1951). Harcourt, Brace & World, Inc., for a passage from THE LETTERS OF EZRA POUND, edited by D. D. Paige. Copyright 1950 by Harcourt, Brace & Company, Inc., New York; and for a paragraph of FROM ANOTHER WORLD by Louis Untermeyer, New York (1937). Holt, Rinehart and Winston, for selections from THE COMPLETE POEMS OF ROBERT FROST. Copyright 1916, 1923, 1928, 1934, 1939 by Holt, Rinehart and Winston, Inc. Copyright 1936, 1942 by Robert Frost. Copyright renewed 1944, 1951, © 1956, 1962 by Robert Frost. Copyright renewed © 1964 by Lesley Frost Ballantine—and from IN THE CLEARING, Copyright © 1956, 1962 by Robert Frost. Reprinted by permission of Holt, Rinehart and Winston, Inc. Houghton Mifflin Company, for seven lines from *A Critical Fable* in COLLECTED POEMS by Amy Lowell, Boston (1955); and for a passage from TENDENCIES IN MODERN AMERICAN POETRY by Amy Lowell, (1917). The Macmillan Company, for a quotation from the Introduction by Robert Frost to KING JASPER by Edwin Arlington Robinson. Copyright 1935 by The Macmillan Company, New York. Macmillan & Co. Ltd., and the author's representative, for the twelve-line quotation from *The Golden Room* in THE GOLDEN ROOM AND OTHER POEMS by Wilfrid Gibson. Copyright, London, 1926. New York University Press, for a number of passages from A SWINGER OF BIRCHES by Sidney Cox, New York (1957). Charles Scribner's Sons, for two lines from *Miniver Cheevy* by Edwin Arlington Robinson, in THE TOWN DOWN THE RIVER, New York, (1915, 1941). Mrs. Edward Thomas, for a quotation from the Foreword by Walter de la Mare to THE COLLECTED POEMS OF EDWARD THOMAS (Faber & Faber, Ltd., 1936) and for fourteen

lines from *The Sun Used to Shine* in the same volume; also for a passage from THE
PROSE OF EDWARD THOMAS, selected by Roland Gant (Falcon Press, London, 1948).
Jean Starr Untermeyer, for special material about the poet. Harriet Fox Whicher,
for a quotation from *Out for Stars: A Meditation on Robert Frost in* POETRY AND
CIVILIZATION by George F. Whicher. Cornell University Press, Ithaca, N. Y. (1955).
Associated Newspapers, Ltd., for a quotation from a review by Edward Thomas of
NORTH OF BOSTON by Robert Frost in the London *Daily News,* week of April 18, 1914.
The *Boston Herald,* for a passage dealing with Robert Frost's success in England
and subsequent recognition in America from *Talk of the Town* column, March 9,
1915. *The Christian Science Monitor,* for a special panel on the Book Page entitled
The Poetry of Amy Lowell by Robert Frost, May 16, 1925. *Harper's Magazine,* for
a paragraph from a piece dealing with Robert Frost in the *Editor's Easy Chair*
column by William Dean Howells, September 1915.

To
Clair,
Poet in landscape,
and long a swinger of birches.
With the affection of more than half a
lifetime.

Preface

This book is a labor of love. It began a long time ago, when Robert Frost was Poet in Residence at the University of Michigan in 1926, and I, as Poetry Editor of my high school paper in Ohio, was privileged to attend one of those sessions he conducted, which was somewhat less and a great deal more than a class. I was already in love with the work of the poet in the four volumes he had published by then; but he gave me an appreciation of poetry as a force in the world at large that has stayed with me ever since. It goes without saying that I have always been a devoted Frost reader, and the fact that my devotion is duplicated by countless others speaks for itself. This book, then, is based on an intimate knowledge of, and deep feeling for, the poetry of Robert Frost, and is offered as a tribute to his courage, his indomitable will to overcome the obstacles in his path during the long struggle for recognition, and above all, to his song.

It was my good fortune to be able to visit Robert Frost in his home in Ripton, Vermont, during July, 1962, when I received first-hand information concerning the poet's early life—his childhood in San Francisco, his boyhood in Lawrence, his young manhood in Derry. The anecdotes here included were told to me as we sat in the poet's log cabin and talked of all manner of things. The dialogue throughout is direct quotation wherever possible. I did not take notes except in a few instances, because Frost did not like to have people take notes, even at one of his lectures, while he was speaking; he was more interested in having the listener grasp the *essence* of what he said rather than record the words, only, perhaps to misquote him afterwards. "Poetry is my cause," he often said, and he wanted as wide a distribution of his poems as possible.

I had received a grant from the Huntington Hartford Foundation, and after I took up my Fellowship, I wrote to Frost, asking for specific information concerning his "run-away wanderings" in the South in 1894. His reply gave me details of his ramblings (except for the days in Kitty Hawk and Nag's Head, North Carolina, for that "stretch is made a poem of"). It covered the experiences he had from the time he left New York through his return trip, and was contained in a letter dictated to his secretary during his hospital convalescence in December, 1962. I could not secure permission to publish the letter, but the material is to be found in Chapter V, entitled "In Limbo."

While at the Foundation, I was able to consult the Frost files in the Henry E. Huntington Library at San Marino, California, which included the early letters from the poet to his first sponsors, the Wards, editors of *The Independent*. I also had access to the private library of E. M. Harvey, botanist and plant pathologist at Pomona College, which contained a number of first edition volumes of Frost. For the new material in the book, however, I am indebted to the poet himself.

I wish to thank Mrs. Theodore Morrison, Frost's secretary, for arranging my visit in Ripton, to express my appreciation to the Huntington Hartford Foundation, and to the many others who made this book possible.

Contents

ROBERT FROST: THE AIM WAS SONG

Chapter 1

INAUGURAL POET

He was the first inaugural poet. It had taken nearly ten generations for the nation born out of revolt to realize that poetry was as
valuable to the "general welfare" of its people as the wheels of
industry. It was now January, 1961. The poet had been born
nearly a hundred years before, and that had been almost a hundred years after the nation was born. His white hair whipped by
the sharp winter wind, he had smiled whimsically, half-pleased,
half-skeptical, as he listened to the introduction of "Robert Frost,
our national poet," by one of the day's dignitaries. He was always
incredulous when he heard the string of former honors reeled off:
four times winner of the Pulitzer prize for poetry; recipient of the
Gold Medal for Poetry, National Institute of Arts and Letters; of
innumerable honorary degrees from colleges and universities; and
twice the subject of resolutions passed by the United States Senate
on his birthday.

Bundled up in a burly gray overcoat, he stood at the lectern
("a shaggy, bardic figure," one of the papers called him) glancing
briefly at the sea of faces in the privileged audience at the inauguration ceremonies. It was just before the new President was to
take the oath, shortly after midday, but the weather was bitterly

cold for the capital city, and the wind that riffled the poet's unruly hair rumpled the edges of the manuscript he was holding up to the harsh light. His knotted, muscular hands trembled as he began opening the pages, trying to flatten them against the lectern.

"Poor light," he muttered good-naturedly, amused at the hitches that could take place during the highest government ceremonies when the elements chose to be unco-operative. In the middle of the opening prayer by Cardinal Cushing, the heating apparatus concealed in the lectern had short-circuited, sending forth ominous puffs of smoke that brought anxiety to the faces in the audience until the cause was determined. Now the glare from an unshielded sun, doubled by the white banks of snow—strange sight in Washington—in addition to the sharp gusts of wind, made it almost impossible for him to read. Just as he was ready, the top sheet of the manuscript was lifted and blown to the ground. Someone retrieved it immediately and handed it up to him.

"Thank you." He took it, fingers shaky with age, and waited another half-minute or so before he began to decipher aloud, in halting tones, the hastily written verses he had composed as a tribute to the incoming administration out of gratitude at having poetry brought into the affairs of state at long last.

He had a reputation for wit, founded on years of performance; he was master of the *bon mot,* bordering on a wisecrack but never descending to it. Newspapermen coming to interview him could always be sure of hearing some sort of quip, whether they made use of it or not. During the primaries preceding the presidential election, some reporters had sought him out, pelting questions at him, political and otherwise. Asked if, as indicated by his poems, he thought New England was in process of decay, he had replied laconically, folding his hands over his paunch, "Well, I don't know; our next President will probably come from Massachusetts; we have a number of able Congressmen; we've produced one or two good poets—if New England is decaying, it's the richest compost heap in the United States!" Not one paper had printed his remark, but he delighted in repeating it whenever the opportunity arose. The press had, however, reported that Robert Frost had come out in favor of John F. Kennedy and after the national conventions, Kennedy had thanked the poet for "nominating" him.

The two had become acquainted when Frost was appointed Consultant in Poetry to the Library of Congress in 1958. The Senator had long been an admirer of the poet's writing, and after late conferences was fond of quoting the last lines of a famous Frost poem:

> But I have promises to keep,
> And miles to go before I sleep,
> And miles to go before I sleep.*

In planning the ceremonies for the inauguration, it had been agreed that Frost, as "a great New England poet," should be included, and a telegram of formal invitation to read from his own writings was sent to the poet at his home in Cambridge.

His answering wire to Kennedy was characteristic: "If you can bear at your age the honor of being made President of the United States, I ought to be able to bear at my age the honor of taking some part in your inauguration. I may not be equal to it, but I accept it for my cause—the arts, poetry—now for the first time taken into the affairs of statesmen. I am glad the invitation pleases your family. It would please my family to the fourth generation, and my family of friends, and, were they living, it would have pleased inordinately the kind of Grover Cleveland Democrats I had for parents." Highly individualistic, he liked to describe himself as an "unhappy" Democrat—unhappy since Cleveland left the White House in 1895. Yet he was deeply moved by the invitation and felt that the day was a kind of homecoming for him.

At first they had wanted him to write a poem for the occasion, but he told them occasional poetry was not his style, so after consultation with Stewart Udall and others, Mr. Kennedy asked him to read a poem he had written some twenty-odd years before, in the thirties, when, through the dark pain of depression, Ameri-

---

* "Stopping by Woods on a Snowy Evening."

cans came into a new consciousness of American history, of their country's worth . . . a consciousness that deepened when democracy was threatened by the scourge of dictatorship from Hitler. Called "The Gift Outright," the poem did not appear until 1942, in a volume called *A Witness Tree;* but the poet had read it before the Phi Kappa Society at William and Mary College, just two days before Pearl Harbor, on December 5, 1941.

After publication, the critic Randall Jarrell proclaimed it "one of the best patriotic poems ever written in our country," as well as one of Frost's best shorter poems. The lines, though unrhymed, were strictly metered, as always. ("I would as soon write free verse as play tennis with the net down," Frost was fond of saying.) When, a few days before inauguration, columnists came to him asking for the exact meaning of the poem, he demanded humorously, "You want me to say it over in other and worse English?" and gave them little satisfaction. At Kennedy's request, he did, however, consent to change the form of the verb in the last line, putting it in the future instead of the conditional tense. The line, referring to "the land," read, in the final printed version, "Such as she was, such as she would become": but he had never been sure it expressed all he wished to imply, and many times he had toyed with the idea of altering it. Receiving the request from the incoming President, he repeated the words meditatively, including the change, testing it aloud: "Such as she was, such as she would . . . such as she 'will' . . . become. . . ." He smiled. "I have played with that since I wrote it," he admitted. Kennedy must have sensed the duo-possibilities. "But it is interesting that he wants me to say 'will,' because it is four years ahead that he is going to do something there."

Pressed for a definition of the word "unenhanced," which he had used in the next to the last line, also referring to the land as it had been during its infancy, "The arts do the enhancing," he explained. Citing his present honor, he added, "and this . . . a moment of enhancement." His faded blue eyes lit up. "It is a

proud moment to have poetry brought into the affairs of statesmen."

As he gave voice to his sentiments regarding recognition of the
arts, he grew eloquent, stirred to a creative pitch; and in the end
he had composed extra verses as a kind of prelude to the poem he
was going to present in the ceremonies. He had not had time to
memorize the new lines—he was known to have almost total recall
on the great body of his published poems—but he decided to read
the tribute anyway, since he had composed it. (Apollo was getting
his revenge today; he thought Apollo never did like the poets.)

If only he could see more clearly . . . he struggled on, still halt-
ingly, trying to keep the edges of the paper from curling up in
the wind. This was one of the few times when he felt the weight
of his fourscore years and five—or more—whatever it was; he did
not bother to keep track of his age; he let the public do that. Yet
it was a nuisance, he thought impatiently, not to be able to see.
. . . He continued as far as the line, "This seems to be something
for us artists to celebrate," when he stopped, more in exasperation
than confusion.

"I am not having a good light here at all," he muttered, in one
of his habitual asides at the podium, and the microphone picked
it up. The crowd applauded warmly and his heart responded to
their feeling. The newly sworn Vice-President rose from his chair
and tried to shade the manuscript with his top hat. But the gesture
was of little help and the old poet waved him aside. He held up
the papers for the benefit of the audience. "This," he told them,
"was to have been a preface to a poem I do not have to read." And
all at once his manner changed; he no longer had to depend on
mechanics; his mind and heart he was sure of—as sure as man can
be of his prowess.

Straightening up, he seemed to shed years in a moment. Shoulders thrown back, he began to recite "The Gift Outright" in a
voice from which the stumbling, the skepticism was gone—a voice
suddenly grown serious, and young and resonant. When he came

to the last line, "Such as she was, such as she . . . will become," his hesitation on the next-to-last word was barely perceptible. He finished triumphantly, resuming his seat quietly as the applause rang out on the cold air.

Chapter 2

SAN FRANCISCO SON

He had been born on the opposite side of "the land," in San Francisco, on March 24, 1874. His was a strange, nomadic childhood, blessed by parental love, fraught with excitement and tragedy.

One day, when he was seven, his father had shown him his birthplace. They were striding along Washington Street, not far from the corner of Leavenworth, when his father singled out one of the high, buff-colored brick homes on the hill, whose many narrow windowpanes reflected the western sunlight over the water below at those times that the shifting masses of fog did not obscure it. The boy took two giant steps to keep pace with his father, an expert, even a professional walker, and craned his slender neck to get a better view of the house where he was born; his searching blue eyes found it solid-looking, secure, and somehow appealing, with its two small bays jutting out on either side of the tall doorway. The boy wondered, staring back, why they had not stayed there. The way his father walked, they had already passed the place.

His mother wanted to move to a hotel, his father explained with a faint sigh, followed by the odd scraping sound that came when he let his breath out of his lungs. She was a fine woman, but no housekeeper. She tried hard, but—well, after about a year he felt sorry for her.

Then after another year his mother must have felt sorry for his father, and so it had gone: they were always moving from a rented house to a second-rate hotel, back to a rented house and again to a second-rate hotel, or occasionally a first-class hotel, when the wheels of fortune turned in his father's favor. Rob could already remember living in two different hotels, two different houses. Long summers—stretched beyond the usual length because they had no home to return to, and Rob was not sent to school—were generally spent at some seaside or mountain resort, if not on a farm. His father could not leave the newspaper office of the *Bulletin* for more than a short vacation; he would deposit his mother, Rob, and small sister Jeanie somewhere, visit them on weekends, and pick them up at the end of the season. He prided himself on being athletic, and he wanted his children to have the benefit of outdoor living.

His father, whose swinging gait left him behind if he lagged so much as a minute, called to him impatiently, and the boy took a couple of skips to get in step again. They were on their way to cover a poultry show and cockfight for the paper. He had only the vaguest notion what a cockfight was, but if it were not for his father's ideas on a broad education in the world as being preferable to the schoolroom (plus the fact that he wanted his son's company), added to his mother's fear that Rob was frail and had inherited his father's tendency toward consumption, he would be sitting on a bench in some district school. Last year and this he had begun the autumn term, but had come down with severe colds each time, and his parents, keeping him out indefinitely after his recovery, had decided each time not to send him back.

So here he was, swinging along beside his father toward some adventure, for his father courted adventure and laughed at risk. Like other newspapermen in San Francisco, he carried a revolver strapped around his waist, concealed under his weskit, but ready for the draw at the slightest provocation. If they printed the truth

—or anything to offend an influential figure—newsmen in the raw frontier city of San Francisco in the 1870s and '80s might well be called upon to defend their lives at pistol point. Men still took justice into their own hands. Feuds went on for years, although the raucous days of the forty-niners were fast becoming legendary —tall tales told in saloons, or around the gaming tables, where a man could still win or gamble away a fortune at faro or monte or the roulette wheel.

Legend invested the very ground of San Francisco, and the dust that was always blowing about the town, with the aura of gold. On clear days when the wind blew clouds of dust high into the sky at sunset, it took on the shimmer of gold, and natives swore to their children that some portion of it really was gold. Changing a word in the age-old saw to suit their fancy, San Franciscans would assert, "We all must eat our peck of gold"; and to a small boy like Rob Frost, it seemed as though gold dusted all he drank and ate.

The sails of three-masted schooners entering or leaving the sheltered port on the bay side of the city seemed fabricated of gold in a certain light; and the great seaway to the open Pacific and the Orient that swept between rocky islands, separating bay from ocean, was called the Golden Gate because of the way it shone in the sunset. There were those who talked of someday building a bridge across the Golden Gate—idle dreamers, in the opinion of others.

Between the vapors of the ever-shifting fog, the salt air and sea breeze that savored of far places and transformed the dust, there was an atmosphere of gold about San Francisco aside from its bustling industry and miner's trade. To a boy like Rob Frost, endowed with a fertile imagination, it would not have seemed incredible if he had been told that all the dust was gold. He was apt to make up tales himself as he walked along with his father— or by himself, when, in a year or two, he began to run errands for his father. Looking across the bay on clear days you could see the volcanic mountain Tamalpais, long since dormant, rising above the redwoods in a majestic peak, but who knew when it might start erupting again? Sometimes the boy was sure, or he thought he saw a column of smoke stealing from its cone; then he would run to tell his parents, and they would alert the whole city. (Only the sad fact was that when he did, they never believed him, they never bothered to investigate.) When his eye followed the Mount Diablo range, he saw himself discovering an eagle's aerie and making off with its young before its fierce parent could prevent him; he would tame the bird, train it for some wondrous purpose, but the mother would never forget; she would swoop down and try to avenge her loss by carrying him—Rob (the robber)—off someday. Sometimes he imagined himself roaming the hills of Contra Costa County, a child of the primeval forest, fending for himself like the creatures of the forest; he saw himself strong and athletic, as athletic as his father (before the cough came) and as fearless. Secretly Rob considered himself a coward, but he longed to be as brave as his father.

They turned at the corner of Washington and walked down Leavenworth to Market Street, where they went into a huge barn-like auditorium, with sawdust over the floor, crowded with men standing around in groups, arguing, placing bets on the various matches. By standing on tiptoe, Rob could see over the heads of the men, the small cockpit, on a raised platform with a railing around it, where the fights took place. There were many roosters in crates around the walls or carried in crates by their owners—proud birds—black ones, with an iridescent sheen to their plumage, and pointed red combs; enormous white ones, with tail feathers fluffed out; rusty red, and yellow, and speckled cocks. Plump hens, in as many varieties and colors, were penned in crates of six, all waiting to be judged.

The poultry held little interest for Rob. At the farm on the Napa River, where they had spent the previous summer, he had fed the hens and chickens in the barnyard; and when he grew tired of that, the farmer's wife, Mrs. Bragg, rawboned and brittle, told him to gather the eggs; and when he grew tired of that, he found a way to make it interesting. Quite by accident, he poked a tiny hole in one of the eggs with a nail he had picked up off the barn floor. Struck with an impish idea, he pecked holes in several others, and was delighted when Mrs. Bragg at mealtime expressed concern about some mysterious animal that must be eating her eggs. He repeated the prank just to hear the table talk among the elders speculating about what animal could do such a thing.

But the poultry show had no such possibilities, and the cockfight was all confusion to him. He could hardly see what was going on, and it seemed both stupid and cruel to watch men reach a pitch of excitement over two roosters clawing and fighting each other to death. Cockfighting was prohibited in Massachuetts and many other states, his father said; but in San Francisco, anything that gave rise to betting was a popular sport. To his father, the fact that the sport was frowned upon in New England made it attractive.

Since he couldn't see the fighting anyway, Rob took to examining the faces of the men in the group around them. One of them, so scarred it fascinated him, belonged to a man standing on crutches, wearing a patch over one eye and a bandage on his leg. Rob could not help staring, compelled by the mutilated face: what could have befallen a man so to disfigure him? Suddenly he felt a sharp pain as his father tweaked his ear, hissing an order to stop staring!

Rob rubbed his ear ruefully, and looked away. He was used to his father's quick—and often severe—punishment for bad manners or for some mishap that wasn't his fault, but he supposed all fathers were like that—affectionate and stern or cantankerous by turns. A few minutes later his father went over to the man and greeted him familiarly, asked how he was feeling, and when he would be back on the job.

On the way home, he told Rob the story: the dejected figure on crutches was a newspaperman, victim of a feud started over a scandal story. One of the papers had printed slurs (based on fact) against a big-time gambler and mine operator, questioning his mother's past history, suggesting his illegitimacy. The mine operator, enraged, sent one of his hirelings in the gambling ring to "get" the journalist who, it was rumored, had written the story. He was shot through the head and died. His brother came to avenge his death, but was wounded by gunshot, beaten and mutilated before he could get to the mine operator. This was the scarred man they had seen; it was a miracle that he had survived, but he made it clear that he was not through yet. As soon as he was healed, he would start gunning for the gambler. . . . So the feuds continued.

More than once Rob's father had been in danger of losing his life, but it was all part of the newspaper game, and he could join with the others in the *Bulletin* editorial office, boasting about the time the paper had exposed the stock market and they had to barricade themselves by pushing the files of "leads" against the door to fend off the pistol-fire of outraged manipulators.

W. P. Frost had made many friends among the reporters since coming to San Francisco eight years before. Born William Prescott Frost, Jr., after his father, a mill overseer in Lawrence, Massachusetts, he was a renegade from an old New England family steeped in strict Puritan traditions. Nine generations of Frosts and Colcords, hardy pioneers who battled the Indians to establish colonies—and later the states—along the rugged north-of-Boston coast, had served to produce a changeling in the overseer's son—a young blade who gave promise of a brilliant career when he read his Caesar for Harvard. But he had contrary ideas in his brainy head, and, although he did outstanding work in his first year at college, he was ready to chuck it all to enlist in the Confederate Army, and almost succeeded. He was good-looking, rangy, full of zest and enterprise. To earn a little extra money, he started a tutoring school of his own, and promptly went through his profits in escapades of one sort or another, sometimes with the fairer sex in Boston, sometimes at card games played in secret and semi-darkness in some daring soul's room. In spite of these distractions, he managed to graduate in 1872—*cum laude*—and with a Phi Beta Kappa key to fit in his watch fob.

Not content to settle down after these oats were sown, he refused the post of mill foreman point-blank. He broke with tradition for the second time, and set out to forge his own career in the far west. He could have gone into law, but journalism had more appeal for him.

The melee of carriages, carts, heavy drays, hansoms (his father never took a cab when it was possible to walk), and rumbling farmers' wagons had begun to thin out by the time the story was finished, and they were approaching the terrace of weather-beaten brick houses with odd little balconies across the second story, in one of which the Frosts were living at the moment. Soon the lamplighter would be coming around with torch and ladder to set the gas jets flaring on street corners, and thousands of flickering flames would glow softly from the hillside-city by the sea. His mother had just come from meeting with his sister Jeanie and was hastily putting out a little cold supper in the kitchen. She greeted them apprehensively, putting an arm around Rob's shoulders, but her face broke into a smile of relief when she saw that for once her husband was not out of sorts; he usually stopped at one of the many saloons on the way home.

In appearance still striking, with clear-cut features, a long upper lip, full mouth and deep-set blue eyes, Belle Frost—christened Isabelle Moodie by her Scotch Presbyterian parents—had possessed a pure cameo beauty, as well as intelligence, when her husband first saw her some nine years before. She had come to join the teaching staff at Bucknell Academy in Lewisburg, Pennsylvania, a school he had taken over briefly when he was in need of funds on his way out west. Rob had heard the story from both his parents by the time he was five years old.

Belle Moodie was a Scotch lassie and a bonnie one, for all her six years' advance in age over the temporary school principal. She was born in Edinburgh in 1844, the daughter of a sea captain, whose death, following a few years after his wife's, made the child an orphan when she was scarcely eight years old. Her grandmother had brought her to America to live with an uncle in Columbus, Ohio. As a small immigrant landing in Philadelphia, wide-eyed and awestruck, she was an appealing figure standing beside her grandmother on the docks. (Rob and Jeanie enjoyed hearing about the kind-hearted sailor who gave her a peach; she had never seen such a fruit, and thought it "too bonnie to eat.")

She was brought up in her Scotch uncle's strict Presbyterian household, trained to be a teacher, and had been instructing high school pupils in mathematics for seven years when she received the offer from Bucknell Academy. Something of romance in her nature, inherited perhaps from her seagoing father, prompted her to change the routine of her life. She had recently become interested in the transcendentalist theories of Emerson and the new Unitarianism, frowned upon by her uncle and all staunch Presbyters; here was a chance to get away, to follow her own spiritual bent, to see another section of her adopted country.

She was easy prey for a man who had a well-known eye for beauty, who admired the high order of her intelligence, and was himself brilliant, audacious, brash enough to seek his fortune in the far west. Her Scottish traits, the rare combination of virtue and wit, religious mysticism and preference for romantic poetry, charmed him at once, and before long he began to court her seriously. He knew but two pieces of poetry by heart; the first was the end of Bryant's *Thanatopsis,* and the other a seventeenth-century quatrain, which won her hand before she quite realized what had happened. The lines in a sense epitomized her husband's outlook on life:

> He either fears his fate too much,
>   Or his deserts are small,
> That dares not put it to the touch
>   To gain or lose it all.

What should perhaps have been a warning to her seemed dashing and irresistible, and after a hasty marriage in 1873, Belle found herself back in Columbus, left with her relatives while her husband went on to San Francisco to look for the kind of work he wanted to do.

Almost immediately he landed a job on the *Bulletin*, where the competitive sparring and confusion of the editorial office, the pressure of deadlines, the drama of a real scoop, were meat and drink to his venturesome soul. He sent for his bride, who was more than a little bewildered, not to say unnerved by the raucous customs of San Francisco after staid Columbus and the middle west. It was not safe for a woman to go out alone at night, and even in the daytime she was afraid of running into the "wild boys"—street urchins who roamed the city, terrorizing pedestrians with pranks and petty thievery.

She soon discovered that her husband was not only venturesome, but reckless. After the paper was put to bed, newspapermen retired to the saloons, where heated discussions over a mug of beer led W. P. Frost into politics, which kept him away night after night. Nor could he resist the gambling houses frequented by some of the reporters; the first time he went out of curiosity, but found himself so fascinated by the wheel, dice, and high-staked card games that he was drawn back again and again. If he won, he was elated; if he lost, he was grimly determined to make it up, and sometimes did. It was inevitable that he should fall into the habit of drinking, and Belle's gentle (or vehement) remonstrances were useless; he would not change his ways.

Left to herself, worried, untutored in the wiles of a frontier town, Isabelle Frost turned to religion for help—not to the established faith of her Scotch forefathers, or to the Emersonian doctrines that had swayed her for a time, but to the mysticism of Swedenborgians. One day she heard a Reverend John Doughty, beetle-browed, black of beard, preaching the Swedenborgian gospel; he had traveled clear across the country, leaving his pulpit in Worcester, Massachusetts (and narrowly missing being scalped by

Indians), to disseminate the divine truths from the Swedish scientist turned theologian. As Belle listened to him, she became more and more convinced that this should be her chosen faith. Its founder, Dr. Emanuel Swedberg, as his name was spelled originally, had been first a mathematician, then a scientist, whose visionary outlook led to discoveries in the ways of the universe unknown until his time. Here was a religion offering a direct link with her own life, and she consulted Reverend Doughty for further insight into her private domestic problems. Before she could become versed in the simple, yet profound concepts, she felt that she must try to solve the basic riddle—the financial problem—by some means. As far as she could see, her husband was headed on a downhill path that would lead both him and his family to perdition. From the time their son was born—his father insisted on naming him Robert Lee, after the Confederate general—this mismated pair, drawn together in a moment of mutual attraction and loneliness, seemed to be unconsciously drifting apart. It probably never occurred to Belle that her husband might have stayed home more often if she had been a better housekeeper; and his male ego was too strong to understand a wife's need for more companionship than the babies she had to care for, the house she was supposed to tend.

Rob knew because his mother later told him that in 1876, when he was only two, and she was pregnant with her second child, Belle Frost took matters into her own hands, packed up a few belongings and her small son, and set off on a cross-country trek to Lawrence, Massachusetts, where the elder Frosts, whom she had not met, lived in middle-class respectability (with a stout bank account to back them up). She was confident that when they heard her story, they would offer assistance as well as advice.

She received neither one; but her cold, disdainful in-laws had plenty of criticism to offer. She was shocked and hurt to find that her husband's parents blamed her for their son's downfall, if, indeed, he was going downhill. It seemed hardly likely that anyone with his brilliance (and a son of theirs) should so mismanage his financial affairs that he would fall into the hands of gamblers and cheap politicians. Realizing from the unbelief in their faces that there was no sympathy for her, Belle subsided. Her time was near, and she stayed in Lawrence just long enough in June to give birth to a baby girl, whom she named Jeanie Florence.

She needed refreshment in spirit as well as body before returning to San Francisco, if she could bring herself to go back at all. Taking the two children, she went into retreat at the home of a religious friend, whose patient kindness helped her to heal, and to re-examine her situation. In the fall, she was able to start out once again. She stopped in Columbus to visit her own relatives, before beginning the long trek across the endless plains by laggard, jolting coach.

She had been gone nearly six months. Her husband seemed overjoyed to see her, the daughter he had not yet laid eyes on, and his son. He made a great to-do over them, and took them in a hansom cab to the hotel where he had engaged rooms. He had changed jobs while they were gone, and was now city editor and manager of the *Post*. He talked incessantly, but Belle noticed that his eyes were more haggard than they had been, and he coughed a good deal; every few sentences would be interrupted by the rasping, grating sound that they all came to dread. He was telling about a six-day foot race which took place shortly after Belle had left him. Though he had been given a head start, he was beaten by his closest competitor, missed winning by a hair's-breadth, he bragged; stayed in till the very end. But Isabelle knew the strain had been too much for him. His consumptive tendency had become outright tuberculosis, she was sure, though he vowed he was in fine condition, except for the cough—a temporary matter.

Belle resigned herself to the harum-scarum sort of existence that took shape on her return: the alternating moves from hotels to houses; the long summers that stretched into autumn when she was left alone with the children for weeks at a time; and the evenings in town, when she waited for her husband to come home, hoping he would not be out of sorts again.

For awhile, there were not so many of those miserable evenings. Happy to have his family with him again. W. P. Frost gave more attention to his wife; he took her to the theater occasionally; he had already become friends with James O'Neill, who was making theatrical history in *The Count of Monte Cristo* and had brought his company to the west coast for an indefinite run. Now and then Belle reviewed books for the *Post*—or whatever paper her husband happened to be working for; he switched jobs several times, finally returning to the *Bulletin,* where he remained. Isabelle was an avid reader of novels as well as poetry and religious tracts. She possessed a keen intellect and liked to make use of it. Some of her husband's associates had stimulating ideas—Henry George, for example, who had worked in the composing room of the *Bulletin* for a short time, and who, with his wife, became close friends of the Frosts. Long before his *Progress and Poverty* was published, Henry George was expounding his single-tax theory with such eloquence that he convinced the Frosts to join the movement.

Best of all her reading, Belle Frost loved romantic poetry,—the ballads of "Bobbie" Burns, or the psychic verses of Poe, which could send her into a trance. At such moments, she became another sort of woman entirely; to the delight of her children, she would unpin her heavy dark hair, letting it tumble around her like a cloak, and in dramatic tones begin, "It was many and many a year ago/In a kingdom by the sea," while they shivered with anticipation. Jeanie, who had the gift of mimicry from the time she could talk, used to stand on a stool, her red-gold hair flowing in bright waves down her back like some small mermaid, and recite the verses her mother taught her. Rob, though he listened rapturously to his mother's recitations, was inarticulate in expressing his emotion or his flair for the dramatic, which came out in other ways. He would no more think of reciting than his mother would think of teaching him to spout stanza after stanza. Rob was all boy, his parents said, a creature of the outdoors; if he kept himself fit, he would be an athlete like his father (before the cough came) when he grew up.

conflict

   The boy had only a vague intuitive knowledge of the conflict
between his mother and father—the father he idolized as a para-
gon of manly prowess if not virtue, whom he followed around
with a high heart, proud of being bidden to do so. In spite of the
cough, Rob considered his father in a class with professionals, and
thought of himself—at seven or eight—as a potential walker or
racer. The second summer after they returned from the east, the
family stayed at Nicasio, where Rob rode horseback for the first
time and found a new love in the outdoor world of horses and
skittery colts. Girls' games—like croquet—bored him; he tried one
match, but the little girl he was playing with cracked him on the
head with her mallet for cheating. And maybe he had cheated; he
didn't know. The great redwood forests, primeval giants of the
soil; the mountains; and the plunging sea as the waves broke over
the black rocks beneath the deeply striated cliffs that loomed overhead in antediluvian starkness—these held fascination for a boy of
Robert Frost's temperament. That same summer, when he was five,
he had stood by his father's side at the Cliff House, high over the
ocean, watching a malevolent storm as it approached the land, the
waves breaking wildly, one on top of another; the lowering clouds
seemed to threaten the entire earth with angry punishment, for
what crimes he knew not. Signs of a supernatural wrath were in
that storm. The impression was so strong it was still fresh in his
memory two years later—nor did he forget in twenty, or in thirty-
six years, when it became at last poetic expression,* a childhood
memory made immortal, projected into eternity.

memories

   By the time he was ten, Rob Frost was a necessary adjunct to his
father's career. He was needed to carry legal documents to City
Hall; to run up and down the slanting streets, ringing certain
doorbells to check the voter-registration lists for false addresses
(only the doubtful doorbells of Republican voters were rung); but
most of all, he was needed to accompany his father on campaign
tours for Grover Cleveland. He sat beside his father in the livery-

* "Once by the Pacific."

stable buggy when they drove over the hills to stomp the outlying districts, and would take the reins if a coughing spell came out without warning. W. P. Frost, Jr., who was the Democratic candidate for tax collector, introduced him casually but with unmistakable pride to the other politicos they met on these tours as "My son, Rob," putting his hand on the boy's shoulder. Sometimes he added significantly, "Robert Lee Frost," and the men would laugh and slap him on the back, making jokes about his being born (and christened) a Democrat. The boy smiled, not knowing the difference between Republican and Democrat, knowing only that he felt proud because his father took pride in introducing him.

To the men who met him, W. P. Frost's son did not seem to be much of a chip off the old block. They saw a lanky, dreamy-eyed youngster, whose fair hair blew back from a high forehead, whose prominent nose ended in flaring nostrils, and whose generous mouth (with its long upper lip) was usually pursed, as if he were whistling softly to himself. His exceptionally large blue eyes set deeply under the high forehead, were deceivingly mild and gave him the appearance of being off on a cloud, lost in some boys' world of fantasy. And while this was often true, those who saw him in action, like the men at the *Bulletin* office, who noticed him come and go several times a day, delivering urgent messages to City Hall, checking registration, watching out for his father's coughing spells, thought of him as alert, energetic, enterprising, and considerate. Both estimates were accurate, since he was the product of two singular and definite personalities, both of whom influenced his own individuality.

One side of him was as swashbuckling as his father. He challenged a neighbor-boy named Franklin, older than he, to a race, including a wager.

The match took on unexpected proportions. They set a time and place—each one took a separate block—and each had his band of followers, running in the rear, cheering him on. Franklin offered Rob a head start, but he waved it aside. Like his father, he made a fine show of athletic prowess. But twenty times around a city block was a lot of running, and required more energy and training than he realized. By the fifteenth turn he was winded, but he would not give up. If his father could stay in a six-day foot race, he could stick with a twenty-round-the-block race. He did, with the shouts of loyal supporters, Jeanie among them, spurring him on. Like his father, he lost the race; but he was triumphant at having lost by a narrow margin, and to an older boy, whose stride was longer.

He bragged that he had missed it by a hair's-breadth, borrowing his father's frequent phrase.

His reputation grew, since he never went to school and was seen around town with his father more and more. Some of the "wild boys" so dreaded by his mother, figuring he must be one of them, included him in their pranks and forays, on days when his father was laid up and didn't even go into the office. Rob, inwardly dreading the "bad" boys as much as his mother, was half-pleased at the attention, and felt that he had to test his courage to prove to himself he wasn't a coward. The street ruffians were all as old as, or older than, Franklin had been; if he could keep up with them, he would consider himself strong and fearless.

One day the leader proposed a jaunt to the country to raid the apricot orchards; he had found two big meal-sacks to hold the fruit. Rob was always ready to go out into the open, but they had no luck; the orchards had already been picked and the ranchers had done a thorough job. The leader seemed to blame Rob for their disappointment. On the way back, they passed a slaughter-house, where the squealing of pigs made a frightful din.

Rob remarked that he knew the slaughterhouse well; he had been coming here with his father, who tried drinking the freshly killed animal's blood as a cure for consumption.

Suddenly he received an order to get over the fence and grab one of the pigs!

Without stopping to think, he scrambled up and dropped nimbly on the other side, just behind the squealing, squirming mass; the noise was deafening. The men had their backs to him, and before anybody could turn around, he managed to jam the nearest slippery shoat into the meal-sack, and popped back up over the fence.

His cohort appropriated the bag, and they started off for lower Washington Street, where the combined living quarters and wash-houses, vegetable stands, teashops, and opium dens of the Chinese huddled in a narrow quadrangle of city blocks and alleys between Grant Avenue and Washington. Here the little, slant-eyed men with pigtails down their backs lived in a world of their own and, organized in tongs, fought bitterly among themselves for power to rule the underworld. W. P. Frost had covered more than one battle between the Sum Yops and the Sue Yops, the largest tongs —newspapermen could always find "copy" in Chinatown—and when he had visitors from the east, he would hire a policeman to take them through the evil-smelling dens, where opium, smuggled into the country, was openly dispensed for a price.

The average "Chinaman" ran a washhouse, and boys growing up in San Francisco found it a lark to stand outside, heckling with laughter the hiss of the yellow man's spit on the iron as he labored over some white man's frilled shirt front. After a while, he would get annoyed, then angry, and, letting out a stream of Chinese, would threaten them with his raised iron if they didn't move away. Rob had frequently been one of a knot of boys at this pastime, but today they had business with the laundryman and went inside. At first he eyed them suspiciously, but when he saw the pig offered for ninety cents, he seized the bargain and asked no questions.

Outside again, the instigator doled out Rob's share of the ill-gotten gains—a contemptible fifteen cents, but Rob did not even think of objecting, nor did he feel resentful toward the leader. He spent the money on a small burning glass in a novelty shop, and felt himself the richer.

It was growing late by now, so he hurried home; one thing both parents were strict about was the rule that he must never play out of doors after dark. When he came in, his father was lying on the tufted leather couch in the living room; his mother was reading the latest Swedenborgian tract that had just come by mail from Massachusetts. Jeanie, who had run to open the door when she saw him coming, announced that Rob was home. His father asked fretfully where he had been so long; when the tuberculosis gave him a bad day, the buccaneer in him faded.

Something told Rob not to mention the recent escapade. He said truthfully that they went to the country for apricots. His father subsided, fumbling for change in his weskit pocket; but Jeanie asked eagerly where the fruit was. Rob's fecund imagination was at work. He told them they had two bagsful, but a great bear came along and snatched them away.

Jeanie giggled with delight, but his mother called his name warningly, "Rob . . ." and his father demanded sternly for him to come here and, reaching up, boxed his ear soundly. His mother did not interfere; both of his parents viewed with Victorian alarm the habit of make-believe that could so easily lead to lying. (His father, for all his extravagant nature, was a stickler for facts: raiding for fruit, a universal prank of boys from Maine to California, was understandable; and his mother did not approve of fantasy outside the printed page of poetry. Their son was always coming home with tales of his encounters with animals that seemed highly improbable.)

Rob admitted that they didn't find any apricots. They thought they saw a bear, but were not sure. His father said shortly that he suspected as much and asked him to run on down to the corner and bring him a bucket of beer before the daylight was gone.

No sooner had he left the house than Rob, like Icarus, was carried away on the wings of his imagination, and was with difficulty brought back to reality by the swinging doors of the saloon, the task of buying the "bucket o' suds." He held the change in his hand because his pockets had holes in them (or were stuffed with a miscellany including the magnifying glass, a nail, some acorns, and two green apricots he had picked up from the grass). Halfway back down the block, he dropped a dime, which rolled into the crack of the wooden sidewalk and was lost to view. He put down the bucket and wondered what to do. Farther up the block, there were a few loose boards, but at this spot all was smooth and tight as the planked street. He had received a thrashing only a few days before because he had brought home less change than his father expected; it wasn't his fault—he had just begun to learn simple arithmetic and the rudiments of reading from his mother, who felt it was high time—but the fact that he couldn't figure correct change had made no difference to his father, who kept right on caning him. If money had not been so tight at the moment, he wouldn't be afraid of another beating; but when funds were low (from either his illness or gambling) W. P. Frost was irascible, unpredictable.

Rob could hardly bear to think of telling him he had lost the dime. He might make up a story—he checked himself, rubbing his boxed ear. His parents' concern over his constant game of pretend had its effect on the boy's conscience. The trouble, Rob reflected as he made futile jabs at the crack in the boards with his nail, was that he himself was never sure which stories were true and which a figment of his imagination. The summer before, when they were staying just outside Santa Cruz, in the foothills of the Sierras, he had had several adventures, but he so loved to create a sensation that no one, including himself, knew how much —if any part—of the stories to believe. He declared he had seen a rabbit run over a bridge he had built across the brook, but it might have been only wishing. One incident stayed in his mind with startling clarity. He had cut through a deep redwood forest to visit a boy he had played with on the beach; he wanted to see the huge tank that the boy's father had hewed from one of the big trees for holding spring water. On the way home, just as he was crossing the bridge, an enormous bird, with fierce eyes and claws, had swooped down upon him, circled around his head, seemed ready to seize him in its great talons and fly off to some unknown sphere. Rob, his breath drawn in, had dodged at the crucial moment, and the bird circled away, mounting into the sky. Was it an eagle? Perhaps the one whose nest he had robbed? Then he remembered that he had never robbed an eyrie, except in make-believe. This, however, was a real experience, he was positive; the bird might have been a chicken hawk . . . but no, by the time he reached the house in Santa Cruz, he was positive also that the bird was an eagle. He ran the last quarter of a mile to tell the amazing story—he had almost been carried off by an eagle, which, at the last minute, had veered away on another course. Why? What could it mean? But, as usual, neither of his parents believed the tale. What would an eagle want with a boy? His father made light of it, his mother soothed him, and both cautioned him not to get carried away by his own fancies.

It would not do at all to come home with some far-fetched reason for losing the dime. He decided he would try not to pretend any more, even to himself, unless he knew he was pretending; then it would be all right. He was not having any success in loosening the sidewalk; he had better go and confess.

Luckily, his father had fallen into a doze after a severe coughing spell, and did not hear him come in. Fearfully, Rob told his mother in a whisper what had happened. She was almost as distressed as he; gathering him into her arms, she murmured above his head the prayers she had just been poring over in the tract. Before she could finish, his father, waking, called to Rob and he went in to face the consequences.

He blurted it out in one breath how he had lost a dime down the sidewalk crack.

Perhaps because of his mother's prayer, perhaps because the brief sleep had brought a change of mood to the sick man, his father gently drew Rob down on the couch beside him and forgave him.

And the next day his father felt so much better that he took them all on a horsecar ride out to Woodward's Gardens. Rob, fascinated by the sad, wise faces and comic antics of the monkeys, stood in front of the cage for some time after the rest of the family had moved on to other attractions. Curious to discover the reactions of two little creatures right at the bars, he took out his burning glass and focused the sunlight first on the nose of one, and then the other. The monkeys blinked, puzzled, and blinked again, but when he came closer, one of them reached out and snatched the lens from his hand. More interested than regretful, he watched them scramble to the back of the cage with his burning glass, where they conducted their own tests, breaking it in the process. This was an experience he knew was real, but he did not mention it when he joined the others, and he kept it to himself until long, long afterwards.

The following week his father was back in the throes of the political campaign, stomping for himself as well as for Grover Cleveland. He had cards printed announcing W. P. Frost, Jr., as the Democratic candidate for tax collector. Thumbtacks were stuck in the cards, and it was Rob's delightful duty, as they made the rounds of saloons, to try to drive them into the ceiling by hurling them up with a silver dollar. The two would start out in the morning, often boarding one of the new cable cars (still a novelty, though the first cables had been laid several years before), and ride to the top of the run; then, working their way back on foot, they made stops all along the street. They usually managed to reach Levy's on Bush Street just at noontime, where Rob, sitting at the free lunch with a glass of soda (colored by a squirt or two of raspberry flavoring), was urged to help himself to the heaping bowl of shining white (peeled) hard-boiled eggs or the round salami slices or the outsized sardines, hauled in down the coast at Carmel and brought to Meigg's Wharf by small fishing boats. Since Levy's offered the finest free lunch along with the liquid refreshment for sale, newspapermen in general and those backing W. P. Frost in particular made it their unofficial head-quarters. In the genial atmosphere at Levy's, they "plotted" territories and wrote campaign speeches, clarifying the issues at stake. It was rumored that the bosses in Tammany Hall were going to engineer the nomination of Hancock instead of Cleveland at the Democratic National Convention, but W. P. Frost, as delegate to the convention, was advised—and pledged—to stick to his guns and vote for Cleveland's nomination.

Rob paid little attention to the earnest discussions at Levy's, but he was as excited as Jeanie the day the whole family—even his mother, who was finally won over—proudly made the trip to Oakland, where they stood beside Frost's friend and political backer, Colin Boyd, waving farewell and Godspeed! to Father, a handsome figure in his new stovepipe hat and cutaway. In spite of the ardor of the Cleveland Democrats at the convention, Hancock was nominated. Cleveland was advised to run independently, and W. P. Frost strained his energies to the breaking point electioneering up and down the state. Rob accompanied him on some of the tours, meeting men of the world, seeing the California country as he had not seen it before. He rode on fire wagons and marched in torchlight parades. It was a kaleidoscopic kind of existence that young Robert Lee Frost led—bright bits of color, embracing experiences all the way from the sordid to the spiritual—all of it stimulating to his curious, aware, yet innocent mind and heart. And if a vague melancholy pervaded it, the feeling came because of his awareness, his extraordinary, unrecognized sensibility and perceptivity.

With a divided party, it was hard to make any headway in California, largely Republican since the Civil War. On election day, Cleveland won the Presidency, but California went Republican right down the line—and W. P. Frost went down to defeat.

Although he tried to accept it with his usual bravado, he was a broken man; his cough became alarmingly worse. Rob accompanied him to the stockyards two or three times a week now, watching the sick man gulp down the warm blood with grim determination, but the practice was of small benefit, if any. Other cures were discussed and some tried; W. P. Frost even considered moving his family to the Sandwich Islands for a time. But it was no use: he was a dying man, and he knew it. Without telling his wife or anyone in the family, he cashed in his equity in various insurance policies amounting to $20,000, in the hope that by gambling judiciously, with a system, he could double the money and so provide for his family after he was gone.

He kept up the flamboyant search for health as a cover. The summer following election, they all camped out in a tent on the shore at Sausalito, alongside a rollicking bunch of "Bohemians" from the *Bulletin,* who took the ferry across the bay twice every day, and spent the evenings making merry on the beach. Rob and Jeanie laughed at their antics—one night the men built a big funeral pyre, and with mock solemnity went through a ceremony of "burning their sins"—but Rob could see that his mother was troubled, uneasy over such heretical jokes, and his father's gaiety forced and grim.

Although the boy joined in the pretense that the lost health might be regained, Rob feared for his father because of the reckless attempts at a show of strength. Every day he would insist on taking a long swim way out beyond the piers into the bay.

Rob was to stand guard, he would say, half joking, half serious, in case he had to call for help. He would plunge into the surf, and with desperate, energetic strokes push on farther and farther until he was no longer visible; and the young lifeguard, watching from the sand, was in an agony of suspense until he saw his father's head reappear, and watched the flailing arms and legs as the sick man, his energy drained, beat his way toward shore and dragged himself up on the beach. Gasping, he would bid Rob fetch the "medicine bottle" from the tent, while he lay inert on the warm sand.

The summer passed—a mixture of gaiety and sadness, the joy of living outdoors, the wonder and wildness of the Pacific, watching the stars over the night sea, and the ships passing in and out of the Golden Gate all day. The family moved into a small house when the weather grew too damp and foggy to camp out any longer. His father faded visibly, day by day, during the winter months; early in May, his strength ebbed completely. He was lying on the couch one evening, talking only now and then to his faithful friend Colin Boyd, who visited him nearly every day.

Calling for Rob, his father spoke softly, feebly, to him; above all, he wanted his son's solemn promise that he would never venture into the streets at night to play.

Rob promised, and kept his word.

A little later that evening, his father died in the arms of his political backer and friend. Colin, many years his senior, came to the door of the dining room, where Belle Frost was reading quietly to Rob and Jeanie, to tell them sorrowfully that W. P. Frost was gone, at only thirty-four years of age. It was the 5th of May, 1885, and Robert Lee Frost had just turned eleven.

In the days that followed, they learned what had happened to the insurance money. Instead of being doubled, or even increased, every cent of the equity in $20,000 had been lost; the small bank account that Belle managed to maintain out of household expenses had barely enough in it to pay, besides their fares, for transporting the body back to Massachusetts. It was a bleak little procession of three that boarded the railway coach, accompanied by the black coffin, bound for its resting place in Lawrence, some three thousand miles away. The cars were stuffy; the long journey seemed endless; and every time they had to change trains, the knowledge that the black box held all that was left of the bold, reckless, beloved, yet baffling personality of his father, struck Rob afresh. As he watched his mother, dressed in black, seeing to the coffin for the third or fourth time when they changed in Chicago, Rob saw that she was calm and composed, and he somehow felt comforted, strong. Not until many years had passed did he realize how sad and difficult that journey must have been for her.

Chapter 3

ATLANTIC SALT

The Colcord-Frost clan were respectable, upright Puritans—hardworking, thrifty, "purse-proud," as New Englanders said. To Rob, the darkened house of his grandparents in Lawrence, spotlessly neat, stuffed with heavy dark furniture—antimacassars on every chair, settee or sofa—was oppressive and cheerless, entirely in keeping with the cold reception given to the three weary, dust-laden travelers from San Francisco. The relatives, who had gathered at Grandfather Frost's for the funeral, stood in front of the fireplace, officially lined up; next to Grandfather and Grandmother Frost—impressive in their best black—were Great-Uncle Elihu Colcord and Great-Aunt Lucy Frost Colcord (Grandmother's brother had married Grandfather's sister); and, from Amherst, Great-Aunt Sarah Frost Messner. Rob and Jeanie and their mother were greeted by each of the five in turn with a stiff handshake and a brief forward motion, cheek not quite touching theirs, that was meant to be an embrace.

Then Grandfather Frost, most formidable of all, as tall as his son had been, with a ramrod stiffness to his back, spare, stern, unsmiling, led Rob to wash up at the copper sink before supper, and followed him clear into the bathroom to make sure he didn't clean himself on the towel. To an eleven-year-old accustomed to being accepted almost as an adult by the worldly men in San Francisco politics, his grandfather's surveillance was humiliating, but he was too tired—and too awestruck at the moment—to protest.

Lawrence itself, as they moved in funeral procession next day through the smoky cobblestone streets of the town dominated by the great mills where the spindles never stopped turning, seemed as far removed in spirit as in miles from the carnival city of San Francisco. The graveyard was on a hill in the outskirts; by the time they reached the Frost family plot, where his father was buried after a brief ceremony, Rob realized that the colorful gaiety of his birthplace, grim though it had often been, had turned to the somber gray of a sooty mill town.

Once the funeral was over, Grandfather Frost put the daughter-in-law of whom he still did not quite approve through a series of questions about the lost insurance money, and why Belle had not done something to prevent his son's rash deed. Grandmother chimed in, echoing his disapproval with added force. It was a regular inquisition, Rob thought, listening to them; it seemed hard to believe that his father could have been the son of this stern-faced judge who was trying his mother.

But Isabelle Frost was not one to cower before her in-laws. She answered their questions quietly, factually, neither defending nor blaming herself—or her husband—for what had taken place. The way she stood up to them gave Rob and Jeanie a feeling of confidence and pride. Nine-year-old Jeanie, whose red-gold hair had grown till it cascaded below her waist, voiced her sentiments against their grandparents' household as soon as they were alone, and Rob backed her up. It was just as well that they were all invited to Aunt Sarah Frost Messner's in Amherst for a few days, according to custom.

But the atmosphere there was not much different, and Belle Frost did not wish to make her children conform to unnecessary Puritan severity. When they returned to Lawrence, she considered what to do. First, Rob must get his education; as an eleven-year-old who had never attended school, he had to take placement tests. He was given arithmetic problems in Roman numerals and asked to name all the inland rivers in the United States, questions he could not possibly have known. Bewildered, confused by the quick change in the pattern of life, he did not even try to answer, and was summarily set down as a beginning pupil, at the second- or third-grade level.

His grandparents advised starting him in at once, but his mother held off. She knew Robert had great capacity for learning, but unless he was rapidly advanced—and she could not imagine the Lawrence school allowing him to skip a grade or two—he would be seventeen before he even entered high school. Besides, the children were already growing restive under their grandfather's watchful eye, and she could not blame them. As the weeks passed, the prim household became more intolerable, and one day the climax came unexpectedly. It was in the spring, and Grandfather Frost, who prided himself on the fine display of hyacinths and tulips in his front garden, happened to look out of the window and see a little Irish boy from the shantytown where the immigrant mill hands lived standing suspiciously near the walk holding a bouquet of the flowers in his hand.

Telling Rob and Jeanie to stay there and look out the window, he took his cane and went out. Without stopping to question the boy (he had not actually seen him picking the flowers), he grabbed him by his ragged collar, pinned him in a powerful grasp so he couldn't move, and as Rob and Jeanie watched, he beat the poor child unmercifully. Jeanie closed her eyes tight and stamped her feet, and Rob went white, something very deep in him revolting.

After that their mother could not hold them there, and she knew it. She had been making inquiries about the possibilities of teaching in a district school, and now she applied to fill a recent vacancy in Salem, New Hampshire, just over the Massachusetts border. The pay was not much—nine dollars a week, for the thirty-six weeks of the school year—but they would manage, with the odd jobs that Rob could get during the summer and on Saturdays.

She received the post, and within a week or so, the small family of three were packed up and moved into a couple of furnished rooms in a Salem lodging-house. At least here they would be by themselves, away from Grandfather Frost's domination.

Rob and Jeanie both attended their mother's school. Belle Frost had ideas of her own about teaching, some of them born when she was tutoring Rob in San Francisco, and now she could try out her scheme in a full school of thirty-four pupils. Her method was to seat the children according to ability, giving in-individual instruction as much as possible, and reading aloud during some hour of the day. If she looked gaunt and hollow-eyed, if a perpetual strand of hair strayed over her forehead, it was because she threw herself into the work, drove herself day and night. Yet she enjoyed it, and under her plan she could give Rob the special schooling he needed to catch up with the others of his age.

He made rapid headway and before long showed signs of surpassing the other twelve-year-olds. He was proving good in nearly everything, his mother wrote proudly, defiantly, to his grandparents. Rob himself was surprised at the way he absorbed learning as soon as he began to study; it was as if he had been thirsty without knowing it, and he began to drink in knowledge all at once, insatiable. When summer came, Belle Frost, on her own at last, reverted to the nomadic way of living she had known in San Francisco. There was little to keep her in the lodging-house; the New England summer was brief but beguiling, so she moved into the northwest wing of a decrepit farmhouse outside Salem, run by an ancient couple who kept the sheltered southwest wing for themselves, and needed a boy like Rob for chores or extra help during the haying. Here he read his first book to himself all in one gulp, nestled in the new-mown hay; it was a tattered copy of *The Scottish Chiefs*, which he had noticed on the mantel-shelf and borrowed from the farmer's wife. He had heard the history of the Highlands read aloud many times by his mother, but now it was as if he were uncovering a hidden treasurestore of words and meanings, part of the inner world that belonged to him and no one else. Absorbed, he read on, oblivious of the soft-scented hay-mow, or the ache in his arms from racking the hay on which he lay. As fast as the men on top of the load pitched down their heavy forkfuls to him that morning, he had stowed it away, not letting them get the better of him.

At first he thought he must be mistaken in feeling that they meant to bury him, piling it around him in a fiendish rush, but then he realized they were testing him, goading him to see if he was fit to be a farmhand. The fighter in him rose to the challenge, and though he almost lost his balance under a fork-tossed load a few times, though he might choke on the dry straw-dust, he stuck it out, and mopped the hayseed from the back of his neck just like the men when the job was finished. He had survived his initiation, and he knew it—not by the reward of words of praise or approval, but by the silent acceptance he received when they asked if he'd be helping with the haying at the next farm over the hill.

He quickly learned that there was an unspoken code among the farmers and the hired help—a good farmhand knew his business, didn't have to be told to do it better or faster (especially if a storm was coming)—and woe betide the farmer who made the mistake of giving orders. He would find himself without any help at all. They were a tight-lipped lot, farmers and helpers alike, whose feelings showed through actions rather than words. Unless he knew the code, a farmer might insult a hand, and never know it till the man walked off the job or took out his anger with his pitchfork in half a dozen different ways, some of them like to kill.

But Rob was not figuring out the ways of New England hill folk as he read on and on, lost in the pages of Scottish lore, of the heroic deeds of the Higlander chiefs. He forgot everything until he heard Jeanie calling him for supper, when he looked up to see that the tree shadows over the shorn meadows were long, and a red sunset proclaimed another hot day on the morrow (so the old farmer had told them). He had not quite finished the book, but he closed it up; he knew the end. And the main thing was that he had discovered the joy of reading to himself, for himself. He always liked to hear his mother read, as she did that night, after they had their "halesome parritch" and milk. The dishes could sit on the table while three more mystery romances from the tales of George MacDonald were unfolded and the baying of bloodhounds filled the farmhouse wing. But his mother, even though she was not much of a hand to housekeep, had precious little time for reading aloud, and if he could read a book in an afternoon, the way he had today, he could lose himself in the world of imagination any time he pleased.

After the haying, the fine hot weather continued, and Rob was of a mind to go swimming in the pond the boys on the next farm had told him about. All morning, when the farmer did not need him, the schoolwork with his mother kept on, because he had so much catching up to do, but sometimes in the afternoon he was free, and on a particularly warm day was setting out to find the swimming hole, when the white-bearded farmer called him back. They had to grease the bearings of the grindstone and sharpen the scythe dulled by the mowing, he said. Bitterly disappointed, Rob was ready to tell the old codger the scythe could wait, it was too hot; but some command in the beady eyes that peered at him over gold-rimmed spectacles made him turn in the direction of the yard where the grindstone stood, symbol of a grueling job. So all afternoon, he had to "drive" the wheel and drive it hard while the old man got on with the scythe and rode it just as hard against his turning, pressing the blade against the stone. Lucky for Rob he had to slosh water from a tin can over it every so often or his arms would have broken under the strain. The sweat poured down his face and back, and he wanted to cry out that the blade must have been sharpened to a "creepy" edge after half an hour, but the aged rider was never satisfied. The whine of the creaky machine went on and on.

Before the summer was over, Rob ran off and went swimming once or twice—chores or no—and learned the pastimes of New England country boys—the thrill of "swinging" the supple birches, unlike any outdoor joy he had ever known; the mischief of raiding a blueberry patch before anyone else found it; the quiet pleasures of lolling on the bank of a stream, watching the butterflies dance above the heads of blossoms, learning all unconsciously the names of wild flowers and where they grew.

In the fall, the family returned to the village for the school year, and Rob looked around for some sort of job to help out. He found one at the corner shoe shop—after school and on Saturdays. The cobbler showed him once how to insert nails into holes in the heels of shoes, and he followed instructions perfectly—even to holding the nails in his mouth (a practice he neglected to tell his mother); he worked with a mouthful of nails several hours a day, but he never swallowed or inhaled a single one, no small feat for a lad his age, the shoemaker said. The few dollars that Rob earned during the term, or any other time, he put right into his mother's hands without questioning the matter. She needed every penny to pay the rent, to buy their clothes and shoes. Nor did Belle stop to question her right to take it, to manage the finances from start to finish; she did not ask for details as to the nature of the work, as long as he stayed well. That Rob can do anything, she would say to herself with a little smile, shaking her head. (The next spring, just after his thirteenth birthday, he worked in a factory "behind a big machine, run by a big man"; it was a dangerous process, but he didn't let his mother know—or lose a finger.)

On Sundays, Belle went to the Swedenborgian church regularly here, and the two children attended its Sunday school. The religion based on science, founded by a man who had been mathematician, engineer and astronomer, had broad appeal for a boy interested in outdoor things, and the wonder of the stars soon found its place ahead of many other interests in his humming brain. His schoolwork raced along—even his schoolteacher-mother was surprised. His odd jobs and heavy work, his contact with rough characters of farm or factory didn't seem to hamper his intellectual growth any more than the politicians and habituées of San Francisco saloons had harmed his innocence. His ever-curious mind, alive to experience, to fact as well as fantasy, allowed him to integrate elementary book learning with everyday living. He explored the possibilities of daily events just as he had explored the reaction of the monkeys at Woodward Gardens; it was an attitude he had been endowed with at birth, and one which he was to keep all his life.

In good part, his mother's way of teaching led him to advance at such a pace, and with such naturalness and ease that he never felt pushed. Under her tutelage, he was ready to enter high school just two and a half years after beginning to study.

His mother suggested that he go to Lawrence, since county schools left much to be desired, and Rob was just as well satisfied. Their neighbors in Salem clucked their tongues at the extra expense of the interurban coach trip twice a day; but his grandparents, to his surprise, approved the plan wholeheartedly. His grandmother cut down one of his grandfather's suits for Rob, and the old gentleman himself came forward with an offer to pay for his transportation every week; after school, the boy could come to their house and help with chores until traintime. It was a good plan.

With the first term, the budding intellect of Robert Lee Frost burst into full flower as both scholar and leader. His teachers recognized in him an extraordinary student, and his classmates not only accepted him as a "regular feller," but looked to him for guidance or advice in personal matters. He could always see both sides of a question, and they trusted his judgment. The Frost-Colcord clan, which had regarded Belle and her two children so dubiously, took a sudden interest in "Junior's boy"; Uncle Elihu was so pleased he presented Rob with a "boughten" suit, his first brand-new long-pants suit.

Lawrence High School, housed in a typical dull red brick building—unadorned, with steep stone steps leading to its portals—stuck by its traditions as an institution of higher learning, emphasizing the classics above lesser subjects, though its standards in general were strict, its teachers unyielding. The spelling and Latin teachers were the most demanding of all—there was no getting by in those courses; like it or not, you had to study hard or fail. Rob's spelling, which had never been good (because his ear was quicker than his eye, his mother said) improved somewhat under such stern supervision. And through the iron-willed classical language teacher, Miss Newell, who brooked no nonsense in regard to temperament, he went much farther than mere mastery of Greek and Latin grammar. If No-nonsense Newell was adamant about assignments, she was also ardent in her admiration for Latin poetry, a fervor she was able to instill in her students, particularly one like Robert Frost, whose sensitive ear for the sound of words picked up the nuances of Latin poetry. He found himself fascinated by Latin verse forms, going beyond his assignments in Virgil every day without realizing it.

He studied until late at night and took odd jobs on Saturdays. His mother was able to go out more often; she attended single tax meetings, and was even persuaded by her old friend Henry George to make the trip to Boston for their banquets. The socialistic theory of taxation seemed sensible to her, and during Rob's first semester she read Bellamy's *Looking Backward* to him and Jeanie after supper. It was a fabulous tale of a man who went to sleep for fifty years and awakened to find an ideal world, run by socialism, but Rob was rather bored with the notion, and much preferred the stories in Virgil's *Eclogues*. He didn't hestiate to tell his mother that he thought socialism boiled down to everybody looking after Number Two, and his strong individualism objected. "It's harder to look after Number Two than Number One," he observed, "for how do you know what Number Two wants?" His mother could see that he had a point, and she did not argue with him; at fourteen, Rob was entitled to his own opinions.

Although he knew from the comments of his teachers that he had passed all the tests with high marks, which were not given out, Rob had no idea he was head of the class of '92 until his second year. He found out where he stood one week when his work wasn't quite up to par. As head of his class, they told him, he must set a good example; or they reminded him that several others had shown promise of being head—a girl, for one.

No name was mentioned, but he had an idea it might be Elinor Miriam White (whose father had once been a Universalist preacher, but deserted to become a wood-joiner; he was a descendant of Peregrine White of Revolutionary fame, and he let everyone know it). Rob had noticed her during study period. She wore her hair in a single braid, wrapped round her head like a coronet, and there was something regal about her profile outlined against the sunlight from the study-room window; her dark eyes were thoughtful, her mouth serious, and sweet. He asked his friend Ernest Jewell about her. Ernest, a senior, who was editor of the school paper—the *Bulletin*—knew the whole student body, it seemed, and was always ready to help out a fellow. Before too long Robert Frost became acquainted with Elinor White; and before much longer, he was taking the farthest way to Grandfather Frost's every afternoon, so he could walk Elinor home.

She was one of the few girls at Lawrence High whom he could talk to and know that what he said was understood. Elinor had brains; she could exchange ideas with him without bursting into self-conscious giggles; yet when her laughter came, at rare moments, it had a lilt that made his heart leap and he thought there had never been a girl as attractive as Elinor White. One day in spring they had been discussing Prescott's *The Conquest of Mexico* all the way to her house; Rob had been reading the book in history class, and was moved by the valiant but tragic efforts of a small group of Indians, who just might have turned the tide for themselves in one dark night of battle, but didn't quite make it. He was still visualizing the sad fate of the Montezumas when he left Elinor; and whether it was because she had been such a sympathetic listener or whether his soul was so stirred by the story, he did not know, but he was suddenly aware of a strange whirling in his brain—a bringing forth of words he did not know were there. He hardly knew where he was going.

"There was a wind and a darkness," he said afterwards. He had never written a poem before, and as he walked, it appeared like a revelation, and he became so taken by it that he was late at his grandmother's.

Luckily she was upstairs, so he sat down at the kitchen table, took out his school notebook, and began to write as the words flowed—a long heroic narrative ballad, straight off, making no changes in the stanzas as he had heard them along the way—like a voice from some unseen Power. (For always it would be the sound of poetry that took him, the music arising from the spoken sylla-ble, word, and sentence—aside from the seed, the idea planted in a poem.)

He called this first attempt "La Noche Triste," and the next morning laid the sheets of notebook paper—uncopied—on Ernest Jewell's desk. His friend was surprised that Rob wrote poetry and asked if he had any more.

Rob said eagerly that he might have before they went to press. He wanted to try himself again, quickly. And the April (1890) issue of the *Bulletin* printed "La Noche Triste," along with a fragment, the beginning of a Scottish ballad called "Tenoch-titlan"; both were signed Robert Lee Frost—for all the world of Lawrence to see. The boy who was already known as scholar, leader, athlete, like his father before him, now proved to be a poet as well. With the excitement of his discovery came an inner relief: he knew unconsciously that, like his father, he could choose the path of writing, never mind how thorny it might be.

The next year, the question of his class leadership became a school issue, and he was in distress: rivalry was strong between the Greek and Latin teachers, and Miss Newell kept proclaiming Rob as the head of the class, while the other teacher put forward one of her pupils; at times the publicity bothered him so that he could hardly study. And by his senior year, the situation was maddening because Elinor popped up as his foremost rival. He was elected editor of the *Bulletin*, and had to give a lot of time to assigning articles, making up the paper and writing a piece himself (by far the easiest task) every week. The contributors were so slow in bringing him copy that he finally could not bear it; he wrote the entire contents of one issue, signing the articles with a variety of pseudonyms, and sent in his resignation as editor. But his studies had suffered, and one day the Principal, himself a classical scholar, who was Rob's Greek and Roman history teacher, stopped him after class. He was a large, easy-going man, "smoked as a ham, scholarly and lazy—very pleasant," Rob thought.

"Do you realize," he drawled, "that Miss White is catching up— she may get the valedictory?"

"Give it to her now," Rob burst out involuntarily. He was tired of being nudged, and he didn't want Elinor as a rival, anyway.

No, the Principal said, he couldn't do that, it was only the middle of the term; and in the end he called it a tie. So both of them had to prepare speeches, and Rob did not object; the valedictory would come in handy later, he thought. His literary ambitions were growing, and his ideas were his own; he had no tendency to ape any other writer. He chose for his valedictory address the ponderous title, "A Monument to After-Thought Unveiled," and, quite naturally, some of his remarks dealt with leadership: "Not in the strife of action is the leader made," he wrote, "nor in the face of crisis, but when all is over, when the mind is swift with keen regret, in the long after-thought. The after-thought of one action is the forethought of the next. . . . It is when alone . . . that men form those habits called the heroism of genius, and lead the progress of the race." He spoke of "the supreme rise of the individ- ual . . . a life from self for the world" as "the aim of existence."

". . . The poet's insight is his after-thought. It is of varied heart-beats and converse with nature. And the grandest of his ideas come when the last line is written.

"Life is an after-thought: how wonderful shall be the world? that is the after-thought of life. . . ." His classmates might not understand what he was talking about, but that didn't bother him. "My idea was," he said later, "tackle the subject—say it the best you could—make your own troubles and get out of them. Nobody around me had thoughts. I scorned opinions from the beginning. I wanted ideas; wanted to use a figure."

Elinor's topic was "Conversation as a Force in Life," and the two valedictorians rehearsed their speeches together. Rob also wrote the class hymn, set to music by Beethoven. Graduation day exercises took place at the end of June, and the Lawrence *Daily Bulletin* for July 1, 1892, carried a full account of the event, including the unusual double valedictory, and thumbnail sketches of the charming young pair who spoke. Rob was graduating at exactly the age he would have been on entering, if he had accepted his rating on the placement tests! Elinor in her graduation gown looked almost like a bride, and he could easily imagine himself the bridegroom.

But afterwards he hardly had a chance to talk to her. They were crowded away from each other by hordes of congratulators and then their families claimed them. Rob's grandparents, his great-uncles and aunts, sat beside his mother and Jeanie during the program, pleased and satisfied that Robert had made such a brilliant record in high school. They had no doubt that he would expand it in college.

For his grandparents had offered to send him to college. It was Grandmother Frost's idea, and she chose Dartmouth; Rob's mathematics teacher had suggested that he apply for a first-term fellowship at the Hanover college, and his grandmother was afraid of the drinking at Harvard. (She needn't have worried, because Rob hated the taste of liquor from the few sips he had had on occasion, and would probably not have been tempted as his father had been.) Everyone took it for granted that Rob would be only too happy to have the chance to go to Dartmouth.

But the young man himself was not so sure. Now that the fanfare of graduation was over and high school was a thing of the past, he began to doubt himself and his powers as a writer. He worked on a farm most of the summer, which gave him little chance to see Elinor, and many hours to meditate. Why should he go to college, when all he wanted was to create, on his own? He had enough of literary, academic background. But then the vague, overwhelming doubt would wash over him in dark waves, and he was quite sure he would never be a writer. By the end of summer he hardly knew who he was, or what, if any, his purpose in life was. Perhaps it was because his book learning had come too fast, and he could not face the thought of sitting through any more courses for a while; he had absorbed more education in half the time—just six years—than most students covered in twelve years. He had gobbled it up, and the feast had left him sated. But more likely his confusion came simply from the fact that the fever of the creative artist in its initial stage was bringing upheaval to his whole being, as it must to any man struck by the germ.

This was not clear to him; he thought if he could talk to Elinor, she would understand. When he saw her, however, just before the fall term opened, she had suffered no such doubts about going to college, and could not grasp his; she felt it was essential for both of them to have a college education. A few days later, she trooped off to a sectarian school in New York State—St. Lawrence—along with other dutiful daughters of Universalist families. Rob, realizing that he could not see her till Christmas anyway, packed his grand-father's old satchel and took the rumbling interurban to Hanover.

Chapter 4

THE DUSTY HALLS
OF DARTMOUTH

The college town of Hanover, its streets lined with urn-shaped elms forming a Gothic arch of branches overhead, shading the mellow old buildings of the campus with yellowing leaves in the autumn sunshine, was outwardly appealing as Rob Frost went slowly up the walk toward his room in Wentworth Hall. Marked especially in his mind was the library, housed in Wilson Hall; he had a feeling he was going to need the book-lined shelter behind the carved, Romanesque door.

His room was hardly inviting—sparsely furnished; heated by an open coal stove gaping at him from the wall opposite the narrow iron bed; and poorly lighted with a single window over which hung a cracked green shade. For this he had to pay $26 a year. Board was $2.50 a week. Tuition was $90 a term, but because of the fellowship which he had won, and because he was to be a monitor, Rob paid only $10. Dartmouth college directives for 1892 were severe in the extreme; students were required to attend sixteen sessions of prescribed studies a week, daily college prayers, and public worship on Sunday forenoon. There must be no drinking whatever. The curriculum was limited; Rob was enrolled in Greek, Latin and mathematics; English, or literature, was brought in only incidentally, if it happened to come up in connection with Latin poetry; freshmen were not permitted to take elective courses. (The "not permitted" list on the bulletin board in Dartmouth Hall had hardly changed since the building had been completed a hundred years before, in 1791.)

Relief from stringent rules was bound to take the form of violence in class customs and traditions; the salting down of freshmen (with hard rock salt); savage rushes in retaliation, in which Rob was a party to more than one fist fight with sophomores; and other kinds of hazing filled the first few days. His chief cohort in these attacks was Preston Shirley, frail in body but wild in spirit, who had the room next to his, and became his best (and only intellectual) friend at Dartmouth. Thin and wiry, suffering from a number of ailments, Preston did not sleep well, and he soon formed the habit of dropping into Rob's room at night; "he was the life of the place in many ways, full of old family and Dartmouth traditions, the more roughhouse the merrier." The two planned practical jokes, shared escapades.

It was Preston who put Rob onto the rowdy custom of "wooding up" the professors they didn't like. The mathematics teacher, who was a backbreaker, had assigned so much work that no one could complete it, and Preston, giving Rob a nudge, began to pound his feet on the old floor-boards of the classroom; Rob did not hesitate to join in, nudging the fellow next to him, and inside of a few seconds the whole roomful of freshmen was stamping out a noisy protest. Clouds of dust arose along with the rhythmic, insistent clatter, until the red-faced professor, hands over his ears, ran from the room and down the hall to the president's office, howls of derision echoing at his heels.

"Just an old college custom my grandfather taught me," Preston explained to Rob, wiping his eyes, weak from laughter, as the boys bolted class and left the building.

The acting president himself was the target of a battle royal because of rules laid down at one of the weekly Rhetoricals for seniors, held in chapel and attended by the entire student body. The attack was started by an upperclassman and taken up immediately by the others, Rob and Preston in the forefront. First someone's cushion went flying through the air, then wooden footstools, books, sacks of salt-filled dust left over from the hazing followed— anything they could lay their fingers to—and forced the Head to scurry out of the chapel, dodging flying objects right and left. In vain did he try to shout over his shoulder at them to remember they were gentlemen.

Fraternity rushing began; Rob was invited into Theta Delta Chi, and joined; he had no money for extras like initiation, so Preston, who was rich compared to him, paid the fee. But an incipient poet is no fraternity brother, nor can he force himself to be, Robert Frost discovered very soon. He did not enjoy the company of rumpus-makers all the time (though if there was a fight, he was among the first to get in it), and he said as much to Preston when his friend wanted to know why he wasn't going to fraternity meeting. Then began their late-evening "confabs" when the two sat up till all hours, sounding off on religion, politics and history in high old talks so vital to the young. Since drinking was forbidden, they sat up all night gorging a box of Turkish paste, if they felt like having an orgy.

Rob's aversion to the hale-fellow-well-met atmosphere grew, and he stayed away from meetings altogether. He also felt "a large indifference" to his teachers—mostly because he wanted instinctively to be at the top of the system, himself a teacher, and not an everlasting pupil underneath; the wild, school-free days of San Fran-cisco came back to him; he thought of his father, not bleakly, but warmly, as if his parent-companion were still alive. He remembered his father's theory about California and the west, surpassing all other areas; he remembered a map his father had laid out, on the floor of a San Francisco hotel room, showing the eight areas of power into which he thought the States would eventually be divided. Fumbling, Rob tried to put his feeling about California into verse. A fragment, perhaps never a poem, but he set it down:

> Europe might sink and the wave of her sinking sweep
> And spend itself on our shore and we would not weep.
> Our future is in the West on the other Sea—

And of that other Sea, he wrote another fragment, remembering the terrible, wondrous storm he had witnessed from the Cliff House. He kept a single couplet:

> The clouds were low and hairy in the skies,
> Like locks thrown forward in the gleam of eyes.

In the crisp weather of late October, he walked among the fallen leaves listening with his inner ear to the metered lines his memory sought to create. He paid little heed to assignments, even Virgil; but one day, the classical language professor, whom they called "Clothespin" Richardson, quoted a line from Shelley:

> Where music and moonlight and feeling are one

and Rob sat up as though flashed awake in class. Richardson urged his charges to look up the poem, read it all. The next day, Rob, on one of his meandering walks, sauntered by the bookshop and stopped to browse. On a neglected rack, he saw in a row of paper books, Palgrave's *Golden Treasury*. He took it down and began thumbing through the pages. There was Shelley! . . . and Keats . . . and Tennyson, and all those golden-tongued poets in one volume, treasure galore. He could hardly spare the change from the weekly allowance his grandparents sent, but he bought the copy and bore it with him to the inviting woods outside Hanover, where, with his back against a tree, he read avidly all afternoon.

He returned there often—not always to read, and not only during the day; he liked to walk through the woods alone, accompanied only by the crackling sound of the dry leaves as he shuffled along, sometimes in the late afternoon, sometimes at night. (He had begun taking night walks during the past summer on the farm, and he found as he moved through the night air that the cool darkness—relieved only by distant star or gentle moonlight— led his thoughts more easily in the poetic way; and he felt serene, never scared by eerie nightsome sounds.)

He cut class, stayed away from fraternity meetings altogether, and, except for the occasional talks with Preston, stuck to his own company. The Theta Delts were perplexed: Rob Frost had seemed as gregarious as any of them in the beginning of the term. A group of wags finally knocked on his door in Wentworth Hall one morning and wanted to know what he did in the woods—*all alone.*

"I gnaw wood," he told them, cocking one eyebrow and pursing his lips in a sudden stubborn quirk. He closed the door in their faces.

When the chill November rains came, he took to spending more time in the library; about the middle of the month, happening to stop at the magazine rack, he picked up a copy of the *Independent* and found a poem on the front page. He stood stock-still, reading: "It was a sort of threnody called 'Seward,' by Richard Hovey, a friend of Bliss Carman, and a celebrated Dartmouth graduate. The subject was the death of Thomas William Parsons, translator of Dante's *Inferno,* friend of Longfellow."

The poem itself was not exceptional, but the fact that a publication existed, "anywhere in my native land," he thought rapturously, that offered a means of publishing poetry, was a complete revelation to him. He noticed that there was even an editorial about the poem, and he moved to the nearest table, where he read it "with rapt amaze." He turned back to the cover: it was Number 2294, the November 17, 1892, issue of the *Independent.* He marked the data down in his notebook and his mind, as if on this day he had sighted a goal he was determined to reach.

And from that day, college life, the routine of sitting in dusty classrooms under some professor's thumb, became more and more irksome to him. He let everything slide; he was no college boy, and, like his mother, "no housekeeper either." After the cold weather began, he had to build a fire in the open coal stove if he wanted any heat; but he "never emptied the ashes—just let them pile up on the floor until they reached the door." His mother finally had to send up an old high school friend, Carl Burrell, from Lawrence to dig him out.

His listlessness continued; he missed Elinor, whom he saw briefly at Christmas; he didn't know if he could stick it out till the end of the term or not. Then his mother, who had taken on a new school in Methuen and was having discipline trouble, wrote, telling him she needed him to take care of some big, brutal boys she could not manage. It was an ideal excuse, and he seized on the obligation to his mother to justify running away in his own mind. He knew it wasn't the real reason, but he told himself he had to go.

He said nothing to anyone else—except Preston Shirley, the only person he said good-by to. His friend was sorry to see him leave, but made no move to dissuade him; he knew well how unhappy Rob had been. They sat up all night carrying on a turbulent, high-pitched battle of wits and saying good-by to each other.

The next day, Rob took his few belongings and left Dartmouth without even notfying the Dean's office; the term was not quite over. In one hand was his grandfather's satchel, and in the other he carried the cherished copy of the *Golden Treasury*.

Chapter 5

IN LIMBO

"I did take hold of my mother's school," Robert Frost related with satisfaction; "bought some rattans and caned those unruly boys good and plenty." They needed it, for his mother, usually capable of keeping order by her manner of sweet, quiet command, was at her wits' end to know what to do next. And Rob needed some action after his lethargy at Dartmouth. His energy, unexpected in the tall, rangy figure, took the unruly boys by surprise, and subdued them completely. He won their respect and kept it all the while he was assisting his mother at the Methuen school. She did not reproach him for taking French leave of Dartmouth before he had completed his first term, and she tried to understand what his inner concentration on writing poetry meant to him at the moment, and to his destiny. Of the latter, she was far less aware, he thought, than Elinor would have been; but Elinor was away at college, and he could not talk to her until summer.

His grandparents, however, made it plain that they were bitterly disappointed and out of patience with him. The elder Frost was hurt—that Rob should so treat a grandfather—one who had sincerely offered a college education to a promising valedictorian—put the would-be poet out of all repute in Lawrence. He could not hope to explain his case to them if he tried till doomsday. A cloud of puzzlement hung over him when he went to return his grandfather's satchel; he saw that they looked on him as "an obstinate, indecisive young fool." Maybe he was, but he had to feed the fire burning inside of him.

He read, he *studied* the paper copy of the *Golden Treasury,* found favorite poems, and pored over them as if to discover the hidden seeds of their greatness. Now and then he jotted down a few lines of his own, as he had done at Dartmouth—a couplet here, a quatrain there. Certain forms, like the ode, appealed to him more than others. He began rereading his high school pocket copy of Shakespeare. In between his teaching hours, he read, and thought, and read, and, somewhat shyly, wrote.

When the school year ended, he had to look for a job. His grandfather, hoping this would stabilize the errant grandson, made more than one offer to set him up in business. But Rob refused them; he would rather take odd jobs, the way he always had during the summer. In the fall he could still do elementary teaching along with a job; he applied at the mills for minor spots, wherever they could fit him in. His ex-classmates in Lawrence (like Ernest Jewell), as well as the Frost-Colcord clan shook their heads sadly at his strange behavior; Rob Frost, the head of his class for four years; class poet, valedictorian extraordinary, was proving himself a lazy ne'er-do-well, an aimless intellectual.

Let them think what they liked; if this was folly, it was his to pursue, not theirs. Moreover, his mother didn't mind his odd jobs. She believed in any honest work. She was with him all the way.

Summer came, bringing Elinor home from college; an honor student, she had passed the freshman finals with flying colors, and next year would be a sophomore. The lovely quality of her face had ripened into real beauty during those months, and, though she was the same age as Rob—nineteen—she seemed more mature in many ways. She listened with her sweet seriousness to his hopes and ideas, to the few lines of his poetry that he read to her as they sat on the porch swing at her parents' home in Lawrence. She

sensed that genius lay at the roots of these slender shoots, yet she
hesitated to voice her feelings beyond a certain amount of encouragement, which she gave with full sincerity. They exchanged ideas
as they had in high school, but with the subtle difference the year
apart had made in both. Robert wanted to see Elinor every night,
but she kept him on tenterhooks; her father disapproved of her
seeing one young man all the time, especially one with such a
doubtful future.

Then he couldn't see her anyway for a while, because his grandmother, always so strong in body and mind, was suddenly taken
ill, and died within a few weeks. Rob was at his grandparents'
house a great deal, helping out, like a dutiful grandson.

September came too soon, taking Elinor back to college. With
something of defiance, Rob became a mill hand, and took a full-
time job on electric lights at Arlington, the huge mill halfway between Lawrence and Methuen. He was a light-fixer in the dynamo
room, where the great black blocks generated the energy to keep
the spindles endlessly turning, turning. He had to take care of the
arc lights, replace the carbon as fast as it was consumed. He had
to scramble up tall iron ladders and fit himself into risky angles,
but he was young and agile and was soon sighting fellow workers
down between the belts and machines with shouted jokes about
the work. Even on bright days when the lights were not in use,
Rob, like Ishmael in the rigging of the *Pequod,* climbed up to
his special hideout under the broad belts and read his pocket
Shakespeare for hours.

His schedule was switched to the night shift, where he happily
discovered his high school friend, Ed Gilbert, also a Shakespeare
lover, working as a light-fixer. They found a "bible" copy on an
office shelf, and during the watches of the night, the lines of the
great plays, read aloud with stage diction, could be heard above
the hum of the generators. Sometimes the boys would break off
to delve into the meaning of the lines or confide in each other
their feelings about life in general, still in Shakespearean diction.

The mill work was like a backdrop, a stark setting for the ex-

citing drama of creation that constantly stirred the soul of the
mill hand turned poetaster. The leaves fell, the first snows came;
his mother moved the little family into one side of a square double house on Tremont Street in Lawrence. As Rob walked home
from Arlington in the dawn, his coat collar turned up against the
cold that nipped his ears, he pictured, with sudden longing, the
summertime streams and meadows, himself lolling on the river
bank, his eye lazily following the zigzag course of a butterfly
among the meadow flowers. Then he felt the same queer sensation he had before he wrote the "Noche Triste" ballad; the cold
wind was a shaft of air from some unearthly sphere, penetrating his
brain.

He ran the last few steps; he came into the house, went straight
to the kitchen, locked the door, sat down at the table and began
to write. The lines formed themselves into an ode, the design that
had so inspired Keats and some of the others in the *Golden Treasury*. His sister Jeanie, now a senior at Lawrence, came downstairs
to heat some water, tried the door and banged on it with both
fists when she couldn't get in, but Rob paid no attention. She
shouted she must get ready for school, but it was as if he had been
stone-deaf; he kept on writing, writing; occasionally crossing out
and rewriting. The pounding on the door continued. All the time
he was working, Jeanie tried to batter it down and get in, but he
could not stop. He wrote the poem "all in one go," and as his
pencil flew along the page, he "sensed that something was happening. It was like cutting along a nerve." The opening of the
second stanza,

> The gray grass is scarce dappled with the snow;
> Its two banks have not shut upon the river;

was like a proclamation of his gift for poetry.

He got something there, and he knew it. In the single line, "Its
two banks have not shut upon the river," he found himself at last.
"It was the beginning of *me*," he realized afterwards. Poetry was
"like a blush—you can get something you didn't know you had."

When he finished, he had produced an ode of true lyric quality; and if he realized, too (later on), that a poet's development is "like a waterspout at sea, he has to begin as a cloud of all the other poets he ever read," Rob Frost was just as sure that the core of this poem represented himself and no one else.

He called it simply "My Butterfly" and sent it off immediately to the *Independent;* it was only a little over a year since he had determined to submit a manuscript to that erudite publication. Weeks passed, and in that time, to keep his courage up, he mailed three more attempts to other publications. Then, wonder of wonders, toward the beginning of March—before his twentieth birthday—he received an acceptance notice from the *Independent!* The editors, William Hayes Ward and his sister Susan Hayes Ward, both adherents to classical literature, were inclined toward the poem because it was an ode, and, they mistakenly thought, a product of the school of Sidney Lanier. No mention was made of the date of publication (or the rate which would be paid on publication). Excited, Rob sent back his gratitude for the mere fact of acceptance, and received a note of real encouragement from Mr. Ward. It was the beginning of a professional literary influence in his life, and Rob answered with such eagerness he forgot to check his spelling, even to the name of the magazine. (It appeared in his greeting as *The "Independant."*)

The editors had asked for his background—professional, educational, and literary.

He replied on a sheet of lined paper from his notebook, with a broad-nibbed pen, making bold downward strokes.

In the dignified language of hopeful youth trying to sound worldly, he expressed his pleasure in the note he had received; but he made no secret of the fact that he was young and inexperienced, that this was the first poem of his that any publication had accepted. Nor did he hide the fact that his legitimate education was limited to his high school diploma and the few months at Dartmouth. He emphasized his self-education, however: his avid reading in the realm of poetic literature, his belief that "to love poetry is to study it." He admitted that the few rules he knew were his own afterthoughts.

He ended casually that there would be no objection to using his name with the poem.

He read over the letter, written on both sides of the notebook paper. He smiled to himself at the understatement in the last line. Ever since his Dartmouth days it had been coming on . . . this wish to write things and get them printed; and he certainly had no desire to be anonymous!

Evidently his editors felt that their protégé was in need of academic improvement, to say the least. They advised him to learn to spell the name of their magazine, which brought a doubtful laugh from Rob, who couldn't even remember how he had misspelled it. The worthy Dr. Ward went on to exhort him to complete his college education at all costs, go back to Dartmouth, show more stability. It sounded just like Grandfather Frost, and instinctively Rob rebelled. One grandfather was enough. Next time he would write to Miss Susan Ward, who offered constructive comments on further poems he submitted, and showed that she was warmhearted and wise, as well as intellectual.

There was still no word of publication date, but Rob had real impetus now, and every minute he could spare, on or off the job, he spent in composing or studying poetry. During his lunch hour, he went for a walk in the fields beyond the factory so he could be alone to think, to compose, jot down a word or two; it was spring, and the seedlings of his art were growing like the green fields he headed for when the bells sounded the noon hour; sometimes he wrote to Elinor, following the good news of acceptance with his hopes and dreams of greater achievement. He had seen her only a few times—at Christmas and between terms; he could hardly wait till she came home for the summer. There came a day when he dreamed too long, and was brought back to reality by the first clang of the closing bells for lunch hour; he started to run, but before he reached the gate, the knells came slower, "like the count of fate": if he didn't get there before they stopped, he would be locked out for half an hour, "his time be lost, his pittance docked." He ran like the wind, but just as he sprinted up to the gates, they closed, locking automatically.

For a moment he stood there, "rebuked and unemployed," but suddenly rebellion in him rose high, and he shouted to the closed doors, "You can't do this to me!"

Instead of waiting till the thirty-minute penance was up, he walked out on the job, "a lone striker." It took many years before he could see himself in a clear light, standing there on a sunny spring day, defiant and fed up with rules and regulations. When he did, in the days of many strikes and dark depression, the poem was a monument to mill workers, including "A Lone Striker."

He strode to his mother's school and announced that he was quitting the mill. He would rather teach elementary school, and he would find one for himself. His mother accepted his decision with little comment. Rob's life was his own, as long as he contributed to the household expenses. Within a few days, he had found a post; and although he could hardly bear the commotion connected with orthography, which he, of all people, was assigned to teach in the district school, for the time being it was better than the eternal routine of the mill. Perhaps he would have more time for poetry. A letter of praise from Miss Ward proved he had talent, no doubt of it. He was so grateful for words that were not adverse criticism that he answered her at once, submitting three of his most recent attempts, and pouring out his soul in a letter dated April 22, 1894.

He offered his thanks unlimited, and repeated his own belief in his ability; the scope of his ambition was so broad that his failures only served to justify it! Then, since the lady had asked to know more of him, he gave her a glimpse into his life, intellectual and otherwise. He liked to read novels occasionally—Thomas Hardy, who taught him the "good use of a few words"; Scott and Stevenson, whose prose inspired him with the thought that Scotsmen, himself included, were bound to be romanticists. He listed his favorite poems: Keats's "Hyperion," Shelley's "Prometheus,"

Tennyson's spelled ("Tenneson's") "Morte d'Arthur," and Browning's "Saul"—all poems about "giants."

After such an auspicious beginning, he hurried to confess that his job in the district school was so uncongenial to him that it had become a test of physical endurance; when he wasn't teaching, he spent hours lying around, "consciously sleeping or unconsciously waking." As if this were not bad enough, he added that he was constantly feeling "iratable." He explained that his nerves, so susceptible to sound, brought on the condition, when he could neither read nor write. He did find a few hours for study, however, and assured her that he had great hopes for the future.

He went on to speak of the trials he had had in revising one of the poems he was submitting; he worried about the last line, and "that consonant syllable of mine, 'l', spoils a word"; what should he do with it? "The only thing I can think of is 'eddifying,' which weakens the impression." After a few more deliberations on the wording, he ended abruptly, "Yours by right of discovery R. L. Frost."

His letter made a rather shocking impression on his spinster mentor. For a young man of twenty to confess casually that he spent hours lying around, that he was bored and irritated with his profession, one she considered among the noblest, put her out of patience. From the number of words misspelled, he might do well to study a little in the subject he was teaching. Her words of genteel but firm reproval, sent along with a volume of Lanier and her advice on the poem in question, brought a quick response.

The fledgling poet wrote in defense of his position, hoping to correct the impression of a callow, distasteful youth, which he must have given Miss Ward in his rash remarks. After thanking her for the copy of Lanier's poems, he hastened to tell her that his pride, like that of most provincials who affect Bohemianism and long for experience above all else, saw nothing degrading in teaching. He had sold newspapers on the streets of San Francisco, worked in the mills and on the farms in New England, he told her stoutly, adding that his pride was peculiar.

Then he turned to the subject of his poetry, his efforts to revise the latest he had submitted to her. He had tried unsuccessfully "to induce the passion" that was the spirit of the poem originally; he canceled one line and altered two others, but he was still greatly dissatisfied with it. Nevertheless, he was putting the whole at her disposal. On an impulse, he signed the letter "Really Robert L. Frost," and mailed it at once, lest he should lose his nerve and hold back the poem.

Elinor arrived home from college with further academic achievements to her credit and the upsetting news that she had taken a job with a composer in Boston for the summer. She was full of plans for her stay in the big city; during the two or three evenings Rob saw her, she was so preoccupied with busy preparations (or he felt she was) that she could not give him the consideration or attention he had been hoping, longing to receive. His own achievement of having had a poem accepted for publication seemed to lose its aura of enchantment, its momentousness. His news seemed to pale before her bright plans, and he stood around confused, inarticulate—and awkward, seedy-looking young fellow, vague and dreamy—instead of showering her with all that filled his heart.

She took off for Boston in a flurry of activity; all he could see was the tip of her ruffled parasol as the train pulled out of the depot. He went to work on a farm, and when the haying was over, he had some time for poetry, struggling to rework the fragments he had sent to Miss Ward for criticism, trying to improve his meter and form. In one of her letters she mentioned a meeting in Boston, and he was eager to arrange a time; it would give him a chance to see Elinor.

She did not reply immediately, so he went to the city without an appointment. He got a little job as an agent, trying to sell a Shakespeare reader to the public, to arrange bookings in small theaters for the one-man performances.

Elinor had precious little time to spare for him; he felt lost, frustrated. He hoped at least to meet his editor, and wrote anxiously on August 22nd, hoping it was not too late for a meeting with the redoubtable Miss Ward. If he could get close to someone in her position, it would increase his stature as a writer in Elinor's eyes. In his frantic mood, he misspelled words and pleaded for understanding of his childishness in regard to the revision of a poem he had submitted. Then in the next breath he vowed he was learning to spell, was writing better poetry. He would soon "throw off the mask and declare for literateur mean it poverty or riches." But for all his bravado, he received no appointment with Susan Ward. He tried to make a go of his job; he tried to write some new poems; but he had little success at either one. It was a waiting time and he chafed at the indecision of his life.

Soon the summer was over. A few weeks had shown the determined, *shall*-be poet that he was far less a promoter (even of Shakespeare) than teacher, so he went back to Lawrence; Elinor would be there shortly, as she had to get ready for her third—and, she hoped, her final—year in college. Perhaps he could settle things between them before she left. . . .

He was doomed to disappointment again. Afterwards he told the story simply: "Then she came home but when I called on her she did not want me to come in—the president of her college was there. He thought I was a fool! I must have looked awful to Elinor. I looked worse than unpromising—everybody was broken up by the way I *looked*. I had no sense of being defiant—I just went this vague way. . . .

"As a result of that evening I quit—I was persuaded at last that Elinor did not love me. I went off to Boston for a day and was really convinced."

He made his meager report to the agency he was working for —and resigned. He didn't know what he wanted to do—outside of writing—and at the moment he didn't care; all he knew was that Elinor did not love him. As he wandered around the Common, he believed beyond doubt that life would never turn out right.

When he came home in the evening, he found that his mother was holding a religious meeting for Swedenborgians in her schoolroom, as she often did. Perhaps it would bring him some comfort; he stopped in and sat down quietly in the back row. Some fifteen or twenty people were gathered together to study the doctrines to which his mother was dedicated; yet as soon as she saw him, she called out to him and came over to put in his hand a letter from Elinor. Surely his love was star-crossed, but it was still alive, vital to his very existence.

To maintain that existence was constant trial. He made an attempt at newspaper work, as a reporter for the Lawrence *Sentinel;* his father had been a newspaperman, after all, and it would mean writing—of a sort—for his livelihood. The work, however, was a far cry from the creative art he longed to master; moreover, he was distracted with thoughts of Elinor and went about his assignments in desultory fashion, preoccupied with the problem of showing her, showing them all. He went to the job printer near the *Sentinel* office, and arranged to have a volume of his poetry published at his own expense.

It was a very small volume called *Twilight,* the first (and only) printing, just two copies—one for each: Elinor and Robert. That was all. He picked out covers of pebbled leather for his book and pages of fine linen. He selected for the contents five of his best poems so far: "My Butterfly," "Twilight," "Summering," "The Falls," and "An Unhistoric Spot." When he came to call for the copies and the printer put them into his hand, he felt an elation flooding through him like the tingling of an electric current in his veins—if his first volume had been gilt-edged and hand-tooled, it could not have been more valuable in his eyes.

His plan was simple, and he set out for St. Lawrence College with a high heart one fine October morning, ready to prove to his love that he was worthy to stand beside her. He rode the train to Canton, New York with jubilant impatience singing in his heart.

When he proudly presented his tenderly nurtured offering to his girl, however, she accepted it with cool gravity, distant as the New Hampshire hills. She would be glad to show the book to her professors in the English department—she would say no more.

Which of them had taken her from him? he wondered. He was convinced her mind was on someone else. Then came the blow to his whole being: the professors railed at his poetry; the five poems he had so carefully selected, when read aloud, had invoked nothing but good-natured ridicule for the hayseed poet—ertswhile farm hand, mill hand! Let him study, let him learn a little more—

But he had heard enough, he had learned enough. Stunned, blinded by rage, he took the little volume, his first published work, and tore it to pieces with his own two hands.

He could not go back to Lawrence. He could not face his family; more than that, he could not face himself as the world outside must see him; he would run away. . . .

He headed south, "out of time," out of his mind in pain and anger. Down through the Adirondacks, the Appalachians, the eastern Smokies. His meager funds gave out soon after he left New York, yet he kept going blindly south, blazing his own trail in

> a pathless wood
> Where your face burns and tickles with the cobwebs
> Broken across it, and one eye is weeping
> From a twig's having lashed across it open.

He didn't know or care where he was going, he just kept on and on; he didn't let anyone know where he was, he sent no address. He bartered for bread with the small store of energy he had left, swallowing his pride with the morsel, doing any job at all, it didn't matter. He had wanted to show Elinor, now he wanted to hurt her someway. He tried drinking—drunk on applejack, on corn liquor —but it only made him sick, and he was sick enough at heart as it was.

He finally came upon a southern city—Elizabeth City, and then Kitty Hawk—where some were kind to an emaciated, ragged young man whose blue eyes were still burning with outraged wrath but whose body had been pushed to the point of exhaustion.

That year was a depression year, and he had found plenty of company, unwanted, as he made his way on foot along dusty roads toward New York City; people from mill towns were scurrying to the city in the hope of getting jobs; they were everywhere Rob went—on the railroad tracks, on the freight cars. Hardly knowing what he was doing or saying, he walked with them, he rode the rods with them; much as he wanted to, he found it hard to get away from them. It was Election Day when he got to New York City, and with most of the few dollars he had in his pocket, he bought a boat ticket and "sailed" away as far as those few dollars would take him.

He got off at Norfolk, wandered aimlessly around the docks awhile, and finally set off on foot again, down through the Dismal Swamp on a one-plank path; it was dank, neglected woodland, wild and eerie, but he was too angry and heartsore to be scared. Then he veered toward the shore again and "picked up another boat for Elizabeth City." He had no money for a ticket, so he paid his fare by "helping a little"—swabbing the deck, relieving the stoker. When the boat docked, he leaped

> out and down along
> past Elizabeth City

in the neighborhood of the now-famous Kitty Hawk, on the beach at Nag's Head. Here he

> fell in among
> Some kind of committe
> From Elizabeth City

a passe of duck-hunters perhaps, who were kind to him and fed him, and gave him a swig from their flasks; included him

> Like a little brother
> In their revelry.

They bade him stay, but that night he stole

> Off on the unbounded
> Beaches where the whole
> Of the Atlantic pounded.

Here he "fell in with a lone coast guard" and walked along the beach with him in the moonlight and listened to the sad story of Theodosia Burr, daughter of a traitor.

He strayed back to Elizabeth City, not knowing where to go when he got there, and wandered into a saloon, where he knew he could get a free lunch for the price of one beer—all he had in his pocket. From his childhood days in San Francisco, when he made electioneering rounds with his father, he had learned to be friendly with barkeeps. Here the genial saloonkeeper who struck up a conversation with him tried, and almost succeeded in getting the runaway a job, "either as a teacher in Mr. Sheep's Academy or as a reporter on Mr. Lamb's newspaper." Rob, drowsy with beer and the long hike he had taken, half-homesick in spite of his lingering hurt, was fuzzy in his mind and didn't really care. . . .

He set off on foot again without bidding anyone good-by, taking odd jobs for food, sleeping whenever he got tired. Soon he came to a great lumber camp, larger than any he had seen up north. The camp boss said he could work for his food and a night's lodging, so he joined the lumberjacks, "a lot of mighty men, mostly colored," and spent a great night in camp, and could have stayed longer if he had wanted to, but he didn't know what he wanted.

He turned north unconsciously, aimlessly, without much more object in life than he had in going south. A job here, a job there. Somewhere near Bull Run, he stumbled on a tramp's jungle just as they were starting their fitful fires for the rank coffee and beans they offered him. They were all manner of men, he found—whatever made them hoboes would make a history by itself—and he spent an entertaining night listening to "all sorts of stories by daring travelers about their travels"; some were brutal, some were funny, all were lawless in the sense that they were bound to no set of rules by government. Here, too, he might have stayed, but "partly shy and partly scared," he "fled a free society." Reaching the law-abiding city of Baltimore, he got a job in a grocery store; and there, somehow—it might have been through a note he did not even know he had written—his mother located him and sent for him to come home.

By the first of December, he was strong enough to look the world of Lawrence in the eye again.

He saw the issue of the *Independent* lying on the hall table as soon as he came into the house on Tremont Street—there, on the front page, was his poem, "My Butterfly. An Elegy by Robert Lee Frost." How impressive it looked! He read it over and over, gloating. He glanced at the date: November 8, 1894. If he had waited a week or so, he would not have needed to run away; he would have thrust the magazine under the noses of those professors like a rapier! He laughed with fiendish delight at the thought, but sobered immediately; what must Miss Ward think of his silence?

He sent her a long letter of gratitude and explanation, telling her where he had been for the past four weeks or more—he could not calculate exactly how long it was because he had been "put out of time for a little while." Without revealing the cause of his trip, he implied that it had been made in a mood of desperation. But he wanted Miss Ward to know how deeply he appreciated the sight of his poem published on the front page of an important periodical like the *Independent*. His enthusiasm, always "verging on egotism," soared and would have spilled over the letter in a fountain of self-praise, but that he assumed an attitude—usually one of despondency—in order to be dignified. He admitted that in this way he always confused himself trying to be modest; and now he could not refrain for long from expressing his sheer enjoyment of his poem, as if he had written it lately and not eight months before.

He closed with a paragraph of his feeling for sound as an element of poetry, "one but for which imagination would become reason." In this way he justified the use of dialect, as contributing to the illusion and giving "the artist the courage of his imaginings." He cited the influence of sound on Kipling; he, Rob Frost, was so fond of sound that he wished Kipling would write more poetry!

His final sentence was a promise to send one or two more poems when he found time to revise them.

Both Miss Ward and her brother were moved by the young poet's eager appreciation, his artless comment, "And the poem does look well—don't you think it does?" Such a spirit deserved continued support, and, as an initial step, Miss Ward aranged the long-sought meeting in Boston, at the new North Station, with the added purpose of delivering in person a fifteen-dollar check in payment for "My Butterfly." Rob was both excited and shy at the idea of this first encounter with his editor, but from the moment he met her, the robust spinster, warmhearted and highly intelligent, put him at his ease; they were friends, colleagues. It was a friendship that would last many years.

Rob could stand up straight again, strong enough to vow that he would not be thrown off balance again. His mother and Jeanie had shared his joy of professional publication, and his grandfather, if a bit grudging, admitted that the irresponsible Rob must have some talent, or a magazine like the *Independent* would not print his poem—on the front page, moreover.

Still in a glow of inner strength, it was a determined Rob who tramped through blinding snow to Elinor's house when she came home for Christmas—who demanded to see his love alone, to thrash things out. His copy of the *Independent* in hand, he confronted her with the proof of his ability to write poetry; let her show that to the St. Lawrence professors who had snubbed him! Then a turbulent scene ensued, stormier than the blizzard that raged outside the living-room windows. And when it was over, Elinor White was engaged to Robert Frost, no shilly-shallying about it.

For her part, once the betrothal was firmly fixed, Elinor caught the fever of conviction from Rob; let her father object all he wished. He could say nothing to change her mind. Her teachers had told her she could graduate from college in three years if her marks kept up, and when she left after vacation, it was for her final term. Robert and she would be married some time after graduation.

Rob was at greater peace with himself than he had been at any time since his own graduation from high school. He was still restless as far as his work was concerned, and soon after the new year gave up his job on the *Sentinel*. Reporting was distasteful to him. "Too much prying into the affairs of others," he said.

Before his twenty-first birthday, he was teaching in a district school once more. His girl was his—and he his girl's—and his mind was free to create poetry.

Chapter 6

A FAMILY ENTERPRISE

In the fall, Belle Frost embarked on a daring venture of her own: she took a house on Essex Street in Lawrence and opened a private school. Jeanie, whose record in high school was a close rival of Rob's became her assistant; and the two who were

> less than two
> But more than one as yet

made up the rest of the faculty. Rob taught arithmetic, Elinor taught French, both dreaming of the day they would be wed.

About twenty pupils came every day to the long classroom, formed by two rooms across the center of the house. Above the fireplace was a blackboard, on which a different poem appeared each day, to be copied into notebooks and learned by heart. Here Rob's mother made her last valiant stand for personal expression in a life marked by self-denial and the constant strain of suppressed worry. Her pupils came to love the carelessly dressed, spare figure who stood before them every day, holding the little school together with her calm, quiet manner, lightened by the gleam of humor in her blue eyes. "Her frame was angular, rather loosely knit," one of them, Clara Searle, described her long afterward, "the type of figure we associate in a man with Lincoln . . . the large, broad brow of the thinker; the eyes deep-set, somewhat cavernous, blue, with a humorous kindly twinkle; a large, generous mouth. The heavy graying hair was coiled at her neck, and always a stray lock detached itself." Her eyeglasses never stayed put. Her shirtwaist and skirt were never quite held together by her belt. Her fingers were usually caked with chalk dust, which now and then left a smudge on her face when she pushed back the straying strand of hair.

Just outside the schoolroom door, her fat little dog Keno, who followed her everywhere, lay comfortably snoozing until classes were over. At the far end of the room, a few chairs faced a desk in front of three long bay windows; here the arithmetic class met the first thing in the morning. Luckily, the door from the dining room opened directly into the bay, so that Rob, who was always the last to finish his morning coffee and toast, could go right in to his desk, still with the aroma of buttered toast around him. The children were always waiting for him when he finally opened the door and sat down casually opposite them, his blue eyes vague with dreams. As soon as he began the lesson, however, he became alert, and he gave his pupils the same sort of attention his mother did, treating each child as an individual.

He would explain a problem two or three times to a little girl or boy who didn't grasp it at first, but occasionally he lost his patience. Once Clara Searle insisted stubbornly, after several examples, "I can't understand it; I can't, I can't!"

He came back at her sharply, "Yes you can, Clara Searle, if you want to, but you have made up your mind that you won't see it." And his small pupil, surprised, subsided meekly.

Over in another part of the schoolroom, Elinor was sounding the syllables in beginning French, and Rob strained to catch the music of her voice over the multiplication tables one of his charges was reciting. Elinor's gentle gravity, the purity of her profile, the sparkle that would flash unexpectedly in her great brown eyes, made of the waiting months a constant taunt, but propriety demanded that at least a year elapse between engagement and marriage.

Eventually, in December, 1895, the three months passed, bringing the wedding day, with the first deep snows, the whirling blizzards of the year before; but today no similar storm raged inside, only a deep joy between the two who had so early walked into each other's lives, now linked, they hoped, for all time by bonds of love and faith. Both had barely come of age, and the years stretched ahead of them, full of promise of riches known to them alone. Half a dozen poems were all they had to start with—"The Flower Boat," "Now Close the Windows," "Waiting—Afield at Dusk," "Hannibal," "The Trial by Existence," and "Revelation" —but the handful represented a mine more valuable than silver or gold, to their way of thinking. Never mind how much Elinor's father might frown upon the match from a practical standpoint!

The two continued teaching in the little school on Essex Street, removed from the problem of finances by Rob's mother, who, as always, handled the purse strings. The family faculty of four worked well together, following Belle Frost's lead in directing the minds of pupils to the best advantage of each. Rob did not have to use his rattans to keep order. If a discipline problem— or an academic one— arose, Belle, accompanied by Keno, made a friendly call at the home of the child in question, and the matter would be straightened out amicably to the satisfaction of all, including the pupil. Scholarliness was rewarded with books to fire the imagination of young minds, pointing them toward a taste for literature.

In spite of his mother's zeal, however, Rob could not be content with elementary teaching. His brain was occupied with iambics rather than multiplication tables. He had Elinor as an ally now, and even when he could not produce a poem, he kept up the struggle, confident of her approval, her joy in reading the verses he did complete. By now he was used to the lulls, followed by pickups. Whatever came of his creative moments, he had to push on, to proceed with his headstrong folly, brooking interference from no one, whether he was a puzzle to everyone, including himself, or no. He was not sure yet what he was about, except that he enjoyed writing poems above anything else; and he knew he could write at least a little poem. That much he was certain of, though he might have small sense of direction or destiny yet.

Periods of discouragement were inevitable, however, even a month after marriage, when the passion of his love ran high, and on one hand life was brimming with happiness. Around the middle of January (1896), he sent a frustrated letter to Miss Ward, along with a few fragments of poems, on which he had struggled unsuccessfully and finally given up. "I fear I am not a poet, or but a very incomprehensible one," he concluded sadly (and not quite honestly), hoping the lady would correct him on his estimate. Surely it was not for him to condemn his own poems; let the editor do that if she must; he would be more than grateful just to hear from her.

Six months later he was still writing in the same vein. School had closed, and he had slept practically around the clock for a whole week, so he felt quite rested physically, but his spirits were low, and he had moments of dejection when he considered himself a failure. Striking a rather theatrical note, he told Miss Ward that he was anxious to publish one more poem before he died.

He enclosed two poems, one of which was accepted for publication in the August 20th issue of the *Independent,* a matter of rejoicing for the young couple. Elinor, for her part, realized on her wedding day that the poet (Robert Lee Frost) and her lover-husband Rob were one and the same man, and there was no dividing his loyalty to his art. The old saying, "with his head in the clouds," which her father frequently used in reference to Rob, certainly applied, yet she did not censure him for his other-worldliness—not even when their first child, a boy, was born on September 25th, and Rob, though pleased, hardly seemed aware that the event was of great moment to her. He helped her choose a name—Eliot—for the baby, but he did not bother to announce its arrival to Miss Ward until December, in an afterthought: "As nothing that happened matters much and as most of my thoughts are about myself I am always at a loss for likely subject matter. I am the father of a son if that is anything. . . ." Elinor knew instinctively that it would always—must always—be this way with Rob, and she accepted her fate unhesitatingly, for she had married a poet—and, she believed with all her heart, a great one. She read his latest poem, "Caesar's Lost Transport Ships" in the *Independent* on January 14, 1897, with deep pride.

She had given up her post in the school just before Eliot's birth; Rob kept his until the end of the spring term; but they agreed it was difficult to raise a baby in a private school, and the young couple wanted to be by themselves, anyway, now that they had become a family. The summer found them and the baby in a rented old house at Salisbury Point, where Rob relaxed after the long school year, read the classic poets, and wrote his own metered lines (mostly pentameters) when they came to him. Now and then he and Elinor pondered over what to do next. Teaching in his mother's school was hardly a lifetime career. How was he to earn a living?

He was in the attic one rainy day reading Tacitus, when all of a sudden it occurred to him: since he had experience in elementary schools, why couldn't he go to college for his degree and become a college teacher? He went downstairs, where Elinor was bathing the baby, and talked over the idea with her. They discussed the pros and cons of the move while the baby kicked and crowed in his bath, wrapping his small fingers around the forefinger Rob held out to him. The upshot of the matter was that Rob decided to apply for admission to Harvard. As if to strengthen his claim, his latest poem, "Warning," was published in the *Independent* on September 9, 1897; he was practically a "regular" in the magazine!

His letter to Dean Briggs, which gave a complete account of his educational background (including his retreat from Dartmouth, unglossed), received a favorable reply, and Grandfather Frost offered to pay the tuition, while Elinor's mother, who had always been fond of Rob, rented a house in Boston for the little family. Rob enrolled as a freshman in Greek and Latin, Philosophy, and the standard freshman English A; he tried to get out of the last, but "comp." was mandatory for all beginners. The course, taught by Alfred E. Sheffield, brother-in-law to another poet-in-embryo, T. S. Eliot, was a nuisance and a bore. Rob was far beyond a daily theme, and detested both the class and its instructor. His tall, lean figure, the evanescent gleam of humor lighting up his moody, sensitive face, the deep blue eyes shining or scowling by turns, puzzled and unnerved Sheffield. When Rob handed in a copy of his poem, "Now Close the Windows," the instructor lifted a haughty eyebrow and asked whether this was written for his class.

Rob shook his head, unperturbed. It was a substitute for the daily theme, he explained briefly, mentioning one or two of the poems the *Independent* had printed.

"So we have published poetry, have we," Sheffield's tone was sarcastic, snide. To him, the idea of a freshman who showed professional talent was insubordinating, and he was inclined to discount the value of the work.

Rob did not deign to answer him. The next class was Greek, the subject he was most interested in mastering, one of the main reasons he had returned to college. His fascination with classical verse had not lessened in the five years since he was graduated from high school, and he made a brilliant record which won him the prized Detur, highest Harvard honor in the classics. In view of the fact that he did not have much study time because of a little teaching job in a North Cambridge public school, which he took to help out financially, he did remarkably well during the first year.

Not that he was a campus leader; it was too late; he was a family man for one thing, and his marital status set him apart from most undergraduates. He felt a shyness amounting to diffidence with the fancy-free freshmen, and was too deeply in love with Elinor to want to overcome it. He made friends with only two of his fellow-students, both on the same bench with him in Latin class. One was a Negro (who sat on one end) and the other a white Southerner (who sat on the other end). Robert, seated somewhere in the middle, had a certain affinity for both because they were as devoted to Latin poetry as he.

As a result of his record, Robert Frost won, as he said, a "big scholarship" for his sophomore year at Harvard, but for some reason (he did not know why, at that time) nothing went well during his second year. He could not seem to get back into the routine of college life. He did not continue his teaching job in Cambridge, but kept leaving town during the term to look after his mother's school in Lawrence; she had begun to fail in health, and was having great difficulty in holding her own as an experimentalist in education. Rob was torn between helping her and furthering his own education, between working to become a scholarly professor and a creative artist.

The second conflict, subconscious, not recognized till later, proved too much for him. "A feeling of suspended animation" came over him, as it had at Dartmouth. He was restless, possessed by "a spring-fever sort of puzzlement" again. He went around in the same sort of daze as before. He knew Elinor was pregnant, expecting another baby in April, and he would have to have some means of livelihood for their increasing family; but he could not make the situation seem real. Instead, the fever became real, physical as well as mental. He became "terribly sick, as if something were very wrong with heart or stomach. Trouble in the solar plexis." Elinor, none too strong herself, and with small Eliot to care for, was glad to have her mother's help in nursing Rob. But he did not respond, and finally had to resign from the sophomore class at the end of March, to the Dean's regret.

"The doctor thought I would die. He sent me home to die."

Through the haze of fever, he watched Elinor prepare for their departure; then, just before they were to leave, the baby arrived—a daughter Lesley, born on April 28, 1899.

*   *   *

Still not quite realizing what had happened to him, Rob began the slow climb back to health on a small chicken farm belonging to relatives in Methuen. The doctor had suggested that the fresh air and quiet of the country might be the single hope of recovery from the strange malaise that was torturing the young poet who could not find his way.

As the network of nerves deep inside his body began to calm down, under the healing influence of routine physical labor—mixing the mash, gathering eggs, tending the barnyard flock from peeps to pullets—he began to see clearly again, began to think poetry again, and to feel the urge to express himself. If he and Elinor could be by themselves, the impulse might crystallize into word-song, but here, under the roof of older relatives, he felt confined within the daily chores. Sometimes, when he and Elinor went for a ride in the wagon after taking the eggs to market, they looked around the countryside for a likely farm—one just large enough for Rob to work and have time left over for poetry—but the kind they had in mind was hard to find, and they had no money to buy it anyway.

Life kept badgering him. In the fall, Belle Frost became seriously ill with cancer; she could not open the school, but, hoping to recover by the second term, went to a sanitarium in Penacook, New Hampshire. Her pupils, who could not wait for their education, enrolled in other schools, ending the experiment on Essex Street. In looking back on his mother's courageous attempt, Rob wondered if he should have stuck with the school. "It just might have been a success," he thought bitterly. That much he might have done for his mother.

She did not improve, and as the first winter of the new century was ushered in, Rob and Elinor went as often as they could to see her. In the spring, as they were driving back one afternoon, they came upon a small farm—thirty acres in West Derry, New Hampshire, only twelve miles from Lawrence. Neglected and run-down, field daisies and dandelions from the meadows spilling into the front yard, a little rise of ground between the clapboard house and the road, the place had immediate appeal for the young pair who pulled up to read the roadside "For Sale" sign. The thirty acres included an orchard, fields, pasture, woodland, and spring— all for $1,800. Elinor and Rob Frost looked at each other and knew they had found their farm.

Often and often they passed by, every time they went to see Rob's mother, and each time the place in West Derry seemed to be more their own. But how to buy it?

In the middle of July, tragedy struck their lives like a thunder-bolt: Eliot, their first-born, not quite four years old, was suddenly taken ill and died within a few days. Both were grief-stricken; Elinor was inconsolable. No man, even the sensitive Rob, could find words that would soften the blow for her. It was not man's province to understand the deep secret sorrow of womankind over loss of a first-born. They harried each other, trying to find a way out of darkness.

If relatives had not been hovering (and at the same time frown-ing) over them, it would have been easier. Both longed to escape to the little farm they had found in Derry; but how to make it really theirs? Rob, having twice failed his grandfather in making good the backing the old gentleman had provided for his educa-tion, could not bring himself to present a third request. Instead it was Elinor who, almost with relief, found the strength to make the initial approach. With Puritan directness, she asked Grandfather Frost outright if he would buy the farm for them. Surprisingly, he agreed at once. But before the matter was settled, he wanted to get things straight with Robert.

"Shall I give you a year?" he asked his grandson. "I know what you are up to," he added with a shake of his white head; no use beating around the bush about the fact that Rob wanted to write poetry. "Will you settle down if I give you a year to try this out?"

And Rob, elated by the prospect of escape to peaceful solitude, "struck a great auctioneer's pose, and dared him with: 'Give me twenty, give me twenty!' "

But in his heart he hoped it would not take that long.

Chapter 7

THE CHOSEN WAY

Then all was peace—the sort of serenity the two had been searching for since their marriage. The isolated life in Derry, the sight of gently rolling hills and slender valleys, threaded with meandering streams, brought the sense of peace so necessary to the poetic turn of mind. The move was made during the Indian-summer weather of early October (1900), when fields were already brown, and withered curls of cornstalks were beginning to crumple over the bright heads of pumpkins; but the prospect of the future lent a springtime fragrance to the air that Robert and Elinor Frost breathed as they went about settling in their first real home.

The house itself was not unusual—typically New England, the bay windows across the front; the sheltered comfortable side porch, shaded by an apple tree; the long narrow ell, connecting the kitchen with the barn; the outhouse on a pleasant knoll some distance away, all stood for rural life in the New Hampshire region around the turn of the century. At night the only light they had (except when the moon shone brightly through the windows) came from kerosene lamps and the rosy glow of the coal stove. Yet the young Frosts settled in with a sigh of glad relief and went

76

about their chores with the happiness of those who have escaped
to life from a small room where they had been suffocating.

Up to now, all their living arrangements had been temporary;
the farm gave them a feeling of permanence. And when Rob's
mother died in November, only a month after they had moved,
the step he had taken became all the more final; he knew he could
not go back from the fate he had chosen. Belle Frost was only
fifty-six years old when her "trial by existence" closed, and her son,
at twenty-six, was just beginning to test his will to live by his creative art. Whether he would succeed or not, only time could tell;
but no matter if it took twenty years or one, he meant to allow
himself full opportunity.

To be sure, his distant goal made of him a dreamy-eyed, indif-
ferent farmer who worked the land by fits and starts, who reversed
the ancient farm routine and milked "the only cow" at midnight
and 1 P.M. so that he could study, wrestle with words, shaping the
contour of a poem while other farmers slept; sleeping late while
they shaped the contour of the land. His neighbors scarcely knew
him, except by the strangeness of his farming, the reputed glow
of the kerosene lamp in the kitchen window (reported by those
who chanced to pass on rare occasions when they were out late)—
a yellow gleam that lit his reading sometimes until dawn.

Oh, he did his share of farming, but when he ploughed a field,
the furrows might run zigzag; when he planted, the seeds were
buried with apple blossoms, a "spring-time passion for the earth."
His air of abstraction might puzzle his French-Canadian neighbor
when they met to mend the stone wall between the properties, but
Rob did not mind what others thought. "I am the most unconscious thing," he admitted to Elinor. "I never know where I am
when things are going on." She smiled, knowing what he meant.
When the warm winds came, she shared his feeling for the outdoors, and both of them took fresh delight in their home, their
pastoral isolation from relatives. They sometimes felt they should
make an attempt at being lonely and remorseful, but they could
only sit side by side, looking like a pair of roguish, impertinent

angels. Try as they might, they could not feel "forsaken," the poet declared happily in meter.

In lines as yet unwritten, he cried out "to the thawing wind" to "burst into his narrow stall"; he welcomed the teasing zephyrs that swung the pictures on the wall of the corner where he worked, rattled his scribbled pages, and scattered his poems across the kitchen floor. "Turn the poet out of door," he called jubilantly in his heart.

He and Elinor traversed the obstinate "west-running brook" on the road to Derry; they gathered rose pogonias from the "saturated meadow" where "every second spear Seemed tipped with wings of color," and prayed "that in the general mowing That place might be forgot." Or, if Elinor could not go with him, Rob would bring her an armful of flowers as "the measure of the little while" he had been "long" away.

It was as if their love, so nearly blighted by well-meaning but meddlesome interference and tragedy, was blossoming anew, with a fullness neither had known before. This was "the time when after doubt Our love came back amain," as the poet was to sing in "A Line Storm Song."

During the day, Rob might spend a morning "amid lolling juniper reclined," summoning his muse when he should have been mending walls or mowing; but as a rule, he managed, albeit in haphazard order, to get his farming done. Then at night, when the chores were out of the way and the house quiet after bedtime, he would take two books from the shelf—the well-worn high school copies of Shakespeare and Virgil's *Eclogues* that he had always studied—to sit reading, now and then jotting down a few metered lines or images in the nickel notebook he carried around in his pocket. Outside, the hush of after-dark was broken only by the hoot of an owl or the sighing of the wind in the trees against the house. Elinor often sat up with him in the rocking-chair they had brought from his mother's house; her hands were busy with thread and needle as she patched and darned and "made-do" the family clothing from one year to the next. She spoke rarely, knowing full well that these were Rob's best hours for concentration; but she was an eager listener if he felt like reading—perhaps a scene from *Coriolanus* or *A Winter's Tale,* or a dialog of Virgil.

Occasionally, he would try his own words out loud to see if the rhythm was right; but he did not like to reveal, even to Elinor, the bits and pieces of syllable and sound that went to build the structure of a poem. As soon as it was complete, he was more than ready to put it to the test of speech, but until that moment the workings were too deep a part of him. ("You have to be secretive to secrete anything," he would often say.) When Elinor, too worn out with the day's household cares to stay awake any longer, dropped off to sleep in the rocker or went upstairs to bed, Rob would study on by himself, until his straining eyes refused to follow the print before he blew out the lamp and followed her to their room above the kitchen.

The poems came slowly, and he made no frenzied attempts to hurry them. If a month passed, or two, or three, without a finished product, he kept his patience; he knew it would come eventually. If the struggle between train of thought and mechanics of meter became unsolvable, unendurable, he could always get perspective on it by stepping out to gaze at the stars or going for a walk in a nearby wood, breathing in the fragance of new-mown hay (or in winter, the freshness of new-fallen snow). A nighttime country walk was all he needed to clear his head.

Sometimes, after weeks of meditation on a theme, the poems came "all in one go" like his earliest attempts, and then he would send them out quickly, hoping for a speedy acceptance; but more often than not, they came back, unwanted, unrecognized even as promising. One of these, "Bond and Free," a four-stanza work containing an intricate rhyme scheme, and one of his most subtle love lyrics, bore the word "Rejected" like a burning brand in red on the face of the cherished composition itself. Unable to bear the disfigurement, he hid it away for the day he felt strong enough to send it out again, if such a time should ever come. At these moments, it was Elinor who stood firm, comforting him and shielding

him as much as she could from the unfeeling world outside, re-
newing his faith in his poetry by her own.

Yet she kept him down to earth, reminding him gently to milk
the cow or fetch a pail of water from the spring when the "dauntless wings" of thought carried him too far afield for the human
touch.

And if, occasionally, they had their differences of opinion, the
incident jolted them into recognizing the individual in each,
though their lives were so closely bound together. It served Robert
as inspiration for a touching love sonnet, "A Dream Pang"— an
immortal note of reconciliation after a lovers' quarrel. For they
were still young lovers, passionate yet reserved, who could not
bear to be more than a little apart:

> I'm going out to clean the pasture spring; *
> I'll only stop to rake the leaves away
> (And wait to watch the water clear, I may):
> I shan't be gone long.—You come too.

Late that summer (1901), Grandfather Frost died unexpectedly,
leaving the farm property to Rob on a ten-year holding basis, at
the end of which he would be given title, but not before. The old
gentleman had been canny enough to provide a will which would
insure that his errant grandson stayed put at least ten years—more
than enough time to prove his mettle, yet only half as much as
Rob had dared him with. Now the last parental influence was
gone—for during the past few years his grandfather had been like
a father to him—and Rob was really on his own.

The second winter set in early, bringing heavy snowstorms that
piled in drifts over the dooryard, isolating them even from the
comforting barn, which seemed far away in the swirling whiteness.
The howl of the wind against the east window, the creeping cold
at night as the fire died, brought an unwonted dread of the havoc

---

* From "The Pasture."

the elements might wreak. In the dead of night, Rob recorded in a powerful ode, "Storm Fear,"

> I count our strength,
> Two and a child, . . .
> And my heart owns a doubt
> Whether 'tis in us to arise with day
> And save ourselves unaided.

They could not live alone forever. A man in a farm had need to know his neighbors; he could not live fully, could not raise a family, without a helping hand in times of stress or danger; an exchange of work in times of pressure like the haying season.

And when, in the spring, the flower-strewn meadow had blossomed again, Rob, working alone, feeling alone, went to

> turn the grass once after one
> Who mowed it in the dew before the sun,

and sighted (through the questing flight of a "bewildered butterfly")

> A leaping tongue of bloom the scythe had spared
> Beside a reedy brook the scythe had bared,

it was "a message from the dawn." That single "tuft of flowers" taught him that "henceforth" he "Worked no more alone." Then it was that he came to know the strong sturdy farmers down the road—the Berrys, the Lowes, the Websters, and, on the other side of the apple orchard, his French-Canadian neighbor who insisted that good fences make good neighbors.

The same spring, it was a neighbor with a newly installed telephone who rang for the doctor in a hurry when Elinor gave birth, ahead of time, to a son, whom they called Carol. The Frosts, like their farmer-neighbors, proceeded to enlarge the family with a new baby almost every year; after Carol in 1902, came Irma in 1903; and Marjorie, born at the time of the maple-tapping in March, 1905. For Elinor, child-bearing meant being tied to the house, burdened with domestic drudgery; the only assistance she received was from the few relatives who came from Methuen or Lawrence to help out during her lying-in periods; and they marveled at her patience, her quiet, good-natured acceptance of her lot with Robert. She did not seem to mind the bare cupboard or the meager stores in the cellar, little more than potatoes and carrots. They wondered, too, how a man with the brillance Rob had shown could be content to plough and plant and till the land, to mow and reap, and do the barnyard chores; it was not right; indeed, it was shocking, the relatives contended. They never thought to ask if Rob was writing poetry, or he to tell them. Someday they would know because the world would tell them. . . .

In the spring of 1905, however, his serenity received a jolt: coming in from the fields, he found the grocer waiting to assess his old horse for the over-delinquent grocery bill. He had to face the fact that he could not go on being a poet-farmer. He would have to be more than that—or less; he did not want to give up either poetry or farming. He had recently begun a new form of creative expression—narrative poems, full of dramatic power, the conflict of human emotions—works that sprang from his long study of the *Eclogues* and were based on New England legends he had heard around the countryside, jotting down notes in his copybook (pulled crumpled from his pocket when something rich turned up). He had completed three such poems—"The Black Cottage," "The Housekeeper," and "The Death of the Hired Man"—and he was eager to try his hand at more of them. Farming gave him the time and the seclusion to do so, but the sort of farming he did could not provide for his family.

That night he and Elinor held one of their casual conferences after supper in the kitchen, while the children played on the floor until bedtime and Elinor was nursing the baby. Rob could always go back to teaching—not full time, but to increase their income so they could stay on the farm. (It was an amusing paradox that as a farmer, he had to go to work elsewhere to pay the grocery bill!) There was old Pinkerton Academy, two miles away on the hill above the village. Perhaps the minister, Charles Merriam, whom

Rob had come to know through Susan Ward, could arrange some way of introducing him to the faculty. (Then Lesley asked if "Papa would read them a story," and the parley ended.)

At the next meeting of the Derry Village Men's Club, which happened to be ladies' night, Mr. Merriam asked Robert to read his poem "The Tuft of Flowers"; but Rob, suddenly timid at the thought of facing an audience to deliver his own lines, requested the minister to do it for him. The reading was forceful, full of feeling; the villagers were held by the artistic account of the way Robert Frost had been "scared away from life and crept back to it through this poem." The last couplet—" 'Men work together,' I told him from the heart, 'Whether they work together or apart' "—was followed by a moment of silence and then a burst of applause, a spontaneous call for the author to take a bow. So this was the starry-eyed, queer farmer who was seen milking or ploughing at the oddest hours—a poet, to be sure! The Pinkerton schoolteachers who were present marked him for their faculty, and by the fall term, he was a member, registered as a part-time teacher of English—two classes a week, at a salary based on $200 a year. (He was offered a full-time post, which would have earned him $1,000 annually, but he preferred to keep as much time for himself—for poetry—as possible. With this schedule he would have five free days at the farm, to do as he pleased—that was the pith of the matter!) He could always depend on the apple orchard to yield a good part of their income, so he was not worried.

The routine set up in the autumn of 1906—if such it could be called—marked the beginning of a lifelong pattern of teaching and writing, with farming a haphazard third. It was a pattern that allowed him variation of form and color; it kept him in touch with humanity when he was apt "to hide too well away."

Twice a week he took the two-mile walk to the red-brick Academy building (topped with a central tower, like a sentinel of learning on the hill) which, in its old-fashioned dignity, appeared to send an architectural frown down on the casually dressed, hatless instructor with the wind-tossed hair, who came running up the high brick steps at the last minute before the tardy-bell rang. Rob, as usual, found himself a nonconformist within the confines of formalistic, institutional teaching, but he made no effort to conform. Because of his late hours of creative effort, he never could get up early enough to take his turn at leading chapel, as Pinkerton teachers were supposed to do; the mere thought of it terrified him, so he simply forgot about it. He initiated his own methods of teaching—inherited from his mother's school—with his opening class, by announcing that he never gave assignments for themes; the students must draw from the well of their own thoughts, their own lives, emphasizing "what was common to experience, but uncommon to expression." Most of them looked blank, but one boy asked what he meant.

He thought a moment, rumpling his already tousled hair. He wondered out loud, Could one of them, for instance, make him see pigeons on the street: their primly laced lavender feet, their iridescent necks, the way they poked their heads in walking . . . ? His eyes twinkled at the stares on the faces of his pupils. Yes, that was what he meant, he told them; they should write about something familiar as if they were seeing it for the first time.

His originality, his informality, soon won him popularity among the students. They never knew what to expect, and that made it fun to attend English class. He might have them write a composition (on a subject of their own choosing) and then not even look at the papers, as he did one day when he came in and found a stack of themes piled high on his desk. At the thought of plodding through them all, grading pencil in hand, his "native indolence" overcame him. He confronted the class with characteristic straightforwardness.

"Anything here anyone wants to keep?"

They shook their heads "no." So he asked them again and they said "no" again.

"All right. If you don't value them enough to keep them, I don't value them enough to want to read them."

And he threw them all into the wastepaper basket.

"I am no perfunctory reader of perfunctory writing," he added, more perhaps to justify his laziness than to explain his action to the astonished faces in front of him. (That was one way of "Scaring a class so they want to find out what you've got to say.")

And if there were a few raised eyebrows among the teachers at Mr. Frost's unorthodox methods, most of the faculty admired his individualism, his daring to act as he saw fit, to reverse the order of the English teacher's responsibilities. The first duty was to self, he said; the second to books; and the third to students. Yet he gave the students the kind of attention they enjoyed and needed, to find themselves. He dumped the textbooks and grammars, and read to them from Palgrave's *Golden Treasury*. He got them to read aloud stories like Mark Twain's "Jumping Frog," Hawthorne's "Mr. Higginbotham's Catastrophe," and Stevenson's "Bottle Imp." Such hilarity never had been heard before in the staid halls of Pinkerton's.

For all his brashness, he was not too sure of himself during the first few months; and when, in December, the teachers suddenly turned cool to him, he wondered if he had carried his unconventionality too far. It was directly after publication of his latest poem to be accepted by the *Independent*, "The Trial by Existence," which dealt with the poet's concept of the soul. He found it hard to believe there was any connection between the poem's appearance and the fact that the other faculty members barely spoke to him in the halls, yet there must be.

Puzzled, he tried to figure it out, and finally consulted his friend, the minister. Had the teachers questioned his orthodoxy, he wondered, or just his sanity? Or perhaps they could tolerate his misspelling Derry (for his faulty orthography ran to place names also), even less than his grafting Schopenhauer upon Christianity," as he had done in "The Trial." Local pride was more easily offended than religious principle, he supposed.

Dr. Merriam, with a smile, informed him that he was wrong in both his guesses. His colleagues on the faculty were offended simply because he had not stated that he taught at Pinkerton! The explanation struck Rob as being so absurd that he immediately wrote an account of the whole episode to Miss Ward: "Mr. Merriam says that I was twice wrong. I had made myself unpopular by the simple act of neglecting to give Pinkerton the credit for harboring the poet that wrote the poem. It was too funny. But while it lasted and I was still guessing, I was rather miserable. . . ."

The incident showed him the prestige of published work, and he determined to send out more poems; perhaps he would even have the courage to try the rejected ones a second time, at different magazines. In any case, he was relieved to know that his teaching methods were not under attack. He continued to stir up young minds, to make them feel and enjoy the experiences in stories they read aloud in class. It was fun, even slightly improper, to act out scenes instead of parsing sentences of literary classics, as they had always done—and still did—in other English courses. Robert Frost's pupils came to class expectantly, almost with an air of conspiracy.

He decided to go a step farther and suggest producing plays professionally, for a paying audience in the schol auditorium; he would direct them himself. The students took him up in delight, and he got real performances because they understood—they felt— the humor or pathos or tragedy of the lines. At first comedies were presented—*The School for Scandal, The Importance of Being Earnest,* and Milton's *Comus.* In the course of production, the young actors picked up a knowledge of eighteenth-century society, the world of Oscar Wilde, and the precision of Miltonian verse without realizing it. They hired animal masks for the rout scene in *Comus,* and the chairman of the school board himself volunteered to get the use of the silver communion service for the magic banquet. The following term brought a most successful production of *Macbeth* and other Shakespeare plays.

In extracurricular activity, the new instructor did not confine himself to theatricals. He took any Pinkerton boys who were interested on botanical (and philosophical) hikes, sharing their inmost thoughts on life. Nor was he above joining in athletics; he frequently served as pitcher or coach on the baseball team. And with his childhood training, he could challenge any boy on the track team.

One of these boys, an athlete as well as scholar, was John Bartlett, whom Rob spoke to on the football field one afternoon while he was watching the team practice. John happened to be standing next to him for a moment, so Rob casually asked a few questions about Devil's Den, a curious rock formation nearby, which the boy had described in a theme. John answered the new teacher rather shyly, but Rob caught the gleam of real interest; he could see that John was a fellow with ideas, and said so in an offhand way. It was the beginning of a lifelong relationship between the two, which included Margaret Abbott, from Derry Depot, one of the girls who sat at right angles to the boys in Rob's class. Like Elinor, she was an honor student, and valedictorian of her class; and, like Elinor, she was putting John through the same sweet torment that Elinor put Rob through in Lawrence High School days. Robert Frost could not help taking an interest in such a pair, once even to the point of patching up a lovers' quarrel between them. Sometimes he walked home to Margaret's house with them; sometimes he brought them to the double house where the Frosts lived temporarily one year, for a visit with Elinor.

(And after they were married, the young couple turned to the older for advice on all manner of things from having children to article-writing.) In the past, no Pinkerton teacher had shown such a personal interest in students without patronizing them, and they responded by entering into the projects he proposed with real pleasure.

His own children were not neglected because of his new occupation; on the contrary, he spent a great deal of time playing with them, looking after their education, outside of the *abc's,* which Elinor taught each and every child in turn, almost as soon as they could talk. It was her province to take care of the children, including their earliest learning. Lesley, the oldest, was given a notebook (like Papa's) when she was five years old, and encouraged to write something in it every day, either from real life or her child's imagination. Rob took pains to explain metaphor to her—without labeling it—and praised her figures of speech. He often read poetry to the children before bedtime, occasionally even his own (or he would write verses especially for them), but he never let them know he was a poet. They never saw him write—except for those notes in smudgy pencil that he scribbled in his copybook. They did not see him when the poems were made, late at night.

None of the children went to school at the usual age. Rob and Elinor knew enough of district schools to realize that they could give the children a better background for higher learning at home than by sending them off at an early age to be at the mercy of minds less equipped than theirs to teach the very young. Those like Belle Moodie were rare, and Rob was not going to risk his children's early training in the hope of running onto another educator like his mother.

In the early summer of 1907, another baby was born, a little girl (Elinor Bettina) who lived only four days. To Elinor, who had never completely recovered from the loss of her first child, the death of the sixth was a continuation of a grief she would never forget. Rob, trying to console her, felt inept once more; try as he might, he could not make her understand his own deep sorrow. Out of their struggle, eventually, came a penetrating, poignant eclogue, "Home Burial," in which the poet struck at the heart of the conflict that could tear asunder two who were in all else so close together. In the poem, the young husband pleads:

> "Let me into your grief. I'm not so much
> Unlike other folks as your standing there
> Apart would make me out. Give me my chance.
> I do think, though, you overdo it a little."

The young wife breaks in with the accusation that he is sneering at her. And he protests heatedly:

"I'm not, I'm not!
You make me angry. . . .
A man can't speak of his own child that's dead."

She counters:

"You can't because you don't know how to speak."

And she chides him for talking about "everyday concerns" right
after the burial. Their deep-set emotional difference remains un-
resolved to the end of the poem: and so it would be with Robert
and Elinor Frost. Rob, realizing that Elinor refused to be consoled
now (in 1907), as she had after the death of their first-born, did
what he could to help her by taking the other children off her
hands as much as possible, keeping them diverted, with games and
stories, from worrying her with too many questions about "baby
Elinor," whose life had been so quickly snuffed out.

He showed five-year-old Carol how to fix a homemade wagon
the little boy had broken, and suggested that the girls lend a hand,
to learn a bit about carpentering, too. (Lesley was seven, Irma
four; tiny Marjorie, at two, tagged around after all of them.) He
took them for walks in search of wild flowers. He wrote a poem for
Lesely, and a story about a small boy very much like Carol. It was
called "The Lord Protector" (and was set down in Rob's notebook
along with his random observations, colloquialisms, odd names
and country tales he picked up from the neighbors). He read it
aloud as they all sat under the apple tree by the side porch:

"Once there were three little girls who were afraid of almost everything when they were away from home, engines and electric cars and
automobiles and road rollers and bears and giants and cannons. But
when they were at home they felt perfectly safe because they had a
little brother there just a little bit smaller than they were who was a
great hero. He always walked about with his chin close in to his neck
and his fists in the pockets of his new trousers. He kept almost whistling.
All about the yard, like bones in front of a lion's den, were scattered
the sticks and clubs that none but he could wield and the carts and
boxes and things he had broken by not playing with them gently

enough. When he heard a wagon coming down the road, he would come to the barn door to let people see that he was on guard. As long as they went by it was all right. He had a terrible smile, a terrible smile. He made the three little girls feel perfectly safe even at night."

Rob had written the story as much to make the children over- come certain fears as to entertain them. They were all afraid of the dark, though neither he nor Elinor had ever shown such trem- ors. In an effort to cure them, he took the older ones for night walks, allowing them to stay up beyond bed time if they would go. Or he would try bribing them—daring them to go down a dark road alone: he would place a dime on a tree stump more than half- way along the path to the Berrys' and say: "The first one to go keeps the ten-cent piece." But sometimes nobody made a move, and he would tease them for being scared, until finally Lesley or Carol would feel bold enough to make a dash for it.

Occasionally a poem was created to allay the children's needless fear of the dark: "Locked Out" (As Told to a Child), which began:

> When we locked up the house at night,
> We always locked the flowers outside
> And cut them off from window light.

As they grew older, the children came to feel that the dark could be as friendly and familiar as the day, but one thing that always scared them (a little, Lesley said) was the sight of tramps! Tramps, appearing suddenly over the hill, or coming up the road at dusk, stopping at the pump for a drink, perhaps begging a meal and a night's lodging. And though Rob often let vagabonds sleep in the barn or the back kitchen, he was careful to slip a bolt inside the house proper. One night just as the light was fading, he was play- ing with the children on a blueberry knoll, "reading them some- thing rhetorical like 'Ye Mariners of England' through a self-made megaphone, when a tramp came by and went to the pump for water." The children shrank involuntarily, leaning toward Rob, and were so distracted (by anxiety mixed with curiosity) that he

stopped reading; always interested in the stories of these travelers
on foot, he ambled over to the pump, followed at a safe distance by
the little troupe. As it turned out, the man was on his way from
Sidney, Australia, to London to see his wife. "He'd left her in her
father's care because he thought her father could take better care
of her than he could. . . ."

Some of the stories figured in poems; or the incident itself
might make a long poem like "Two Tramps in Mud Time," written years afterward, during the thirties.

Later in the summer, when hay fever began to plague him
("since the ragweed dusted," he wrote to Miss Ward, "I have done
nothing and written nothing . . ."), Rob decided it was time for
the family to take a vacation from the farm. Elinor, still quietly
sorrowing for her loss, and worried about Rob, had not been
away from the house for a single night in seven years; and in all
that time they had not been invited out for a single meal. She
never complained; her family was her life; her husband's art her
own deep joy; but there came a point when drudgery could sub-
merge the spirit, not by reason of the tasks themselves, but because
of outside misfortune such as she had suffered.

Hearing that Henry Ward Beecher, also a hay fever victim, had
found relief at a resort in the White Mountains, near Bethlehem,
Rob packed a bag and went up to Northern New Hampshire to
reconnoiter. He found all thirty hotels in the region "plumb full
of boarders who had come for fishing and climbing and blueberry
pies." He went into the drugstore for some white grapejuice, his
favorite drink, and, in his words, was looking around, sizing up
the other customers, in the course of which he met a man named
Fitzgerald, who was a hotelkeeper in the resort country. His hotel
was full, unfortunately; but seeing the disappointed look on the
poet's face, he recommended his cousins, the Lynches. They had
a big farm, which stood high out of the village, to the north; he
indicated the road outside the drugstore; it was quite a walk, he
said. But walking was a pleasure to Rob, and the house, reward-
ingly, "viewed on all creation." Lynch was a gloomy old Irish

patriot, who still nursed a deep grudge toward England, and his wife was quite a crusty character. But the new boarder had a way with him, and before long, she agreed to let Mr. Frost bring his wife and children.

Promised "a couple of rooms upstairs and a share in the kitchen," Rob went back to fetch the family. Loaded down with luggage, and surrounded by the children, journeying by train and trolley, Rob and Elinor were quite confused by the time they had to change at Holyoke. After waiting for what seemed an hour on the right street,

> A trolley car they hailed
> Went by with clanging gong
> Before they guessed the corner
> They waited on was wrong.

Afterwards, they laughed about it, telling the Lynches around the dining room table; but they were a weary "Rogers Group" by their dusty clothes and drowsy children, and very glad to be at the farmhouse on the mountaintop at last.

The clear, dry air was bracing, the view boundless, the people congenial company. ("There were lots of Lynches and lots of Fitzgeralds and we liked them and they liked us," Rob said.) The children rejoiced in the freedom of mountain life, the pony they could pet or ride, the playmates they found—for the first time in their lives—among other vacationers. Rob, as always, discovered for himself the stuff of poetry here, sometimes lyric, sometimes dramatic, even tragic. (Right down the road from the Lynches, a young boy had lost his hand in the teeth of a "snarling" buzz-saw, and died from shock and loss of blood before the doctor could save him. Robert Frost's realistic account in " 'Out, Out—' " seemed to him so "cruel" that he never read the poem in public.)

For the most part, however, the Frosts felt they had found a paradise, and Rob, hoping to persuade Miss Ward to visit them, sent her a glowing description of the place and the life they led, which ended, "People here go down to the surf at Old Orchard and return the same day like Freedom rejoicing in each of the two mighty voices, one of the Sea, one of the Mountains."

They stayed at the Lynches as long as they dared before Rob had to be back in Derry for the fall term at Pinkerton. Early in November, he was writing in a reminiscent mood to the household in the mountains, ". . . How long ago and far away Bethlehem is already. Our summer was one of the pleasantest we have had for years." Not quite believing in the reality of it all, he recalled the snug, downhill dining room with the view over five ranges of forested mountains, the talks under the hanging lamp, the tea-inspired Mrs. Lynch suddenly grown sociable, and wonders like the towering ridge of the blue black Lafayette that made the summer memorable. "There is a pang there that makes poetry," he told his friends. "I rather like to gloat over it."

He frequently used the phrase, "Poetry is gloating," but he could not enjoy that pleasure as fully as he wished—classroom duties took too much of his time. Yet he could hardly expect to teach less and still receive a salary; it was a vicious circle, but for the moment he was not going to change the pattern he had so lately achieved.

Christmas was coming along, and he had pleasanter problems to worry about. Every year the children were given large copybooks early in December, for the purpose of writing anything they chose—poems; stories; a record of the most important events of the past year (this time, the summer in northern New Hampshire would undoubtedly fill the major part of the older ones' pages); or anything they had learned in the last twelve months, whether it was the *abc's* or some remarkable fact in American history. The books were proudly presented on Christmas morning, gifts from the children to Mamma and Papa.

On their side, Rob and Elinor always had homemade presents waiting for the children when they came downstairs early on the holiday. This year Rob decided to carve different little animals out of birch wood for each child, and on Christmas Eve he was still whittling away, while Elinor took the final stitches on a pair of mittens for Marjorie. They spoke softly as they sat by the fire, she in the rocker, and he in the morris chair he had kept from the furniture in his grandfather's house. It was two in the morning before he completed the pig he was working on for Carol, and, holding it up for Elinor's approval, concluded it should have a pen. Late as the hour was, he picked up another block of wood and went on whittling until light began to show in the east window. Elinor, tired and drowsy, sat there with him, but went to sleep as she rocked. She woke at dawn, to find that Rob had just finished the pigpen!

He enjoyed making things for the youngsters, his spirit of fun bringing forth inventions for his own pleasures as well as theirs. Spring flowers, always so slow to come in New England, seemed later than ever the next year. When there was still no sign of blossoms at the end of March, he "made some out of paper and put them down the roads on April Fool's Day." And if the neighbors saw him strewing the bits of colored paper along the path, he paid them no heed—or if he did, it was to give a friendly wave, inviting whoever wished to ask just what he was about.

Like his father, Rob wanted his children to be able athletes. With his training, they became not only first-rate walkers, but early learned to climb great trees (as well as swing the slender birches) and ropes and trapezes, which he put up in the barn. Boylike, Carol would show off his strong muscles; and Lesley, fleet of foot, was an expert skater and ready runner, whose prowess later nearly won her an Olympics rating.

The books he chose to read aloud to the family circle of five, seated around him in the evenings (the children usually on the floor), provided entertainment and education at the same time. The list included his favorite adventure stories and histories: from his high school days, Prescott's *The Conquest of Mexico;* Melville's *Typee* and *Omoo,* exciting and poetic; Hakluyt's *Voyages* (from which the poet fashioned a "Rhyme," "The Discovery of the Madeiras"); Darwin's *Voyage of the Beagle;* the *Odyssey;* *Robinson Crusoe;* and more than once, the American classic he

thought comparable to Defoe's, the bible of New England natural-
ists, *Walden*. Every so often he would read Thoreau's pithy volume through once more for sheer pleasure.

Lesley was the first of the young Frosts to be sent to the West
Derry district school, some time after her ninth birthday, and
then it was a reluctant decision on her parents' part. Both Rob
and Elinor would have preferred to educate their children entirely at home; since their first home after their marriage had been
a school, the attitude did not seem strange to them; but Lesley
longed to go to school, like the other girls she had met. In the end,
she was given permission—and a bicycle, to ride back and forth!—
the envy of the other pupils in the little rural schoolhouse.

By 1909, the "pang that makes poetry" had deepened to the
point of demanding more attention. Rob determined to get his
teaching time cut down, but just as he was about to request
fewer hours, he was approached with the suggestion that he apply
for the principlaship, which was open at Pinkerton's. The prospect of such a post startled him—Heaven forbid that it be offered
to him.

"You really don't want me—no degrees!" He told the committee
that came to him. "That would not look well in your prospectus."

His logic put them off; but the new principal, Mr. Silver (an
alumnus who had the necessary degrees), was so impressed with
the poet's distinctive method of teaching that he asked him to
speak at a state teachers' convention, which only increased his
reputation in the profession. Morrison, the state superintendent
of schools, called Robert Frost the best teacher in New Hampshire—it was embarrassing. His "laziness" brought him nothing
but laudatory comment and advancement.

When Mr. Silver, within two years, was appointed head of the
State Normal School in Plymouth, not far from the White Mountains, he persuaded Rob to come with him as psychology and education teacher of schoolmarms in the making. But in agreeing to
accept the new job, which meant moving, abandoning farm life
for a time, Rob warned Silver: "For one year, just one." He would

not commit himself to stay longer. The urge to create poetry was bedeviling him. Who knew where it might lead?

According to the will Grandfather Frost had left, Rob now had title to the farm, and he considered selling the property, at a profit if possible, in order to have enough capital to concentrate on poetry for a while. He and Elinor thought it best to store the furniture when they moved—all except their two chairs—so that if an acceptable offer came, and they decided to sell the farm, they would be unhampered by possessions, free to make the truly important change which Rob knew in his heart must come.

In the meantime, the State Normal School at least brought a change of subject matter, a challenge to his teaching ideas. He saw no reason why psychology and education should be taught any differently from English courses, and he started out the same way here as he had at the Academy, by telling his first class to get rid of the required, and insufferably dull, textbooks on the *History of Education.*

"Take them down to the basement," he said to the astonished young ladies. "We won't use them. Instead we'll get a few books that have lighted teachers down the ages—Plato, Rousseau and others."

At first he found himself quite alone in his theories, his general attitude toward teaching in Plymouth, just as he had in Derry. He had "no one at all with whom to talk . . ." not the sort of literary, philosophic give-and-take he wanted just now. But one night in December, when he and Elinor were chaperoning a school dance, he met a young instructor from the high school, Sidney Cox, with whom he was to form a literary friendship such as he had never known, though their meeting was hardly propitious. He later described the incident with characteristic humor in his preface to *"A Swinger of Birches"* by Sidney Cox.

"I didn't know who he was except that he looked very teasably young. He didn't know who I was except, it seems, that I looked too old. By saying something flippant about the theme papers he had to hurry away to correct, I angered him to the point of his inquiring behind my back if it was because of alcohol I had got no further up in the world at my age. I was thirty-seven. I was just teaching psychology in the Plymouth Normal School. He disdained to speak to me on the street for a while afterwards. But his seriousness piqued the mischief in me and I set myself to take him. He came round all right, but it wasn't the last time he had to make allowances for me. He worked at it devotedly. . . ."

After he "came round," Sidney often went for long walks with Robert when classes were over for the day. They tramped through snowy woods and over mountain intervals, discussing, arguing, quoting poetry if they felt so inclined. They seldom took the same point of view, but they ended up by understanding each other's attitude, sometimes reaching a plane of agreement, sometimes not; it did not matter. When they returned from the walks, Rob usually took the young high school teacher to the drugstore for a glass of white grapejuice. Or, as Cox himself told it:

"Other times he took me home with him for a dinner of leg of lamb. When the kids had gone to bed he would read from thin, attractive volumes of poetry. . . . Once he recited Thompson's "The Hound of Heaven," his uniquely vibrating voice a flexible instrument for the speech music of many emotions. Tones, he said, pauses and rushes and intensities of sound are more revealing than the definition value of the words. 'Lycidas,' he said, sympathetically read aloud would be stirring and charming if heard through a wall that muffled all the words. He had once recited 'Lycidas,' he said, all of it, alone on the summit of Mount Lafayette."

So they went on, a poet communing with a pedagogue half his age (but before he was through, Robert had made Sidney more of a poet and less of a pedagogue in his teaching); they spun literary yarns, forgetful of time, until Elinor reminded them gently but firmly that they both had early morning classes, and the hour was already too late.

Even after Sidney had taken his reluctant leave, Rob would stay up, trying to give form and measure to the ideas whirling in his stimulated mind. His muse nagged him more than his beloved and devoted wife; soon he would have to give in to the insistent goad. Late in December (1911) he sent Miss Ward a "book of manuscript verse as a peace offering" for having "been such a laggard in letter-writing"; and he explained, "It represents, needless to tell *you*, not the long deferred forward movement you are living in wait for, but only the grim stand it was necessary for me to make until I should gather myself together. The forward movement is to begin next year."

Ten days later, as the fervor for moving ahead yeasted and foamed inside him, he penned a rather urgent note to her. He explained his churning emotions in regard to his career, his restiveness in the new teaching post. "And though getting along in years like other folks, I still find myself young enough to hate and abhor giving up what I have once really set my heart on. So I am coming to have a spoken word with you, if no more than a word." He needed the advice of his mentor, the moral support she would offer, he hoped, to his plan.

The meeting took place in New York, and after his return, Rob found it more difficult than ever to remain at his present post; poetry kept interfering, interjecting itself into his classroom work. "I must tell you," he wrote Miss Ward, "that one day—I couldn't for the life of me say how afterwards—I actually turned a recitation in the History of Education into a recitation of irrelevant verse. But there's no harm done, perhaps even some good. At any rate Elinor and I think so. It will never be counted against you with us that you have encouraged my poor Muse with interest when you couldn't with praise." He included his most recent work with the sentence, "Sonnet on the next page for my Moth and Butterfly book." A casual reference to a poem later recognized as a masterpiece, "Design," it contained even in this early version the filaments of enduring art that eventually evolved.

It traced a dread pattern of death in the weird sight of "a dimpled spider, fat and white, On a white heal-all, holding up a moth"—a unique design of death in white.

With such potent magic brewing inside him, he could hardly be content to plod along in Plymouth, to remain in the rut of the teaching profession for the sake of mere financial security. Yet at times he wondered if he had the right to risk his family's future by uprooting them from native soil and removing them to some unknown realm for the sake of his artistic endeavor. (He and Elinor had been talking vaguely about going somewhere, but until now that was as far as they had got.) The question had conflicting angles, facets that drew him now one way, now another, until he scarcely knew which way to turn. At school his mind wandered (since he could not) so that at times he hardly knew where he was.

One day at the end of classes he went for a long walk in the woods by himself (from the mood he was in, he was just as glad that Sidney Cox had not appeared that day); and as he was returning in the twilight, he had an extraordinary, fateful, perhaps occult experience. He made no claim to mysticism in spite of the spiritual overtones of his realism, but the mysterious encounter with what appeared to be another self, <u>at the juncture</u> of two roads that passed each other, was too significant to be dismissed.

The roads were lonely. He had walked them several times during the winter without meeting a single soul on foot or in sleigh. They were always unbroken for days after a snow or blow, untraveled roads at any time. But on this particular evening, as he came down one he was astonished to see a man, who in the dim light of dusk looked for all the world like himself, coming down the other. The same build, the same intentness, approaching with the same pace to the point where their paths must intersect; unless one of them pulled up, they would inevitably collide. Yet he kept on, feeling as if he was going to meet his own image in a slanting mirror. And as they slowly converged on the same point with the same noiseless yet laborious stride, he felt as if they were two images "about to float together with the uncrossing of someone's eyes." It was eerie, yet he was not frightened; on the contrary, he actually expected he would absorb this other self and only feel stronger for the three-mile journey home. They were almost upon each other; in the fading light there might be a fusion of his two interchangeable, yet separate selves—

But he did not go forward to the touch. He merely stood still in wonderment and let the other pass by. He did so silently, making no effort to speak and find out what could have brought them "by cross-paths to the same point in a wilderness at the same moment of nightfall." When the other had disappeared, he walked slowly back to Plymouth, still wrapped in wonder. He hardly spoke to the children or Elinor, and only late that night could he reveal what had taken place. In a letter dated February 10, 1912, he related the strange interlude to Miss Ward. Speculating on its motivation, he said, "Some purpose I doubt not. I like a coincidence almost as well as an incongruity."

It could not have been entirely happenstance that shortly thereafter Robert and Elinor made up their minds to leave Plymouth for someplace that would provide a better "climate" for poetry writing. Following his curious, mixed emotions during the brief time of that portentous twilight scene, Rob's inner conflict disappeared; he knew now which way to turn.

He and Elinor had held their usual family parleys about the matter, casual, idle talk in the midst of other things, as if the move was of no great moment. First they had thought of going to Vancouver, where Margaret and John Bartlett had gone to seek their fortune after their marriage. From their letters, the Frosts gathered that the province was sparsely settled in spite of a land boom, and was one of the most interesting in Canada. (John kept sending Rob various British magazines like *T.P.'s Weekly* to whet the desire to investigate Vancouver.) Recently, however, the Bartletts had written that living there was growing expensive because of the land boom, so the Frosts dropped the notion. Then one night Rob suggested England. They were in the Plymouth kitchen at the time, Lesley at the table doing homework, her mother standing by the ironing board, pressing a dress for her daughter.

"Yes, let's go over there and sleep under thatch!" cried Elinor, setting her iron on the trivet with a bang like a clap of approval.

Rob was delighted. Ever since he had found the little book at Dartmouth he'd wanted to visit the land of the *Golden Treasury*.

"Let's toss a coin," he proposed, taking a dime out of his pocket and flipping it. Elinor and Lesley watched him, waiting.

The coin chose England. And so they began really trying to sell the farm in Derry, and Rob gave notice at the normal school that he would be leaving at the end of the term—much to the dismay and consternation of the principal: one of his best teachers, leaving—just at the time when the prospects were brightest for his career!

Silver was flabbergasted. He thought Frost must be going to hell, to be so offhand and careless about uprooting four children and leaving a school where he was in good standing as a teacher and earned $1,100 a year. (In Derry he had never earned more than $1,000.) The principal thought his prize instructor must at least have some connections over there, but Frost confessed that he had no letters of introduction, and knew not one soul in England. He simply felt impelled to lose himself among strangers, so that he could write poetry without further "scandal" to his family and friends.

Mr. Silver still couldn't get it, but in the end, when the farm was finally sold and the luggage packed, he was kind. He put the children and Elinor on the train, for Rob had gone on ahead to Boston to buy the steamer tickets. (It cost him $60 apiece for two —$120 for Elinor and himself; the children could go free. The farm brought in $1,100 after the mortgage was paid, which was all he had in hand. Then a small allowance, $800 a year, had come in from his grandfather's estate; that would last another two or three years at best before it ran out. Figuring closely, they could risk it, he felt. Like his mother, he was inclined to be wasteful of the little money he had.)

When Rob went to say good-by to the principal before leaving Plymouth, feeling slightly rueful now that he was actually going, he surprised himself by quoting the Bible—the strong-hearted phrase from Paul's first Epistle to the Corinthians: "Quit you like men." His temerity came from the inner knowledge that he had recently had three poems accepted (after a barren interval of three years): "October," to be published in the *Youth's Companion* of October 3rd; "My November Guest" in the November *Forum;* and "Reluctance," again in the *Companion,* in the November 7th issue. Six years before, still full of doubt and indecision, he had written "Pan with Us," a rather skeptical evaluation by the new-world poet of his own art.

At this moment in 1912, however, the thirty-eight-year-old Robert Frost was giving up a good teaching post, his farm and property, and was uprooting his family to follow the pipes of Pan.

Chapter 8

THE AIM WAS SONG

Several times during the voyage on *The Parisian,* as he made the rounds from bow to stern with the children or sat beside Elinor in a deck chair, Rob had to repeat to himself the biblical phrase from Corinthians, for he had not the faintest notion how he was going to fare in England, and he could not help having misgivings about leaving the post in Plymouth. Their funds were meager; and the only household possessions they had brought with them were a secondhand typewriter they had bought for Lesley, and, as before, the rocker and the morris chair—now in the ship's hold, crated for the crossing in packing cases. Just how he was going to find a furnished house in the country—they planned to raise their own vegetables to save expenses—he did not know; but it would be of small help to worry or to spend time regretting the move.

Consequently, by the time the family from rural New Hampshire arrived in the vast, sprawling city on the Thames, Rob spent very few hours in reverent sight-seeing among the hallowed towers and spires that had seen so much; he was in a frame of mind to act, to begin the forward movement as he had promised. The first night alone was given over to entertainment: passing the Strand on the way to their little hotel near the Victoria embankment, he noticed that G. B. Shaw's *Fanny's First Play* was to have its five hundredth performance that night; and as a kind of spree, because he felt the Frosts had something to celebrate as well as the playwright, he extravagantly bought tickets. The evening made their arrival in England unforgettable.

The next morning Rob set out to search for the right place to locate. With his usual ingenuity, he looked up the author of the "Country Walks" column in *T.P.'s Weekly,* who turned out to be an ex-policeman! The obliging columnist gave him a list of country cottages near London and offered to assist Rob in going through it for a suitable house. The two explored on foot for a few days, walking about the British countryside, conversing as they went, until at Beaconsfield, Buckinghamshire, they found an empty bungalow to let, which could be furnished if necessary. Before it was quite ready, the Frost family were on the spot, ready to move in. Nine-year-old Irma, in her Christmas book that year, included a description of their arrival (at the beginning of September). She called it "OUR NEW HOUSE."

With remarkable precision for a child her age, she recorded their actions from the time they got off the train in the Beaconsfield station and started walking toward the bungalow until they reached the house itself. Stops that had to be made along the way were duly set down: "I must go into the groser's," said Papa, "and tell him to come in the morning." The others went ahead, but she waited for him. By the time the grocer and baker were taken care of, the rest of the family had made a tour of the rooms, including a very dirty kitchen where men were washing the walls, and were out in the small, dried-up garden when Irma and Rob caught up with them. Men had been unloading furniture in the front of the house, so they all went in and placed it around—in the large bedroom and the two small ones, in the sitting room, and the now less grimy kitchen. Even the layout of the bungalow was included in Irma's copybook report.

Her "papa," writing an analytic announcement of their venture-

some move to his aging mentor, Miss Ward, followed with a literary account of their new surroundings.

Their house stood between high hedges of laurel and red-osier
dogwood, within a mile or two of where Milton finished *Paradise
Lost* on one hand, and a mile or two of where Grey lay buried on
the other, and "within as many rods as furlongs of the house where
Chesterton tried truth to see if it would prove as true upside down
as it does right side up." It was only a run to London town. At
night when he went into the front yard for a last look at earth
and sky before going to sleep, he was able to see the lights of London flaring like a dreary dawn. If there was any virtue in location
—but he did not fool himself on that score. "I know where the
poetry must come from if it comes," he said with stern reality.

Almost at once the Frosts settled down to British country life.
The children of course did not go to school, but increased their
education through country walks with their father, who taught
them to look with a sharp eye for differences—and similarities—   *confused*
between their native New England and their ancestors' Old England. Lesley's and Carol's Christmas books were full of description,
plus perceptive evaluations concerning the scenery and customs
of the two countries. Active as they were, they often came back
from a trek over rain-soaked roads with rubbers covered by clay
mud an inch thick; and Elinor would tell them to scrape it off
with a stick before they came in, or leave their overshoes outside.
British housekeeping was no easy task at best, she found.

For one thing, the quaint brick stove which made such an inviting kitchen was difficult to heat; she had trouble preparing
meals on it, and Rob frequently did a good share of the cooking;
he seemed to be able to handle it (and, she suspected, enjoyed having a finger in the pot). At night she set the rocker as close to the
fireplace as she dared; although she accepted the hardships with
her usual calm, she could not help worrying, when she wasn't
meditating about Rob's poetry.

Across from her, reading or writing in his trusty morris chair,
which had just the right arms to support a shelf stolen from the

closet and not interfere with his elbows (all the desk he had for years), Rob sat going over the poems he had selected. Two or three nights after they moved in, he had unearthed from the depths of the family trunk a batch of manuscript poems, stacking them on the floor beside the fireplace. In giving an account of his first poetic endeavors in England, he said:

"I have never written poetry every day. . . . It was just every so often that I would weed out this pile or do something to a poem." In the pile were the poems of his youth, going all the way back to 1892, written separately over the period of twenty years, hardly in a design to be linked together. But he realized as he read through them, occasionally crumpling a sheet and tossing it into the flames, that the majority of them were composed in the years when he thought he preferred nature to people. How unhappy he had been —quite at the mercy of himself! Then, slowly, in the poems after 1902 or 1903, came the swing back toward people; they represented a sort of clinical curve, he thought. By the time he finished weeding them out, he had some thirty poems left unburned. He stuck them in his pocket, and only the next day realized they had a unity by which they might be woven into a book. He got Lesley to type them for him on the Blickensderfer they had brought along, and went through the lot again.

He saw that the poetry itself was pervaded by a furtiveness, an evasiveness. The boy in the lines of verse was too shy to be publicly a poet. Rob would have to write some background notes to tie the poems together.

It was this prose gloss that he worked on as he sat in the morris chair, writing occasionally on the closet-shelf desk for several evenings, until he was satisfied. Then he decided to take the sheaf of poems to the policeman columnist, the only English friend he had so far; they had discussed the "business" of writing, and Rob thought he might know about smaller publishers. (It didn't even occur to him to try the bigger ones.) Selecting a phrase from Long-fellow's "My Lost Youth," he called the book *A Boy's Will*, and went up to London carrying his manuscript.

Automatically the policeman said, "Little books like that cost the author about fifteen pounds." But Rob, remembering his sad experience with the two privately printed copies of *Twilight*, and objecting on principle to such practice, declared vehemently that he would *never* publish a book at his own expense. The columnist then proposed Elkin Matthews, but Rob objected to Matthews as a "vanity" publisher. Next his British friend suggested David Nutt, a name that sounded familiar to Frost. Recalling that he'd noticed something of W. E. Henley's under that imprint, he felt it might be the place.

Setting out from *T.P.'s Weekly* at once, he found the Nutt office, said he had some poems, and wanted to see David Nutt. He had to wait a long time, and then "a strange, lugubrious lady, a French-woman who looked as if she was about to float away," appeared in deep black widow's weeds and said in a funereal voice: "I will speak for David Nutt." Hardly knowing what to think, Rob "just left the manuscript with her" and beat a hasty retreat to the country, wondering how long it would be before he heard a word about his poems. He wondered also, as he told Elinor, why the woman was in such deep mourning; indeed, he did not even know who she was—except that from her imperious manner he surmised she was the publisher's wife. (He did not know then that Nutt was dead and that Mrs. Nutt had also lost her son David by drowning.) Luckily, his suspense did not last long:

"In three days I had a card to come in. I went. The book was accepted!" Robert Frost told the story long afterward. He added, "She never told me anything, though—the relict. Whether she admired the book or why, or who advised her to admire and publish. To have nobody in England to advise or confer with was baffling."

The first fine rapture of having a book accepted in three days' time was followed by myriad doubts, even regret, when a request for a volume of poems came from Thomas Bird Mosher, the American publisher in Portland, Maine. Right after Rob had committed himself to a British publisher!

"The Dea knows I should like nothing better than to see my

first book, *A Boy's Will,* in your Lyric Garland series," he wrote to Mosher. He explained the circumstances, presenting the fears and questions about signing a contract with the firm of David Nutt (he had just learned that the publisher himself was dead). "Why couldn't you have spoken two weeks sooner and saved me all this perplexity?" he demanded. "It seems to me you owe me something in the way of helpful advice for not speaking. Perhaps I can stave off the contract till I can get an answer from you. Have I made a serious mistake in going to David Nutt? Do you know anything about him (or her, if I may drop the business fiction)? Am I too far committed to draw back? I am nearly the worst person in the world in a muddle like this."

One of the things that disturbed him was the "eleventh-hour claim" the publisher made on his next three or four books; and although he said, "I suppose I ought to be proud to be so much in demand; the embarrassment is so novel in my experience," the option clause still troubled him. Wouldn't it seem traitorously un-American to have all his first work come out in England? He did not want to appear to be an expatriate, a poet-in-exile—like Ezra Pound, whom he knew about, but had not met—nor particularly cared to meet. Poetry, the making of his own poems, was Robert Frost's goal; he had three other books of verse near completion (which he called tentatively *Melanism, Villagers,* and *The Sense of Wrong,*) and he wanted to be by himself with them for a while. His aim was song, not the noise of publicized schools of poetry.

However, since one of the necessary evils of being in print was bowing to publishers' regulations, he signed the contract from the Nutt office; for all his doubts and misgivings, the document represented a start in the forward movement he had promised himself.

The terms were hardly generous: straight 12½ per cent, but no advance against royalties. The latter was disappointing, especially for the children's sake—Christmas was not far off, and the family budget had literally few pennies to spare for holiday celebrations. With the three or four pence each was given as spending money, the young Frost band of four marched to the "groser's" in Beaconsfield as they had always done in Derry, to bargain for wooden crates and old cracker-barrel staves to be turned into home-made presents for each other. This year seemed leaner than usual, but perhaps it was because they were far away from home.

For their poet-father, the weeks between acceptance and publi-cation were a waiting time—like being in limbo, between two worlds, left to ponder his future fate in the path he had ('somehow') chosen for himself. At night he worked on the blank verse dramas of New England hill life, which he hoped would follow *A Boy's Will* into print. During the day, as he marketed for Elinor or went down Beaconsfield roads, he might be struck with an idea for a lyric by the sight of "a patch of old snow," the grimy product of England's uncertain winter. And he could not help comparing the lot of the British country laborer with that of the independent New Hampshire hill folk he was writing about. The picturesque, timbered cottages he passed in Beaconsfield housed a life of depri-vation and want that no Yankee farmer—or his hired hands—ever knew.

Robert Frost was no socialist, nor ever would be—individualism was too strong in him; but the outmoded class restrictions that denied a British farm laborer the right to own a cow, a pig, or even a few hens, forcing him and his family to live on a diet of tea, bread and sugar (babies were given weak tea from a bottle with a nipple), aroused the poet's heated indignation. (Rob, even with his limited funds, could afford to buy meat, eggs and milk for his family.) He was bothered no less by the docile submission of the people here to such conditions. The sturdy independence of his Derry neigh-bors gave them the freedom to form a code among hired men re-spected by farm owners the country round. The unquestioned right of hill folk to gather wild blueberries on a first-come first-served basis, no matter who owned the land; the sly courtesies that grew out of the custom, could never exist under the rigid class laws of England. (Prompted partly by his indignation, Rob's poem "Blueberries" subtly pointed up the contrast between the two systems.)

When berry-picking time came in New England, small girls got out their pails and went gathering in their favorite patches as a matter of course. It was first come, first served. Here, Irma and Marjorie were warned by the little girls in the neighborhood when they went berrying to watch out for the game warden, who would dump their pails if he caught them picking. (He was very strict, and made claim as well on any wild fowl wounded by the gentry and fallen in the bushes. Natives in Beaconsfield, unlike those in Derry, could never count on shooting a brace or two of partridge in the fall to help fill the family larder, or in spring, fish as they pleased in any trout stream; they tasted no fish or game fowl unless somebody in the family was a poacher.)

As the winter wore on, bringing no further word from Mrs. Nutt, Rob grew restless and lonely; not that he missed teaching, but he longed for the stimulating conversation of someone like Sidney Cox, some colleague with whom he could compare notes. He had been reading the Georgian poets, and liked the ring of their poetry; it had a common-sense, down-to-earth quality in subject matter— the stories, the tragedies of common, everyday lives; the sounds of common speech. And one day he discovered, quite by accident, a little center of these poets. He had started going into the city now and then, or, more accurately, he liked to steal off by himself occasionally and wander about the streets of London, watching the parade of people with observant eyes, peering in shop windows through the ever-present fog of Britain in winter. One dark morning in late December, he came upon a bookshop he found most interesting: a clerk was arranging volumes of current poetry in the window. Pausing, Rob noticed a sign that announced the opening that night of Harold Monro's Poetry Bookshop. On impulse, he went in and asked if he might attend. The clerk answered politely that the guests were "Invited," but the gentleman might try.

So he did. He hesitated briefly that night before opening the door of the little shop and making his way shyly through the pleasant, buzzing group of poets and art patrons gathered for the unusual event; he wondered whether anybody would question his being there. However, one look at his classic face with its broad brow above the deep sockets of his blue eyes, his slightly impudent nose, and well-shaped generous mouth—and above all, his air of abstraction in spite of his interested glance, marked him as being one of them. So strong was the impression that when he finally reached a seat on the stairway, and sat down beside an attractive woman who made room for him, she immediately asked if he was a poet.

Rob smiled, feeling somewhat reassured, and told her enigmatically that he would "accept the omen."

Her next question was whether he "had a book," which he answered with an emphatic, "No!" He was not going to mention *A Boy's Will* until the book actually appeared.

His charming companion seemed to approve him, nevertheless. She was Mrs. Ernest Gardiner, wife of the eminent archeologist, Rob soon discovered. (Her husband was a member of the Beveridge circle, to whom he later introduced the Frosts.) She presented the man on the other side of her, British poet F. S. Flint, who was greatly interested in an American colleague fresh from the States, and asked a number of questions about poetry circles in America. Flint, who lived in London, and moved in literary company, had recently joined the ranks of Ezra Pound's newly formed poetry group, Les Imagistes. The introductions over, they settled down to listen to a reading by John Drinkwater, after which Flint, picking up his train of thought, asked Rob if he knew Ezra Pound.

"No." (Rob was going to add that he didn't particularly care to meet the gentleman in question, but he thought better of it.)

"Well, you *should*," Flint remarked. He and Rob Frost formed a pleasant friendship that evening which was to endure many years; and within a few days the American poet received a card in Beaconsfield which bore a blasé if not arrogant message:

Ezra Pound, Number Ten Church Walk, London.
At home sometimes.

Rob, reading it, "didn't like that very well." He wrinkled his nose in silent disfavor and handed the card to Elinor without comment. She read it, smilingly shook her head, and handed it back; he stuck it in his vest pocket and forgot about it.

If he was going to cultivate anybody (and Rob Frost was not one to cultivate even the soil very skillfully), he preferred the sponsor of the Georgian group, Harold Monro, with whom he had become friends following the debut of the bookshop. Monro was a poet himself, "but still more the publisher of this group, with his Georgian anthology and his review, *Poetry and Drama*." He was a genial fellow, and soon invited Robert Frost to join him at another meeting-place of poets and critics—St. George's Restaurant. There, having tea, Rob met Wilfrid W. Gibson (innovator of harsh realistic poetry dealing with the miners and other British laborers); Lascelles—to Rob's surprise, he prononunced it like "tassels"—Abercrombie, who proved to be a charming fellow as well as a fine poet; and the person who became his closest English friend, Edward Thomas. With these poets he could exchange ideas, techniques of writing poetry, shop talk on a free and equal footing. They reasserted the importance of imagination, and debated the necessity of experience when creating or describing a scene—which brought from W. W. Gibson the confession that he had never been down in a mine, but had lived among miners enough to know what it must be like.

The months passed, and still there was no word of a definite publication date for *A Boy's Will*, though Rob knew it was to be some time in the spring.

One day in March, he found himself in Kensington, near a sign "Church Walk," which reminded him of Ezra Pound and the unanswered message. He pulled the card (still where he had stowed it) from his vest pocket and, with some misgivings, knocked on the door. "Ezra was at home taking a bird-bath," as Rob put it, "and scuttled into an ornate purple dressing gown." The eminent critic cut an almost comic figure in purple silk and bare feet, yet he was commanding. Annoyed at Frost's impromptu appearance on his doorstep after having neglected his summons for so long, he shot a few questions at his unexpected guest, worming out of him at once the fact that David Nutt was about to publish his first book of verse.

As soon as he heard, Pound decided they should go over to the press and get a copy. He hurried to dress, and away they went. Rob had not even thought of requesting a copy of his book, and when they got there, it was Pound—not he—who took possession of the first copy. ("I had to walk back to his lodgings with *him* holding *my* book!" Rob said later.)

In his small sitting room lined with books, Pound immediately started reading the tender volume, pulling at his beard like a Machiavellian judge, while Rob Frost watched him anxiously, standing on one foot, wondering what the verdict would be. After a bit he caught a chuckle from Pound's chair—perhaps he was getting it?

Presently the critic looked up. "You don't mind our liking this?" he said. Rob, smiling inwardly at the *"our,"* told him to "go ahead and like it." Then Pound advised him that he'd better find a book to read; but Rob had no sooner selected one and was trying to settle himself with it than Ezra said, "I guess you'd better run along home. I'm going to review your book."

It was an abrupt dismissal, making Robert Frost feel rather like a schoolboy, but in the circumstances he did not stop to resent the critic's pomposity. Indeed, Pound's parting sentence filled him with a heady, exhilarating, unreasoning sense of accomplishment all the way back to Buckinghamshire. From the time his first poem had been published—in 1894—only fourteen of his poems had appeared in print, and not one of those had elicited so much as a comment from any critic, let alone a full notice. Now he had a book of poetry in print and it was to be reviewed by a prominent critical authority; for whatever the objections to Pound might be, he was an acknowledged literary leader, not only in London, but in America; he had appointed himself expatriate consultant to Harriet Monroe, who had just begun publishing in Chicago her lively review, *Poetry: A Magazine of Verse.* That Pound's review would appear in the new magazine was certain, and the source of great satisfaction, since Robert Frost's work had been rejected by the lady; he had sent her a sheaf of poems just before Christmas, hoping they would bring in a little extra income. (Later, Miss Monroe protested that she had been out of town—otherwise his offering would not have been turned down.)

Pound, who shortly came out to visit the Frosts, assured them that his review would appear; although Harriet was an old maid, he said, she was far less of a one than the editors of *Harper's, Scribner's,* and the *Atlantic Monthly.* Ezra was a sharp little man, with beady, black eyes and a pointed black beard. His tongue was as sharp as his eyes, and could be charming or satiric as he chose. He was rather disdainful of children as being an encumbrance to any poet imprudent enough to have them, and consequently, the young members of the Frost family did not care for him. But Rob, in spite of his annoyance at the critic's arrogance (soon to become outspoken), could not help feeling pleased at being Pound's latest discovery and, indeed, quite enjoyed his company at first. (Elinor, privately disapproving of Rob's association with the man, made no protest at the moment.)

Pound himself was most outspoken in praise of his new find: "Have just discovered another Amur'kin (Rober Frost)," he wrote to Alice Corbin, assistant editor of *Poetry. "Vurry* Amur'kin with, I think, the seeds of grace." When he had finished his review of *A Boy's Will,* it was longer than he had expected, but he acted to avert any chance of its being reduced by telling Harriet Monroe in his accompanying letter: "Sorry I can't work this review down to any smaller dimensions. . . . It's our second scoop for I only found the man by accident and I think I've about the only copy of the book that has left the shop. I'll have along some of his work, if the book hasn't used up all the best of it. . . ." He sent the notice off without showing a copy to the Frosts, but merely said he was confident it would appear soon.

In the meantime, he took Rob Frost around as his protégé, presented him to people of influence, and happily showed him "London's Bohemia—he was boyish about it." Pound knew the intimate dining corners of Soho, the dens of London's Chinatown, the backstage life of the Strand, the undercurrents of theatrical gossip from one playhouse to the next. He introduced Frost to poet-playwright William Butler Yeats, then in his heyday as chief dramatist of the Irish theater. He and Frost "did not hit it off personally," partly because Yeats dealt with the creative process in a humorless, heavy-handed way which Rob could not abide. For him, poetry writing was a joyous process, even though it might involve a certain amount of struggle in smoothing and polishing; but in the main it had to be spontaneous, a surprise outpouring of music and idea that the poet hardly knew was there. This was especially true of the short lyric. "I'll bet you that I can pick a poem of yours that was written spontaneously!" he challenged Yeats in one of their arguments. For answer, Yeats handed him a volume of his collected verse from Pound's poetry shelf. "Go ahead," he said.

Rob, leafing through, selected a two-stanza lyric about an angel, comparable in length and style to his own "Spring Pools," a poem he did not publish for many years, but the idea for which had come to him after a recent thaw—a fact he mentioned in passing the book back to Yeats. "Do you mean to say you didn't write this all in one go?"

Yeats shook his head solemnly. "That one cost me nine long hours of spitting blood and chewing pencils," he said ponderously.

Frost laughed. "If I had to spend nine hours in spitting blood and chewing pencils over a simple lyric I wouldn't write it—I'd toss it overboard in a hurry!" He exaggerated purposely to make his point. But the dramatist, offended, gave him a look of withering scorn and stalked out of Pound's lodgings.

Ezra frowned on Bob's disrespect of the older established artists, but did not care to quarrel with his protégé right away. Instead, he turned the discussion toward another American poet, Edwin Arlington Robinson, whose *The Town Down the River* Rob had read just before leaving New Hampshire. Both had enjoyed E.A.R.'s character portraits, and they laughed together over the fourth "thought" in

> Miniver thought, and thought, and thought,
> And thought about it.

(He and Ezra agreed that three "thoughts" would have been "adequate," the current critical praise word at the time. "The fourth made the intolerable touch of poetry. With the fourth, the fun began," Rob said.)

But he refused to pay homage to established figures like Yeats or the highly lauded poet-laureate, Robert Bridges. Nor would Rob agree to join Pound's group of Imagistes, although he was friendly with Flint and found pleasure in meeting some of the others—H. D. and Richard Aldington, T. E. Hulme, and Ford Madox Ford (Hueffer) who was the former editor of the powerful *English Review*. They were interesting poets, but they "shortened one another's poetry," which to Robert Frost was tampering. He had to work alone. Pound, to illustrate the aim of the Imagistes, took a poem of his and said, "You've done it in fifty words. I've shortened it to forty-eight." Rob answered, "And spoiled my meter, my idiom, and idea." He would have none of it; nor would he consent to try his hand at *vers libre,* despite Pound's persuasions. Blank verse was another matter: in the "talk-poems" he was completing, he used the medium entirely; but free verse was not for him.

Moreover, Rob preferred the company and the independent concepts of poetry among the Georgians; he admired Abercrombie's *Emblems of Love* and Gibson's *Daily Bread* and *Fires* much more than the *Cantos* that Pound was beginning to write. (Ezra had presented him with two little volumes of his, *Personae* and *Ripostes;* but when Rob said he liked those, Pound backed off with: "But it's all old stuff. I shall not go back to it.")

Rob felt at home with the friends he had found for himself at the Poetry Bookshop—poets who were still trying to make their way, like himself—and he resented Pound's attempts to take him into the Imagistes, to discredit artists he admired. When Pound discovered he was going back to the Bookshop gatherings, he re-

proached him bitterly: "If you *will* frequent the purlieus of literature!"

Pound had a personal hate for Abercrombie: the story was, as
Edward Thomas told it to Rob, that Ezra had said to Lascelles,
"Stupidity beyond a certain point becomes a public affront. I
hereby assume the public's quarrel in your case. My seconds will
wait on you." And Abercrombie, with his irrepressible humor, had
laughed it off by proposing, since he had the right to name the
weapons, that they should be unsold copies of the author's works
at a hundred yards.

Edward Thomas, the man with whom Rob—and indeed, the
whole Frost family—felt a closer kinship than with any other of
their English friends was, at the time Frost first met him, less a poet
than an expert critic of poetry; less a creative artist than an exceptionally good hack writer—or at least, such was his reputation.
It would take a poet with the insight of Robert Frost to recognize
the latent poetic power of a spirit like Edward Thomas; but as
early as Thomas's first visit to Beaconsfield, when he charmed them
all with his tender-sad Welsh songs, his gentle, melancholy face
that could suddenly become mischievous, his trove of nature's
treasures stored in his pockets for the children—birds' eggs or wild
strawberries or thorn-apples—it was apparent to Rob that this new
friend felt the same "pang that makes poetry" in the same things
that he did; and this to him was the essence of a poet.

At any rate, an immediate bond of understanding sprang up between the two, and when *A Boy's Will* finally came off the press in
April, the first review was written by Edward Thomas; printed
anonymously in the *Athenaeum* for April 5, it praised the modest
little volume (which sold for one and six), setting the tone for notices and reviews over the next few months in leading literary
publications like the London *Times Supplement; Poetry and
Drama;* the *English Review;* the London *Bookman;* the *Academy,*
and the *Nation.* Added up, these professional salutes represented
a critical success far beyond Elinor and Robert's fondest hopes during the years of struggle in Derry, when no one paid the slightest

literary heed to the few poems by Robert Frost that strayed into print over long stretches.

His first gift copies went to his first sponsors: to Miss Ward, who had been the most steadfast in her belief that his work would some-day receive the recognition that she had given it from the begin-ning, with the acceptance of "My Butterfly" (which he had included in *A Boy's Will*). He was happy to tell her that the little volume had brought him attention from important figures like Ezra Pound, Ernest Rhys, William Butler Yeats, Henry Newbolt, and May Sinclair.

The other copy was sent to Rob's earliest endorser, Ernest Jewell, who had rather hesitatingly published "La Noche Triste" in the Lawrence High School *Bulletin,* on that long-ago day in 1890. With it Rob sent a revealing note. His words belied the atti-tude that he did not care what his former classmates thought of him. He did care, and he wanted Jewell, above all others, to see the concrete evidence of his ability as a poet.

Ezra Pound's review in *Poetry* arrived in Beaconsfield from Chi-cago about this time—the first American review! It was very long. But Rob and Elinor, reading it together, were aghast at the inti-mate—and often inaccurate—details of their family life the critic had included. "The piece was so personal that Elinor cried," Rob said afterwards. He tried to comfort her by saying that he thought it was "generously intended," that Ezra was trying to give him a start—as, indeed, the article did; and for that, he would always be grateful to Pound. Nevertheless, he was annoyed with the liberties the critic had taken, and as the days passed, he became more an-noyed with Pound's arrogance, his attempts to browbeat his pro-tégés into doing as he saw fit, and his angry retaliation when they refused. The cheekiness of the man was appalling. In the review, he had pounced on his chance to shorten Robert Frost's lines, and that was the way they appeared—no wonder he had not troubled to show the Frosts a copy beforehand!

Now Rob sent an annotated one in a letter to Sidney Cox,

supplying the deleted words and adding comments of his own in brackets. Part of it read:

> I had withdrawn in forest, and my song
> Was swallowed up in leaves ("that blew alway," omitted)

There is another personality in the realm of verse, another American, found, as usual, on this side of the water, by an English publisher long known as a lover of good letters. David Nutt publishes at his own expense *A Boy's Will,* by Robert Frost, the latter having been long scorned by the "great American editors." (The author's surmise—inference from my sad look.) It is the old story.

Mr. Frost's book is a little raw, and has in it a number of infelicities (this is the superior person who objected to "Trial by Existence") underneath them it has the tang of the New Hampshire woods, and it has just this utter sincerity. It is not post-Miltonic or post-Swinburnian or post Kiplonian. This man has the good sense to speak naturally and to paint the thing, the thing as he sees it. And to do this is a very different matter from gunning about for the circumplectious polysyllable. . . . One reads the book for the "tone," which is homely, by intent, and pleasing, never doubting that it comes direct from his own life, and that no two lives are the same.

He has now and then such a swift and bold expression as

> ("And) The whimper of hawks beside the sun.

He has now and then a beautiful simile, well used, but he is for the most part as simple as the lines I have quoted in opening or as in the poem of mowing. He is without sham and without affectation. . . .

Here, as earlier, Rob mischievously deleted a few of his reviewer's priceless words. He tried to feel grateful to Pound for having discovered him, but the autocratic critic got his stubborn Yankee dander up.

The friction between Frost and Pound, although in its pettiness beneath the stature of both men as thinkers and poets, was in a sense inevitable. Pound, who had the insight to grasp the value, the kernel of greatness in *A Boy's Will,* was himself too strong-willed, too powerful a figure, to permit Robert Frost to make his own way into the flowering of that greatness. The egotist in Pound, which served ultimately to destroy the effectiveness, to dim the brilliance of his own work, detracted from his generosity as a critic and caused him to be patronizing, perhaps unintentionally. In the same long review, after the penetrating, if autocratic, criticism of Frost's poetry, he drew a parallel between Robert Frost and "the Irishman who could sit on a kitchen midden and dream stars." An unfortunate comparison, it aroused the wrath and scorn of the Frosts, who considered such an image "stupidly wide of the mark," as Rob said.

Yet, for the most part, Pound could evaluate and appreciate the true poet when he met one, and he knew instinctively that in Frost he had found the makings of a major poet. If he had been able to control his tendency to dominate, which at times amounted to persecution, he and Frost might have enjoyed a rich and lasting friendship. The essential difference between the two strong, complex personalities lay in the fact that Robert Frost did not feel the need to follow the lead of any poet; nor did he hold any desire to assemble a school of followers—a factor of prime importance to Pound's voracious appetite for power.

Each might have benefited from the other if both had been willing to show more flexibility. As it was, the rift which soon came between them was too wide to bridge. Both men were too individualistic, of too prominent an ego, to subordinate their differences in order to preserve the bond of their early friendship.

Before the month of May was out, the more-than-ample figure of Amy Lowell appeared on the London scene, fresh from aggressively won plaudits in Boston, where her book of poems, *A Dome of Many-Colored Glass,* reflected the sentimentality and strict conventional meter of the educated, proper Bostonian. Ready to throw her weight to the side of conventional meter, she noised it about that she would welcome any followers. Rob avoided meeting her, partly because he did not care for her poetry (or her tactics) and partly because Ezra was boasting: "When I get through with that girl, she'll think she was born in free verse."

And as it turned out, his boast was not idle: Amy became a complete convert almost immediately. Unlike Robert Frost, she gave herself over zealously to indoctrination of Imagiste theories by practitioner Pound. She began writing free verse with enthusiastic fervor, and by 1914, had a new book published—*Sword Blades and Poppy Seeds*—entirely in free verse. Pound kept pointing to her as a shining example of the advisability of joining the Imagiste movement, trying his best to nudge Robert Frost into doing the same. But the more he prodded, the less Bob yielded. His own blank-verse narratives were nearing completion now, and all he wanted was the peace and quiet to finish the job. Mrs. Nutt had forced him to sign a contract for the new volume, and had already announced it in her fall catalogue for 1913, listed as *Farm Servants and Other People*. Over this Rob wrote in his bold hand: *New England Hill Folk,* but he was not certain of that title either (and he rejected a third suggestion, *Yankee Eclogues,* from some of the Georgian poets). He would decide later just what to call these "talk" poems. In the meantime, he needed no guidance from well-meaning literary leaders.

He voiced these sentiments, his feeling about his own techniques as opposed to the Imagistes' and his growing antipathy toward Pound, in a letter to Mosher, who had written for permission to use the poem "Reluctance" in his catalogue. Rob gladly gave the necessary consent.

It was July, hot and steamy during the rainy part of the day, so before long, Rob took the whole family northward to King's Barn, a fishing village on the coast of Scotland, facing the rugged sweep of curve, the Firth of Forth. The spot had been recommended by his friend, Mrs. Ernest Gardner, as a place where scholars retreated for study and meditation; and, within a few days, he met on the beach a well-known Scottish man of letters, E. C. Smith, summering there with his family. Parents and children of both families soon became friends. Smith read Rob's newly completed "Death of the Hired Man," with deep interest and saw to it that

Robert Frost met another important English poet, Laurence Binyon, who, in turn, had him to lunch with Robert Bridges. It was then that the poet from New Hampshire, listening to the Poet Laureate of England discourse with solemn incantation on his pet theories of language and poetry, felt his own theories crystallize within him, demanding expression which subsequently came in a letter to Sidney Cox. One passage, which he later used in lectures, was quoted in Cox's book *A Swinger of Birches*.

The living part of a poem is the intonation entangled somehow in the syntax idiom and meaning of a sentence. It is only there for those who have heard it previously in conversation. It is not for us in any Greek or Latin poem because our ears have not been filled with the tones of Greek and Roman talk. It is the most volatile and at the same time important part of poetry. It goes and the language becomes a dead language, the poetry dead poetry. With it go the accents, the stresses, the delays that are not the property of vowels and syllables but that are shifted at will with the sense. Vowels have length there is no denying. But the accent of sense supercedes all other accent, overrides and sweeps it away. I will find you the word 'come' variously used in various passages as a whole, half, third, fourth, fifth and sixth note. It is as long as the sense makes it. When men no longer know the intonations on which we string our words, they will fall back on what I may call the absolute length of our syllables, which is the length we would give them in passages that meant nothing. English poetry would then be read as Latin poetry is now read and of course as Latin poetry was never read by Romans. I say you can't read a single good sentence unless you have previously heard it spoken. . . . Words exist in the mouth not in books.

He would not have been able to give voice to his credo a few months before, but now he was the author of a published volume of verse which, as late as September (1913), was receiving remarkable reviews for a first work—like the one the Frosts found waiting on their return to Beaconsfield from King's Barn. It gave Rob new courage for his convictions (and for the prospects of his forthcoming volume) to read in the *Academy:*

"We wish we could fitly express the difference which marks off *A Boy's Will* from all the other books here noticed. The poems combine, with a rare sufficiency, the essential qualities of inevitability and surprise. We have read every line with that amazement and delight which are seldom evoked by books of modern verse. . . . We do not need to be told that the poet is a young man: the dew and the ecstasy—the audacity, too—of pristine vision are here. . . . No one who really cares for poetry should miss this little book. . . . We have not the slightest idea who Mr. Robert Frost may be, but we welcome him unhesitatingly to the ranks of the poets born, and are convinced that if this is a true sample of his parts he should presently give us work far worthier of honour than much which passes for front-rank poetry at the present time."

He had a hunch that his second volume would fulfill that prediction. In a mood of boyish optimism he wrote in October to Mosher in Maine: "I give you fair warning, I am going to have my moderate success in these islands. The signs are not wanting."

In December his friend Harold Monro published two of the "talk" poems from the manuscript in preparation—"The Fear" and "A Hundred Collars"—in *Poetry and Drama*, among contributions from several of the Georgians, Abercrombie, Gibson, and Rupert Brooke. The distinctive tone of the Frost poems, epitomizing the theories he had voiced to Sidney Cox, set them apart from the others, causing a good deal of speculation as to the identity of the author. Was this Robert Frost a recent addition to the Georgians? A young anthologist and critic, Louis Untermeyer, later told of his experience in coming upon "The Fear" and "A Hundred Collars" in that December issue. He wondered "what Englishman . . . could have written those two poems? . . . There was something beneath local color and far beyond background here; something which, in its very inflection, fixed identity . . . American. It was the accent of common speech and, at the same time, the accent of uncommon poetry. What was more, this was blank verse; yet it was a blank verse so different from the traditional English medium that it had acquired a whole new tone and direction.

"A month or two later the confusion was explained. I learned what has since been enshrined in every American textbook: that Frost's career had been founded on contradictions."

With the new and fateful year of 1914, further notice came to the unique, conversational technique of the "talk" poems that Rob was preparing for his second book, when several of them appeared singly in various magazines. As early as January 15, "The Housekeeper" came out in the *Egoist;* and Harriet Monroe, with some prodding from Pound, had consented to schedule a Frost poem for February—"The Code," which, in a single dramatic incident, depicted the New England hired hand and the unwritten law governing his behavior. Ezra, although at intellectual odds with his stubborn protégé, continued to promote Rob's work in their native land. With mixed feelings toward his "enemy friend," Rob allowed him to send "The Death of the Hired Man," a piece in which he was sure he had "got something he was after," to Willard H. Wright of *Smart Set;* but even with a special word from Pound, the poem was turned down.

Ezra, still optimistic, sent six Frost poems to Ellery Sedgwick, editor of the *Atlantic Monthly.* (Rob had submitted poems to Sedgwick on his own, only to be disappointed, but he hoped that the word of Ezra Pound would make a difference; and surely the reviews of his first book must count for something.) But Sedgwick returned the manuscript with a curt sentence: "We are sorry that we have no place in the *Atlantic Monthly* for your vigorous verse."

"Damn them," Rob said when he heard. And he said it again in telling the story after his second volume appeared. "A few months later these same editors were falling over themselves to get me: *When were they right?*" (There was a practical reason for his being so eager to place his work in magazines: he needed the money for the move they were planning to make.)

In the meantime, Mrs. Nutt was objecting strenuously to any magazine sale of poems to be included in the second volume. Early in March, Robert wrote in a letter to Sidney Cox: "She acts as if she thought I was up to something. Last time I saw her she told me

frankly she thought I had no right under my contract to traffic in
my poetry before I brought it (the book manuscript) to her."

He had decided quite suddenly on a title for the new book, one
more subtle and inclusive than any suggested so far. Since coming
to England, he realized that to the world at large, the image of
New England life was limited to its industrial, cultural, and ship-
ping center; to the average Englishman—and, indeed, American—
Boston seemed to epitomize New England, a false concept that no
poet had corrected thus far—not as he, Robert Frost, had tried to
do in this volume. He sought to present in dramatic poetry the
Yankee farmer as Winslow Homer had portrayed him in painting:
in "truth and honesty," as Henry James had said, so that even
though he might be "damnably ugly," he was an arresting, "attractive" figure, in attributes both individual and universal. The title
of the book, therefore, was going to be simply, *North of Boston,*
depicting life in the hills above the city; and Rob would override
any objections Mrs. Nutt might have.

Lesley was typing the manuscript for him, turning out neat
copies of each poem on the Blickensderfer as he completed the
final revision of the lines. She was capable and quick, full of vitality. With slight coaching from her parents, she could already
read a page of Caesar like a veteran, looking up only a word or so.
At fourteen, going on fifteen, she was also a ready right-hand help
to Elinor, who was no longer tied to the house as much as she had
been during the years in Derry. She sometimes accompanied Rob
at London literary gatherings, and had learned to unbend so far
as to take a cigarette when it was offered—she could at least hold
it between her fingers without offending her Puritan proclivities.

This was again a waiting time, as it had been a year ago before
publication of *A Boy's Will;* they were not lonely any more, but
impatient to be with their friends in Gloucester; and Rob at least
was beginning to feel anxious about the reception *North of Boston*
would get; would the critics understand what he was trying to do?
Would they see New England as he had tried to show it? (He himself "never saw New England as clearly as when he was in Old

England," but perhaps that was because the distance gave a perspective he had not been able to grasp before.) He was tramping around the muddy yard behind the bungalow one murky morning, thinking of the difference in the hill country at home in March, where, instead of yellow fog, a glittering ice storm transformed the scene. Recalling the way the birches looked sent him back in time to the early days when, fresh from San Francisco, he had discovered for himself the suppleness of birch trees, the joy of "swinging" them. Suddenly seized with an idea for a poem, he went into the house, settled himself in the morris chair, and began putting down the words as they came pouring from somewhere within.

The poem, destined to become linked with his name the world over, was among those that took him by surprise, unfolding "by surprise as it went," and written practically all in one go; but when he finished "Birches," he did not give it to Lesley for typing, to go into the current manuscript. Instead he stashed it away like treasure for a later book. Only his beloved Elinor saw the lines. He was not one to squander his poems—or to expose them (as he had exposed "Bond and Free") to the brand of rejection right away.

"I make them in haste and repent of them at liesure," he said in a letter to Marguerite Wilkinson, another anthologist who in a few years would include Robert Frost among the *New Voices* in contemporary poetry.

Eventually, the manuscript for *North of Boston* was ready for Rob to hand in to Mrs. Nutt on the way to the Midlands, where the family was headed by the end of March. Writing to Sidney Cox, Rob outlined the plans. They would make a week of it in London before "we drink silence and hide ourselves in cloud." When he sold the poems to *Poetry and Drama,* he had arranged with Harold Monro to take it out in room rent for the whole family in the upper floors of the Poetry Bookshop in Devonshire Street, which was by way of becoming a threadbare residential club for creative artists. Since Monro was a poet himself in addition to being editor and publisher of the quarterly, he gathered about him the poets who were Frost's friends and enemies. Gibson had

had a room there for about a year before he married Monro's secretary. Jacob Epstein, the futurist sculptor born in New York but now a British subject, whose work was "such a stumbling-block to the staid and Victorianly" was to be across the hall from the Frosts. Rob, who had met him briefly at some of the gatherings in the shop, was eager to talk further with the sculptor whose mind ran strangely on the subject of generation, whose figures were considered monstrosities by many, but who, in spite of all the protests against him, was "reckoned to be one of the greatest living geniuses." Then, too, all the poets in London circles would probably be in and out of the shop. It promised to be a week that Lesley of the children would surely remember.

They also expected to do the city for the youngsters—as much as a poet like Rob Frost was capable of doing a city. He thought there must be a great deal to see in London if one looked for it. For instance, there was the Tower, and—well, he thought "there simply must be something else." He would get a guidebook. Although he took some interest in historical places, he was no sightseer in the accepted sense. People meant more to him than places.

Certainly the people who came and went at the Poetry Bookshop meant much more to the Frosts than the Tower of London or the historic Houses of Parliament. The soot and grime of the city were no more to their liking because of ancient edifices and landmarks than they would be in any industrial town—Liverpool; or Lawrence, Massachusetts. Used to country living, their eyes were on the fair prospect awaiting them in the verdant fields and forests of Herefordshire, where their friends and kindred spirits, the Georgian poets—Wilfrid Gibson, Lascelles Abercrombie, Rupert Brooke, John Drinkwater, and best of all, Edward Thomas—had established a little circle of their own, with a publication of their own, *New Numbers*. There, in the flowering at Eastertide, the hamlet of Dymock (close to which Gibson had found for the Frosts a half-timbered homestead, Little Iddens) was nestled among the surrounding orchards—a rustic and literary haven.

Chapter 9

ENCHANTED RING —
THE DYMOCK CIRCLE

Life at Little Iddens, Ledbury, in the spring of that fateful year 1914, sang with the spirit of the *Golden Treasury,* all unaware of the menacing sword soon to descend over Europe and the world.

Here was the smiling green and gold of pastoral, poetic England that Rob Frost had dreamed of during those dreary months at Dartmouth when, bewildered, he wandered through the woods, perusing his new-found paper copy of Palgrave with increasing wonder and delight. On the day of their arrival, the Frosts were greeted by a golden landscape that flowed beside the river Leaden —"a host of yellow daffodils," thousands of them, dancing in the meadows for miles, from Dymock to Ryton Firs, where Lascelles Abercrombie, who lived there with his family "under thatch," expressed the scene in his line, "Light has come down to the earth and blossoms here."

Just north of Dymock, a couple of miles from Little Iddens, was the ancient thatched cottage of the Gibsons, The Old Nail House, near Greenway—a comfortable walk for Rob and his "band of four," as Abercrombie called the children and Rob, the *tête d'armée.* Close by was the dark green forest of Dean, half-hiding the hamlet of Dymock itself, with its eleventh-century Norman church and primitive Welsh name, meaning "Swineherd's hut"; here one might meet the transient poet-residents, Brooke, and Davies and Drinkwater, perhaps some others at publication time for *New Numbers.* And all about were the rich, well-tended apple orchards of Herefordshire and the neighboring county of Gloucester, the green pasture lands where droves of brown-and-white cattle that bore the place-name cropped the field of grass and lowed softly at eventide.

"Let me try what I can say in a few words about where we are," Rob scribbled in a note to Sidney Cox. "The important thing to us is that we are near Gibson; we are far from any town. . . . We can go almost anywhere we wish on wavering footpaths through the fields. The fields are so small and the trees so numerous along the hedges that, as my friend Thomas says in the loveliest book on springtime England, you might think from a little distance that the country was solid woods.

"We are now in the country, the cider country, where we have to keep a barrel of cider for our visitors and our hired help or we will have no visitors nor hired help."

In one accord, the whole family streamed into the lanes of field and wood; picnics were the order of the day. Elinor didn't even try to have regular meals, but prepared simple cold foods, and spent as much time out of doors as the rest of them. Spring flowers —cowslips—were gathered by the armful. The flowery sunshine of the daffodils was as fleeting as it was heartening; overnight, it seemed, their light was gone. Rob was reminded of another, much earlier poet, Robert Herrick, who had phrased it in the seventeenth century:

> Fair daffodils, we weep to see
> You haste away so soon. . . .

The last stanza of the last poem in *A Boy's Will,* "Reluctance," carried the same feeling one step further by bringing in the end of a love, and in a later poem, a small shining gem composed of four couplets, Rob offered a resolution to the mood; it began:

> Nature's first green is gold,
> Her hardest hue to hold,

and ended:

> So dawn goes down to day.
> Nothing gold can stay.

Their companions, their mode of living in the pastoral setting of Herefordshire, "the most delicately rustic of them all," as Edward Thomas called it, brought the *Golden Treasury* to life for Rob as it had never been, or would not have been, if he had not come to England. It was in the general atmosphere of the place, the poetic aura. No matter if he was planting the vegetable garden with Carol (at thirteen, a young replica of his father), assisted by the three girls, or strolling by himself through orchards fairly bursting with bloom (besides apple, cherry, plum and pear flourished there), the urge to create poetry was upon him, demanding to be satisfied. One day when the air was soft with a shower of fragrant petals shed upon the ground, he sat under a plum tree, forgetful of time, writing the spontaneous love lyric "To Earthward," beginning:

> Love at the lips was touch
> As sweet as I could bear;
> And once that seemed too much;
> I lived on air,

describing the overwhelming sweetness of young love and the inevitable change it must undergo with the passage of time.

His love, mature now, seasoned with the struggle of ensuing years, was no less passionate, but more profound than it had been in the beginning; yet he could speak of it only in poetry; for to him, love was the source of any poem. (Decades later, in speaking of "the figure a poem makes," he said, "It begins in delight and ends in wisdom. The figure is the same as for love.")

It was here at Little Iddens, also, that he wrote the sonnet "Putting in the Seed," which was to be proclaimed by the critic Randall Jarrell one of the most powerful in American poetry, particularly its conclusion:

> How Love burns through the Putting in the Seed
> On through the watching for that early birth
> When, just as the soil tarnishes with weed,
> The sturdy seedling with arched body comes
> Shouldering its way and shedding the earth crumbs.

Edward Thomas came to visit twice during the spring, to share in the talk among the poets, in the idyllic beauty of the countryside he loved so well. Like a benevolent satyr, he bade them all follow him out to listen to "the first abundance of the day-long calling cuckoos . . . the first nightingale song . . . twitched away by gusty winds." (On one of their walks, when Lesley remarked that a flying barnswallow looked like "a bow running away with an arrow," he praised the simile by asking if he might use it in a poem.) Before leaving the second time, he searched for a house in the neighborhood, promising to come back in the summer with his family.

Till then, Rob did a good deal of walking with a Gloucester solicitor, John W. Haines, legal advisor to the Dymock poets, who turned out to be also a leading amateur botanist and lover of poetry. Each had heard of the other before they met, quite by accident, according to Haines. He was meandering through one of the flowery lanes north of Dymock, carrying his botanist's vasculum in case he saw any unusual wild flowers he wanted to take as specimens, when he came upon a "thick-set man of his own age," as he said, of "medium height, with blue eyes and beautifully sensitive mouth, and asked him if he knew where a Mr. Robert Frost lived."

Rob, for his part, had his eyes glued to the tin box in Haines' hand, and was startled to hear his own name. He explained quickly, after acknowledging his identity, that he was a botanist also; and

Haines, introducing himself, said he was aware of that from reading *A Boy's Will*. The two men fell in step, and, with botany as
a binding link, met often afterwards to wander about the countryside—over May Hill, the Leadon valley, and the ridges of the
Cotswolds, hunting flowers together, and discussing poetry. Sometimes they walked at night, and groped by matchlight along the
bank of the Leadon till they found some rare plant they had been
ferreting out; once it was a Spleenwort fern, finally discovered by
a bridge over the river. At other times they searched for Little
Teasel, Lady's Tresses, and Spreading Campanula.

May Hill was a favorite haunt of all the poets, but particularly
of Robert Frost. It was only six miles from Little Iddens—he
could see it from the cobblestone terrace back of the house, where
he often sat revising a poem or taking care of correspondence,
resting the writing pad on his knee. The mountain, a thousand
feet high, afforded a fine view at the top, which, when the talk
flowed freely—as it invariably did with Thomas—evoked the spirit
of the muses; and more than once, the hills resounded with the
ring of poetry recited enthusiastically, spontaneously, from memory. On their descent, the poets usually stopped at a small inn near
the foot, where they relaxed over a country lunch of bread and
cheese and cider, set out on tables under an apple tree.

But for all the "poesy" and simple country pleasures, Rob Frost
could not feel truly relaxed until he had safely passed the publication date for *North of Boston*, April 18, 1914. Anxiety still
sounded a strident note beneath the melody of lines and the chorus
of bird song on his solitary walks through the woods at dusk—
which he sometimes took when "things were going on" inside him.
It was true that *A Boy's Will* had introduced him to the world,
and he had made a good impression; but the real Robert Frost,
the poet of originality, maturity, and insight into humanity, would
stand revealed in *North of Boston;* and there were grave doubts
in the poet's mind whether he would be as well received in his
own striking colors.

He need not have worried. From the first review—and again, it was by Edward Thomas, writing in the London *Daily News—North of Boston* was hailed as a masterpiece of modern poetry, destined to become a classic of its kind. In one voice, the critics accorded Robert Frost a prominent place among the major poets of the world. For the second time, his friend Thomas set the tone of instant recognition when he wrote:

"This is one of the most revolutionary books of modern times, but it is one of the quietest and least aggressive. It speaks, and it is poetry. . . . These poems are revolutionary because they lack the exaggeration of rhetoric, and even at first sight appear to lack the poetic intensity of which rhetoric is an imitation. Their language is free from the poetical words and forms that are the chief material of secondary poets. . . . Many, if not most, of the separate lines and separate sentences are plain and, in themselves, nothing. But they are bound together and made elements of beauty by a calm eagerness of emotion. . . ." This remarkable phrase, which stood out in the long review, remained to signalize the Frostian quality in these and future dramatic poems. And, as if he could not say enough in praise of his American friend's work, Edward Thomas offered in a second review, unsigned, in the *English Review* of August (1914): "Only at the end of the best pieces, such as "The Death of the Hired Man," "Home Burial," "The Black Cottage," and "The Wood-Pile" do we realize that they are masterpieces of deep and mysterious tenderness."

Lascelles Abercrombie, whose critique appeared in the London *Nation* in June, was more analytic, but no less laudatory than Thomas: "His method—we cannot quarrel with it, because in its final result it nearly always accomplishes something remarkable—is to invite us to assist, first, at his careful and deliberate laying of the material for a poetic bonfire; the skill is interesting, and the stuff is evidently combustible; and suddenly . . . we find that a match has been put to the pile. It burns out, as a rule, rather quickly; but while it is burning, substance and fire are completely at one, and at the end we are not left with embers, but with the sense of a swift and memorable experience. . . ." Speaking of the poet's picture of life in New England, he went on, ". . . it is life that has time to look at itself as well as to look about itself. How much of this is due to Mr. Frost's interpretation of New England we, on this side of the Atlantic, can hardly say; but, if internal evidence goes for anything, life has seldom been made into literature with as little manipulation as in this book. . . ."

These were powerful words of praise, and while it might be said that Abercrombie and Thomas were good friends of Frost, they were no less exacting as critics because of it. Moreover, writers who had not met the poet, including those few who could not agree with his conversational approach, concurred that he had revolutionized poetry. Even the London *Times,* "usually so hostile to American verse" (as Amy Lowell remarked), in a variation of Abercrombie's theme, offered: "Poetry burns out of it, as when a faint wind breathes upon smouldering embers."

Rob could not bear to read the reviews as they arrived; it was Elinor who scanned the columns, then happily read them aloud to him. The critical acclaim brought them both deep joy and satisfaction. It was too late for them to feel wild elation; recognition had taken too long in coming. (It was true that Rob had not needed six of the years he dared his grandfather to give him in 1900 when he bought them the farm in Derry; but it was twenty years, almost to the day, since his first poem had been accepted by the *Independent* in 1894. And just three weeks before *North of Boston* was published, the poet had passed his fortieth birthday.)

Yet he did feel a sense of elation when he learned that the Boston *Transcript* had reprinted all of Abercrombie's review in the *Nation* and when his enemy-friend Ezra Pound brusquely demanded a review-copy for a piece in Harriet Monroe's magazine. He felt, as he had the year before when *A Boy's Will* came out, that recognition in America meant more than all the acclaim in the world abroad. Just why this was so it was hard to say, except that love of country was strong in him, and it troubled him to think of his winning a reputation abroad before he was established at home.

But straws were already in the wind pointing to publication in his native land. The article in the Boston *Transcript* had aroused interest in New England; and when Pound's review, entitled "American Georgics," appeared in the December issue of *Poetry,* readers and publishers in the middle west became aware of a new and brilliant light in the American literary scene. In addition, unknown to Rob, Amy Lowell (who was still in London, though she, too, had begun to quarrel with Pound), pricked by curiosity, had discovered her fellow American. As she related a few years later (1917) in her critical work, *Tendencies in American Poetry:* "I had passed the summer of 1914 in England, and there I had heard much talk of *North of Boston.* I well remember purchasing the little green volume at the Poetry Book Shop, and spending an evening reading it with ever increasing delight. On my return home, I suggested its publication to no less than two publishing houses. . . . Mr. Frost's reputation was suddenly made."

Rumor had reached the Dymock poets that as Amy's ardor for imagism increased, her adoration of its dictatorial leader decreased, and she was not only beginning to break away from the fold, but luring away with her for her own Imagist—American version—group some of the most faithful of his flock: Richard Aldington and his wife, H.D.; F. S. Flint; and D. H. Lawrence. She was planning, on her return, to organize the Imagists in America, setting up a center in her palatial residence, Sevenels, in the Victorian aristocracy of Brookline, where she would reign supreme. Pound mockingly coined an appropriate epithet, "Amygisme," to describe her branch of the movement.

Meanwhile, in Dymock, the poets smiled and wrote individually as they pleased, publishing collectively in *New Numbers.* It was a busy center, with poets like Brooke and Drinkwater and Edward Davies (who, with his conceit over his artless nature-poetry, rubbed Rob the wrong way) coming in and out. Most of them depended in large measure on outside assignments—reviews and articles for London papers and periodicals—for their livelihood, and somebody was always having a deadline to meet. (Lesley, imbued with the spirit of the center, started a monthly magazine for the younger generation of the group—one copy, issued every month—with out-side contributions from friends she had made the summer before, the E. C. Smith children in Scotland among them. Irma contrib-uted drawings, and Carol an occasional poem, but he had little time, since he had got himself a job sorting and wrapping the rich Herefordshire apples for market.)

As for Rob, pleased as he was with the reviews of *North of Boston*, he had no idea how the public at large was taking to it, and Mrs. Nutt sent him no word. The "little green volume" itself was attractive, he thought, and followed the format he had wished. He had placed the love lyric, "The Pasture" (the first poem in *A Boy's Will*) in the front of this book, unlisted, before the Table of Contents, to serve as a link between the two volumes, denoting the transition, through love, from the "wind's will" of a boy * to the controlled and seasoned judgment, the insight of a mature man. (And in later years, the young love poem reappeared, unlisted, in the front of every volume of his collected verse, and of the *Complete Poems*, symbolizing the origin of poetry. Significantly, at the front of his last volume, *In the Clearing*, 1962, only one line of the poem was quoted—without the parentheses that had always marked it: "And wait to watch the water clear, I may," placed below the title on the title page.) The inscription in *North of Boston* read: "To E.M.F., This Book of People"; Elinor would know how eloquent the simple words were meant to be.

Before the middle of July, Edward Thomas, true to his promise, came with his wife and three children to stay in the wide wing of the next farmhouse, "three meadows away" from Rob and his family. Their arrival deepened the meaning of the summer, already rich in experience. Edward's wife Helen, a stocky, laughing Welsh-woman, with a forthright, down-to-earth humor in contrast to her husband's intellectual flights and subtle whimsy, proved to be a delightful companion for Elinor; and two of the Thomas children

* Longfellow's lines were:
    A boy's will is the wind's will,
    And the thoughts of youth are long, long thoughts.

—the youngest was not yet walking—were old enough to enter into the activities of the young Frosts (Mervyn, the eldest, was Lesley's age). When a close friend of the Thomases, Eleanor Farjeon, who wrote charming poetry for children, came to visit them for a while, she readily joined the pastimes of the younger as well as the older two-family circle.

As for the two poet-fathers, Rob and Edward, like friends of the mythical past—Damon and Pythias, David and Jonathan—roamed the countryside, one in spirit, one in purpose: to define, to discover the inner workings of their art. It was then that Robert Frost discovered that his friend was more poet than prose writer, as he related in a letter later included in a biography of Thomas by R. P. Eckert:

"Edward Thomas had about lost patience with the minor poetry it was his business to review. He was suffering from a life of subordination to his inferiors. Right at the moment he was writing as good poetry as anybody alive, but in prose form where it did not declare itself and gain him recognition. I referred him to paragraphs in his book *The Pursuit of Spring* and told him to write it in verse form in exactly the same cadence. That's all there was to it. His poetry declared itself in verse form, and in the year before he died he took his place where he belonged among the English poets."

They might spend the morning in a climb to the top of May Hill, declaiming poetry to the four winds as they went, or searching for wild flowers along the way. After lunch at the inn, they might stop at Wilfrid Gibson's, and perhaps the three might go on to Abercrombie's, or make their way back to Rob's, where they sat on the cobbled terrace and, like the Lake poets a century before them, discussed the syntax and sound of poetry. Sometimes they criticized each other's work; sometimes planned new features for *New Numbers*. Occasionally they made day-long expeditions to different spots in the midlands, when their families might come along, forming quite a party, laden with picnic baskets, milk jugs, water bottles and blankets.

For nighttime recreation, it was Rob who suggested poetry-reading by candlelight (most of the farmhouses did not even furnish kerosene lamps); and more often than not, Little Iddens was the scene of single-candle-lit poetry evenings, when four or five Georgians (for Rob was considered "almost" a member of the Dymock circle) gathered together to try their poems aloud (or sometimes reading Shakespeare, as Rob had done in Derry). The children sat on the floor in a semicircle—arms wrapped around drawn-up legs, chins resting on knees—listening, dreaming—and not infrequently giggling at the lines or voices they heard. They might follow with ardent interest Mr. Abercrombie's exciting "Witchcraft: New Style"; but Edward Davies' simple nature studies seemed silly to them. And Mr. Gibson, who later wrote "The Golden Room" in memory of these evenings, and was a pleasant, quiet man, whose ballads often told tragic stories, used such a peculiar high sing-song in his delivery that Lesley for one could hardly stifle the small explosions that burst from her lips. (In vain did Elinor shake her head, so she finally told her daughter, "If you can't control your giggles, just tiptoe out of the room as if you had something very important to do.")

When their friend Mr. Thomas started to read, however, neither Lesley nor anyone else thought of stealing from the room, but listened with joy and fascination; whether he sang or read, whether they understood or not, he cast a charm over young and old alike. Walter de la Mare (another newly published poet, whose work Rob Frost admired), in his introduction to Thomas's *Collected Poems*, captured the rare quality of the man: "His smile could be whimsical, stealthy, shy, ardent, mocking, or drily ironical; he seldom laughed. . . . His voice was low and gentle, but musical, with a curious sweetness and hollowness when he sang his old Welsh songs to the children. I have never heard English used so fastidiously and yet unaffectedly as in his talk. *Style* in talk, indeed, is a rare charm; and it was his. You could listen to it for its own sake. . . . His learning was of men and things at first hand rather than of facts at second or third. . . . What he gave to a friend in his company was not only himself, but that friend's self made infinitely less clumsy and shallow than usual, and at ease. . . . To be with him in the country was to be in one's own native place. . . ."

Small wonder that Rob, whose gifts of personality were nearly paralleled in his friend, should feel so close a kinship to the man whose real talent he unearthed. In 1917, he wrote, revealingly, in a letter to Amy Lowell ". . . the closest I ever came in friendship in England or anywhere else in the world I think was with Edward Thomas who was killed at Vimy last spring. He more than anyone else was accessory to what I had done and was doing. We were together to the exclusion of every other person and interest all through 1914—1914 was our year. I never had, I never shall have another such year of friendship."

1914

The short, happy weeks in July sped by for all of them. It was hard to believe that ominous war clouds had been gathering in Europe since the 28th of June, when the assassination at Sarajevo had startled the world, involving England in a vain effort to prevent war in Europe. Now, almost without warning, it seemed to the Frosts, the guns of August shattered the peace and harmony of the rustic haven, breaking the ring of the Dymock circle. Rupert Brooke, a modern romanticist and perhaps the most dashing of the Dymock poets, who was twenty-seven years old on August 3rd, the day before Britain declared war on Germany, celebrated his birthday by volunteering immediately. Those who were left, trying to cheer themselves with the first false report that the war was not serious and would be over by Christmas, received word from London publications before the second week in August was out that no more reviews or special articles would be assigned until the war was over; the implication was obvious. And one morning a few days later, Edward came over with the news that Chandler, the farmer they were lodging with, a reserve army sergeant, had been called back to service in a Hereford training camp and enrolled for active duty in France. The poets agreed the situation was grave.

As they walked across the fields to Gibson's, breathing the sweet, warm air of the midsummer morning, they speculated sadly on the probable fate of *New Numbers*. When they arrived at the Old Nail

House, Abercrombie was there, conferring with Gibson on the matter; and the four agreed to continue publishing as long as they could . . . at least until Christmas and the December issue proved to be the last.

By August 16, the British Expeditionary Force landed in France and the dimensions of the titanic struggle that was to engulf the world began to take shape. The Thomases were staying on in Dymock for the time being, but Edward was giving serious thought toward enlistment. He spoke no more of the tentative plan he and Rob had made to share a farm in New Hampshire the following summer and, wisely, Rob did not bring up the subject, though he did tell his friend he was thinking of leaving for home, and must cut down on his expenses here some way, at the moment he knew not how.

The war was certainly an ill wind to him, as it was to all the hopeful young writers who were beginning to make a name for themselves. When they learned that so prominent a figure as De la Mare (whom Frost considered the greatest of living poets) lost twelve or fifteen hundred a year by being dropped by the publisher he read manuscripts for, the Dymock poets admitted gloomily that their game was up. There was little hope of publishing any more review articles, let alone books, for any of them, especially Frost, who was not even English.

Indeed, the Frosts were suddenly regarded as rank foreigners —suspicious characters—by their rustic neighbors, who gave small heed to the fact that Robert Frost was a poet, if they knew it. There were queer goings-on at Little Iddens, they thought: candlelight in the latticed windows till all hours! What could it mean? One night a few stones were thrown at the pane close to where Rob was sitting reading. His comings and goings were open to suspicion, too—the way he would run down to London for days at a time, no explanation offered. His New Hampshire accent was questioned. Who could tell if it was really American, or what he was up to?

Rob tried to make light of the attitude, but he knew the Frosts' position was as precarious as their friends', in some respects more so. It was true that his book had been lucky in that it had made its mark with the critics; the reviews had all been "ridiculously favorable," and it received more space than any other book of verse in a long while. The London *Times* gave it three notices; news of the stir it created had already reached New England; he had heard that the Boston *Transcript* carried an article based on the review in the London *Nation*. There were other signs: the Plymouth (N.H.) Public Library bought a copy, and he had received an admiring letter from so remote a village as Stowe, Vermont. The letter, which was from a Mrs. Henry Holt, was to prove significant in a different way, but at the moment Rob considered it merely a note of appreciation from a distant reader. Yet in spite of all this acclaim, his income was at a standstill, and he was at a loss to know what to do.

Lascelles Abercrombie, realizing his plight, suggested that the Frosts move in with them when winter came; by sharing house, the expenses of both families would be cut down. Both Elinor and Robert welcomed the idea, if by then they had not found the fare to go home, or a job to pay for it after they got there. Rob was more and more concerned for the future; his letters to Sidney Cox were harried and undecided. It was a vicious circle, trying to be a poet and a provider for his family at the same time. Almost wistfully he wrote that he really would like a quiet job in a small college where he would be "allowed to teach something a little new on the technique of writing" and where he would have some honor "just a little bit," he said, "for what I suppose myself to have done in poetry. Well, but I mustn't dream. . . ."

Yet he did allow himself to live for a few more weeks in the dream world of poetry and blossoms, as he and Edward Thomas continued their famous talks, their leisurely walks about the countryside. Each knew instinctively that this was to be their final moment of friendship, but neither betrayed the inner knowledge, and both later wrote poems of these strangely serene remaining hours in the face of the stresses surrounding them. In one of the last prose writings of Thomas, *This England,* he presented a rich word-picture of the pastoral, peaceful scenery they both cherished: ". . . now I was here for the third time since the year began. . . . Here I had the consummation of Midsummer, the weather radiant and fresh, yet hot and rainless, the white and pink wild roses, the growing bracken, the last and best of the songs, blackbird's, black-cap's. Now it was August, and again no rain fell for many days; the harvest was a good one, and after standing long in the sun it was gathered in and put in ricks in the sun, to the contentment of men and rooks. All day the rooks in the wheat-fields were cawing a deep sweet caw, in alternating choirs or all together. . . ."

The day-long walks soon lengthened into nighttime, and on one of these, shortly before the Thomas family left Herefordshire—a soft September evening after a rain—the two poets witnessed a sin-gular sight, sensed a mystical experience, immortalized by Robert Frost more than twenty years afterwards in his haunting ode, "Iris by Night."

His phrase painting in the line, "Light was a paste of pigment in our eyes," evoked the mood and color created by "a small rain-bow like a trellis gate | A very small moon-made prismatic bow," and the wonder of the miracle that he alone lived to tell: the rain-bow lifted its "two mote-swimming many-colored ends, | And gath-ered them together in a ring," so that he and Edward stood

> softly circled round
> From all division time or foe can bring
> In a relation of elected friends.

When Edward Thomas and his family were gone, the summer was gone; the golden light gave way to gray as the winter rains moved in, and Rob Frost and his family moved from Little Iddens to share the Abercrombies' house at Ryton Dymock. Now at last they were living "under thatch," as Elinor had expressed it in the Plym-outh kitchen, but the picturesque old house had little charm in the circumstances; the usual tensions arose about the arrangements of joint living, and Rob and Elinor had heated domestic discus-sions about going home, how the fare was to be accomplished, and so on, while in the background lurked the grim specter of the war. After a particularly vehement dispute over the advisability of leaving England at once, Rob flung himself out of the house to tramp in the chill, raw night:

> Out alone in the winter rain,
> Intent on giving and taking pain.
> But never was I far out of sight
> Of a certain upper-window light.

These were the opening lines of a later poem called "The Thatch," in which he described "how that grief started to melt"; it was

> ... the strangest thing: in the thick old thatch,

summer birds were still living, and as he passed along the eaves, his sleeves brushing against them, he flushed birds out of hole after hole, plunging them bewildered into the darkness of the wet ground. Their startled cries, and the fact that they could not go flying in search of their nest in the blackness of night, grieved the poet so deeply that his own grief was greatly reduced.

Elinor was of the opinion that they should sail for home on the first ship where they could book passage, while Rob (stubbornly) wanted to remain in England for a time, until his reputation at home would be established by his success here. As his friends left for the front, he considered enlisting in the B.E.F., but he did not mention this to Elinor. If only he would receive some report on the book from Mrs. Nutt!

In the meantime, he sent a batch of the circular for *North of Boston* to Sidney Cox some time in October, asking his young friend to "scatter" them in the most likely places to build interest in the book. He wrote to Mrs. Nutt, suggesting Thomas Bird Mosher as a possible American publisher, but she retaliated with a curt answer, saying that she did not think much of Mosher and that someone else had signed an agreement to publish in the states —she did not give the name of the firm. Puzzled, half-pleased and amused, half-annoyed, Rob wrote to the Maine publisher in November, just as the British were moving into the terrible misfortune at Ypres. He thanked Mosher for his interest, and informed him that the book was already taken in America.

Toward Christmas, Mrs. Nutt finally sent a summons, inviting the Frosts to have dinner with her. Quiet, reserved Elinor at first felt shy in the presence of the dragonlike lady publisher, but her diffidence was soon overcome by indignation at the suspicion and arrogance Mrs. Nutt displayed. When Rob asked innocently enough how the book was doing, the answer he received was:

"Just like you Americans—all dollar chasers!"

"But, Mrs. Nutt, I am not asking about the money—I only want to know if people like the book," Rob protested, with a glance across the table at Elinor, to show her he was more amused than angry.

Again Mrs. Nutt called him a dollar chaser, and he said boldly:

"If you call me a dollar chaser, I'll go home and keep America out of the war!"

Elinor was possessed by a desire to giggle almost as uncontrollable as Lesley's, but she was still piqued, and she suggested softly, "Rob, I think we must leave; it's getting late."

At that, their imperious hostess bethought herself, and gave them the news she had in store: Henry Holt and Company was to publish the book—*North of Boston*—in America. More than this she did not offer to reveal, and the Frosts were too amazed, too flabbergasted by the whole affair, to inquire about details. They had no idea how it came about unless it was through the woman by the name of Holt who wrote Rob the appreciative letter from Stowe, Vermont, in the summer.

Rob wrote to Sidney just before the holiday: "This is only to say that Henry Holt will supply the book in America. Will you write that on any circulars you have still to send out?" He went on to state their dilemma about leaving: "They say the Germans have made the whole Atlantic unsafe." He did not know if he dared to go or stay.

"If you never hear from me again, write Henry Holt & Co., Publishers, New York, on the circulars and let it go at that."

In a more formal manner, he sent the announcement from Mrs. Nutt to Mosher, again expressing his regret.

The news from the front became more disturbing. The problems Rob had put to Sidney Cox were those that he and Elinor parried day and night, trying to find a safe solution to their quandary as the new year arrived and the guns in Europe continued to shake the world. From the depths of his struggle, Rob wrote to Sidney early in January, giving vent to his feelings. Philosophically, he approved of the war, but he could not like it.

The poetry writing did not cease because of the harassing worry of world conflict. The endless querying itself evoked a poem—"The Sound of the Trees"—"written for Abercrombie," Frost said, feeling that his friend was more than tolerant of the never-ending confabs, which he compared to the incessant sound of the firs outside.

It was another month before he could make up his mind, make arrangements to leave. Then, early in February, he sent a brief message to Sidney, telling him to send no more letters to Ryton-Dymock. They were sailing for home by the *St. Paul* from Liverpool on February 13th.

Thinking of his "closest friend," Edward Thomas, already enlisted, whose literary course he had helped to decide, and tying it up with the recollection of his mystical experience in the New Hampshire woods just before he decided to come to England, Robert Frost found inspiration, just before leaving the country that had recognized him, for one of his most revealing poems. Still living "under thatch" at Abercrombie's, he wrote "The Road Not Taken," in which he presented the scene on that twilight evening four years before, giving it the added touch of the creative spirit that makes art out of reality. With a single adjective in the opening line, "Two roads diverged in a yellow wood," he removed the setting from the realm of strict reality (for the woods in Plymouth had been white with snow); or, rather, he brought to it the force of his inner struggle. His ever-present objectivity enabled him to observe with a smile that someday, in the dim ages ahead, he would be telling this story. He concluded the poem with the combination of fooling and seriousness that was the hallmark of his complexity. Since he "could not travel both and be one traveler," he stood looking down one a long time, and then chose the other:

> Two roads diverged in a wood, and I—
> I took the one less traveled by,
> And that has made all the difference.

Chapter 10

END OF A ROAD

When the long voyage home began aboard the *St. Paul,* a tourist ship stripped for safety according to wartime regulations, Robert Frost, recognized a poet at last, stood beside Elinor with mixed feelings of triumph and apprehension. Besides their own band of four, the Frosts had Mervyn Thomas in tow; Rob had promised Edward that he would see the boy safely to the refuge of British friends living in New England. The risk they were taking increased after a day or two at sea; Germany officially declared its submarine blockade againt Great Britain, which meant extra precautions must be taken; but the young Frosts and their friend entered into the spirit with a will, and were soon adept at donning life preservers, rapid lifeboat drills, and blacked-out portholes at night.

As for Rob and Elinor, the two for whom "The mystic link to bind and hold Spirit to matter till death come" was perhaps stronger than it had ever been, the perilous crossing represented a renewal of the closeness they had always known; the wrangling of the past few weeks over the plans to return was unusual for them. As they sat together on deck, huddled under blankets and heavy shawls against the biting cold of the February sea-breeze, once again of one accord, they could not help gloating over their success in England, the fact that they were returning in triumph. Rob had written "That life has for us on the wrack Nothing but what we somehow chose." They had chosen well; any pain they suffered had been outdistanced by far greater victory than they had dared to hope for in another country.

But would he be so triumphantly received in his own country? Rob wondered. Outside *Poetry,* no magazines had shown signs of welcoming his work any more now than two years ago. The fact that he had won his name across the sea instead of in his native land still bothered him—perhaps irrationally, since he had not set out for fame abroad; he had had nothing to do with it, really. That was as it happened, he told Elinor, who nodded consolingly. Yet, remembering the first meetings at the Poetry Bookshop, and having the need to convince himself, he repeated the words firmly, thoughtfully.

Moreover, he had had no financial success to back up the glory; Mrs. Nutt had not paid him a penny in royalties so far, nor had she given him any idea what arrangements had been made with Henry Holt. The meager funds they had brought with them had been spent for their living in England during the past two and a half years. Rob had just about enough left to take them all to Lawrence, if they boarded the Fall River night boat out of New York right away. He hoped to be able to make some business arrangements through his grandfather's estate for the purchase of another small farm; he and Elinor had decided, in talking things over as the *St. Paul* plied warily through the submarined waters, that they would like to live high up near the Notch in New Hampshire, not too far from Bethlehem, where the Lynches dwelt. Rob had a number of poems in hand, and his head was already singing with the urge to create enough new pieces for a third volume. As soon as the family was settled in the calm clear mountain air, the poems would come pouring out. Elinor was sure he could find them the right place. Rob, however, was not at all sure he could find the means to do it in the first place. In fact, as the ship came in sight of the Statue of Liberty, except that they were all alive, he was certain of very little, save that he was a poet—and a mature one now.

He had hardly made the observation when another stumbling-block presented itself: immigration officers who came aboard just before the *St. Paul* docked, discovered that Mervyn Thomas was under age for legal entry—sixteen—though he was only a few weeks from it; he would have to go to Ellis Island and would probably be deported back to England! Thinking of his friend Edward now in training, Rob was furious—a fine welcome from the land of the free and the home of the brave to the son of a British poet-soldier! However, as Mervyn's sponsor, he was at a loss—literally—to tell the officers he could assume financial responsibility for the boy; he had barely enough for their fare to New England. His "high-hearted penury" as Harriet Monroe described it in a future article, was extremely frustrating at the moment. But he swore by all the gods above, as Mervyn marched away between the two immigration officials, that he would have him released from the misery of Ellis Island by morning. He would find a way!

In this mood, hovering between high dudgeon and despair, the West Street docks looked dreary indeed to Rob Frost and his family as they stood in a huddle on the morning of Washington's Birthday, planning their course of action. Each one, even nine-year-old Marjorie, was carrying a piece of hand luggage, but they were ready to start walking toward the East Side Elevated and a train for Grand Central Station, where they would spend the day in the waiting room. They headed uptown for a block or two, when Rob thought of getting a newspaper to check the sailing time of the night boat, and herded his brood into the next crosstown street.

He stopped at the first newsstand, and while waiting for his change, noticed a copy of the new weekly he had heard so much about—the *New Republic*—dated February 20, 1915. He picked it up and automatically turned to the Book Section: there, the second item, practically jumping out at him, was a review of *North of Boston* by no less a person than Amy Lowell.

He stared at it incredulously for a moment, a little smile, half-pleased, half-skeptical, flitting across his face. Then he told the vendor to keep the change, called to the others and handed Elinor the magazine, holding it open to the place. "You read it!" he said, taking her arm; he could not.

So Elinor, as usual, glanced quickly down the columns and started to read bits here and there, trying to keep the pages from flipping over in the wind as she and Rob walked behind the children, arm in arm. It was something of a shock, and ironic, in a way, that the leader of the Imagist movement in America should be reviewing his first American-published volume just as the leader of the Imagiste movement in London had reviewed his first volume under British imprint; he didn't give a snap of his fingers for the movement in either country (spelled with or without an "e"!). Still, Amy Lowell was an important, influential figure, the sister of President Lowell of Harvard, and principal critic of the latest highbrow review. He caught words and phrases borne on the wind from Elinor's lips: well, he was "photographic," was he? and a "recorder of a dim decaying New England"; he "lacked humor," depicted characters "unchanged by any personal mental process" . . .

Nevertheless, as he listened more closely to find out if Miss Lowell had any praise to offer, Rob realized that the review was meant to be commendatory:

"One of the great interests of the book is the uncompromising New Englander it reveals. . . . And Mr. Frost has chosen his medium with an unerring sense of fitness. . . . He has not been seduced into subtleties of expression which would be painfully out of place. His words are simple, straightforward, direct, manly, and there is an elemental quality in all he does which would surely be lost if he chose to pursue niceties of phrase. He writes in classic meters in a way to set the teeth of all the poets of older schools on edge; and he writes in classic meters and uses inversions and clichés whenever he pleases, those devices so abhorred by the newest generation. He goes his own way, regardless of anyone else's rules, and the result is a book of unusual power and sincerity."

The main thing was: the book was out! The poet-author had to find out more details of publication—why had he not been notified?

With Elinor and the youngsters deposited at Grand Central, Rob hurried to the Holt office at 34 West 33rd Street. Henry Holt, who was then seventy-five years old, was not much in evidence any more, but Mr. Alfred Harcourt, the young manager of the trade department, was in his office. In the words of Harcourt, "a rangy man of about forty, with an extraordinarily sensitive face, appeared at the door of my office and introduced himself as Robert Frost." Almost the first thing the young trade manager did was to reach in his desk drawer and pull out a check for $90. Rob was astonished. Harcourt explained that the new magazine had published "The Death of the Hired Man" in the February 6th issue, and had paid the usual rates for an extract from the book.

To Robert Frost at that moment, the money was like manna: some Heaven-sent impulse must have impelled him to rush down to his publisher before buying passage on the night boat. Now he made a lightning change of plans, and telegraphed the Lynches, inquiring if he could send the family up right away. While he waited for an answer, he settled down for a talk with Alfred Harcourt, who struck him as both a live wire and an intensely likeable, sincere young man.

For one thing, he had a disarming honesty that was a happy discovery for Rob, considering the strained business relations he had known with Mrs. Nutt and her secret machination. In telling the story of the way *North of Boston* had reached the publishers, Harcourt confessed that when the British copy was sent to him by Mrs. Holt from Stowe (Rob's assumption had been correct!) the trade manager took little stock in her enthusiastic recommendation; with the customary disdain of an editor for the literary judgment of the boss's wife, he had consigned the copy to the waste basket. Shortly afterward, noticing it still lying among the discarded papers, something made him retrieve it and rather resentfully to start reading the first lines of the first poem:

> Something there is that doesn't love a wall,
> That sends the frozen-ground-swell under it,

> And spills the upper boulders in the sun;
> And makes gaps even two can pass abreast.

The blank verse, the conversational tone of "Mending Wall," with its refutation of the old adage, "Good fences make good neighbors," pleased the young editor, and led him on to the second selection, "The Death of the Hired Man." The quiet eloquence of its opening had a quality of the stillness of death:

> Mary sat musing on the lamp-flame at the table
> Waiting for Warren. . . .

Harcourt had read on, fascinated.

He did a complete about-face, asked Dorothy Canfield Fisher, a Vermont writer on his trade list, to read the book, and had hardly received her warm confirmation of his opinion before he was writing Mrs. Nutt to see what arrangements could be made. She had hedged, then offered to sell a small edition of one hundred and fifty copies in sheets, for which the Holts had to pay roundly. Harcourt's enthusiasm, however, knew no bounds. He carried the sheets around with him, and bragged to Sinclair Lewis that they were publishing a book of poems by a new American writer that would sell 10,000 copies in its first season. It was then that he had persuaded Francis Hackett, the editor of the *New Republic,* to read the sheets and print a selection in one of the first issues. The small edition had come out in tan boards, and the next month, in March, they were publishing the first truly American edition. He presented the poet with an author's copy—cloth-bound in blue, with gilt-stamped cover. (Opposite the title page was an advertisement for *A Boy's Will*—"75 cents net"—with quotes from two reviews, one of which Rob had not seen, from the *Dial*: "These songs give us the sort of pleasure that we have in 'The Shropshire Lad' of Mr. Housman." Before the first poem was the only prose gloss line he had written for *North of Boston:* " 'Mending Wall' takes up the theme where 'A Tuft of Flowers' in *A Boy's Will* laid it down.")

He had begun this book of people with "Mending Wall" as a symbol of his return to the realm of human beings from the more isolated one of nature, to show that—as he put it in a letter to Braithwaite, poetry critic of the Boston *Transcript:* "I liked people even when I believed I detested them." Now he bid fair to become overwhelmed by the world (the literary "haut-monde," Pound would have called it) of editors, publishers and critics as he listened to Harcourt run down the list of those who were eager to meet him —among them, magazine editors who had refused Frost's poetry. The staff of the *New Republic*—Francis Hackett, Walter Lippmann, Philip Littell, Herbert Croly—wanted him for a Round Table lunch right away. The Poetry Society was making inquiries about him. Harcourt thought he should make as many contacts as possible, and Rob was ready to accept his advice; but first he had to see the family off and try to get poor Mervyn Thomas released. He explained the situation indignantly, and Harcourt nodded, understanding. He would be glad to help in any way if he could.

Elinor accepted Rob's news philosophically, with a mixture of joy and resignation, when he returned to the station and pulled the surprise check of "good poetry-money" out of his pocket. If she would have preferred going to lunch with literary celebrities to transporting their brood to the New England hills, still deep in snow, to facing the rigors of a freezing farmhouse without Rob, she gave no sign. Caring for their children was her sphere just as poetry was his, and if the youngest didn't see why Papa couldn't go with them, it was up to Elinor to help her realize that his role as poet came first. He promised to try to join them before Marjorie's birthday.

He reached Ellis Island around noon the next day, and found Mervyn already being cross-questioned by three judges in a makeshift courtroom. The boy had spent the night in a prisonlike dormitory, among doubtful immigrants and misfits, one of whom committed suicide just before dawn. A frightened adolescent, he tried valiantly to answer the prying questions hurled at him by the authorities, who were obviously in a hurry to "get this over with so we can go to lunch," as Rob heard one of them mutter. His righteous anger spilled over.

"Tell them you don't *want* to stay in a country like this!" he cried out to Mervyn.

At that the judges gave their verdict without further ado: Mervyn Thomas must go back to England on the next boat. Furious, Frost remembered what Harcourt had said and called the Holt office. Harcourt got in touch with their lawyer, who dictated a letter for Frost to give to Fred Howe, Immigration Commissioner. Howe asked no further questions, but released Mervyn to the care of Robert Frost—poet extraordinary, artist of new-found fame.

He could not stay long in New York, however; he had to go to Lawrence to see about his income. And perhaps it was compulsive, but he had a need to visit Ernest Jewell, to make sure his high school friend and first editor knew how much he had accomplished just since *A Boy's Will* was published. Exactly why he cared to be vindicated in the eyes of his old high school mates was hard to say, unless it was as compensation for the fact that neither his mother nor his grandparents had lived long enough to witness his success. (And Ernest had been one of those who was "disappointed" in Rob for leaving Dartmouth—for fiddling around with odd jobs.) Robert wrote to Sidney Cox, who was teaching in Schenectady, on March 2nd, just before leaving Lawrence, expressing his desire to see and talk to his "disciple." Perhaps Sidney could visit them at the Lynches'.

His appeal for funds from his grandfather's estate was not yet settled when he left for Boston, though he had managed to garnish a few dollars for traveling expenses. He was eager to join Elinor and the children, but Harcourt had made him promise to stop in the city and let himself be lionized a little. The experience was still novel, but from the sample he had had in New York, he was not at all sure it was to his liking.

Now he met the redoubtable Amy Lowell and charming Josephine Preston Peabody, both rather formidable patrons, with Mrs. William Vaughn Moody and Harriet Monroe of Chicago, of modern poetry in America. No matter how little he had in his pocket, Robert Frost hadn't cottoned to the idea of patronage from Ezra

Pound, and he wasn't going to accept it from the ex-patriate's ex-disciple. He sparred good-naturedly with Amy on her pet theories, but when, after a cut-glass dinner, she lit one of her black cigars, blew a cloud of smoke and asked point-blank how he liked her poetry, he was at a loss to know what to say, since he didn't think much of it. Nor did he compliment the other patroness-poet, who was Mrs. Lionel Marks in private life, and was said to have found Edwin Arlington Robinson a publisher for his *Captain Craig;* Mrs. Moody was also helping him. Let Robinson rely on these women if he wished; perhaps it was permissible in a cynical old bachelor.

It was in a conventional Boston setting, at a formal, rather chilly gathering of intellectuals, that Frost was introduced to the elder statesman among poets himself. The conversation all evening was more or less of a blur, until, just as they were leaving, Robinson remarked bluntly, "Frost, you look as if you needed a glass of bitters!" They located one, after which things began to warm up: "There were Robinson and I, . . . and the place (near Boston Common) was the Place, as we liked afterward to call it, of Bitters, because it was with bitters, though without bitterness, we could sit there and look out on the welter of dissatisfaction and experiment in the world around us." So wrote Rob Frost years later in his introduction to Robinson's *King Jasper.* "It was too long ago to remember who said what, but the sense of the meeting was, we didn't care how arrant a reformer or experimentalist a man was if he gave us real poems. For ourselves, we should hate to be read for any theory upon which we might be supposed to write. Take the theory that poetry in our language could be treated as quantitative, for example. Poems had been written in spite of it. And poems are all that matter. The utmost ambition is to lodge a few poems where they will be hard to get rid of, to lodge a few irreducible bits where Robinson lodged more than his share."

Such was the sort of talk Rob had enjoyed with the poets in England—an exchange of notes, of creative experience. He admired *The Town Down the River,* and was interested in Robinson's comments on *North of Boston.* Together they guardedly reviewed

Masters' *Spoon River Anthology*, and debated the similarities and differences among the three books of people. He much preferred shop-talk to party chatter, no matter how clever and witty it might be.

The most glittering of the cut-glass dinners was the one presided over by Ellery Sedgwick, editor of the *Atlantic Monthly* and Rob Frost's arch editorial foe, who had turned down only a year ago six of the poems now being hailed in *North of Boston*, in part, as the vigorous verse he had rejected! Sitting at this august table, surrounded by the most brilliant literary lights in Boston, Rob experienced one of the early crests in his public career; it was a sweet moment of retribution, and he relished the flavor of his triumphant return, now a reality instead of a hope. Paradoxically, however, he had moments of wondering what he was doing here in this opulence, when he had hardly enough for his hotel room, and much preferred the country to the city. Moreover, he was objective enough to realize that these state occasions were a babbling confusion of personalities and ideas, so that it was impossible to savor the individual excellence of any particular ones.

He would have enjoyed, for example, much more conversation with two of his table-mates—Ernest Hocking, Professor of Philosophy at Harvard, and his wife, Agnes—with whom he sensed at once an intellectual meeting of minds. Mrs. Hocking, a daughter of poet John Boyle O'Reilly, possessed a birdlike quality that touched him, as if "she was always poised to fly and quivering her wings." But there was little chance to talk, especially since the Hockings had to leave early to attend a Lowell lecture. After the dinner, authors and editors came crowding around with questions about his poetry and plans, and he made up his mind to leave the city as soon as possible.

He was in the North Station the next day, inquiring about train schedules, when he was greeted by none other than Agnes Hocking, who told him she "had regretted not having asked him to tea."

"When do you want me?" Rob asked.

"This afternoon."

"I will be there." As Ernest Hocking related in a letter to a mutual friend: "He came, and we began talking; he stayed the night, he stayed the next day and the next night. When I had to go to class, Agnes Hocking took him on; and when she had to get a meal, I took him on. We had a great time. In three days' time, we had done a fair two years' job of ripening friendship."

Through the Hockings, Rob met informally his one-time teacher in Logic, during the distraught years when he had tried to finish his degree at Harvard. This was Professor Emeritus George Herbert Palmer of the Philosophy Department, colleague of William James and George Santayana. Rob had found him rather stuffy in those days, and his pomposity had increased with age. His logic was, "In a democracy, the greatest poet should be the one read by the greatest number of people. If so, Edgar Guest is the greatest American poet!" He invited Frost to his dignified mansion next to Harvard Yard, showed him the famous Palmer collection of manuscripts, and proceeded to give him some gratuitous advice. Now that Robert Frost was a name, he should write on a grand scale, produce a serious work—an epic, Palmer said. To that end, he offered his ex-student the use of a house next to his summer home at Boxwood. But again Rob stubbornly refused patronage. He must be beholden to no one—except himself.

The mere thought of feeling obligated to write an epic sent him fleeing the cultured city for the rugged country of the New Hampshire hills. He was not happy without Elinor and the children; and he had a need to look on the "Great granite terraces in sun and shadow, Shelves one could rest a knee on getting up—" as he described them in "The Mountain." By March 13, he was happily reunited with his family, but still worried about finances.

Elinor was proud of Rob's reception by the literary world, eager to hear every detail; she was proud of the article in the Talk of the Town column—"the Herald scrap," Rob called it when he sent the clipping to Sidney. Nevertheless, he was as pleased as Elinor with the story, which, reading from a retrospective point of view, took on the tone of a fairy-tale:

"Boston's literary sensation of the day has been the home-coming of Robert Frost. Three years ago a young New Hampshire school-master went over to England, lived in retirement for a while, and published a volume of poems which won him many friends in a quiet way. Some time later another volume of verse went to the same publisher and one morning Robert Frost found himself famous. He was sought on every hand in the circles where literature values count and was acclaimed one of the elect —ranking with Masefield, Gibson, Abercrombie and others of that high grade in the younger generation of British poets. . . . In due time copies crossed the water and appeared in the bookstores and the libraries. Readers began to discuss the remarkable work and ask, 'Who is Robert Frost?' Nobody could say, in spite of diligent inquiry, and *Who's Who* was silent.

" 'You'd better get hold of him,' said a friend to the editor of *The Atlantic*—'he's another Masefield.'

"Then came the news that Frost had just landed in New York with his family, on his way back to New Hampshire, to take up farming again—he had been a farmer as well as a schoolteacher.

"Last Friday they were discussing Frost at the monthly 'shop talk' of the Boston Authors' Club; one of the members, reading from his work, said that Frost was doing for New England in verse what Alice Brown, Mary Wilkins and Sarah Orne Jewett had been doing in prose. Another member announced that Mr. Frost was in Boston that day, and was dining that evening with Mr. Ellery Sedgwick and some literary friends. . . ." There was more, in the same high-flown style. Sedgwick, whom Rob referred to as "mine ancient enemy," was one of those who had asked to see some of his latest work, but the poet was holding off: the time did not seem right—and he did not want to appear too eager, although the fee would have been welcome.

They waited impatiently for some word from Lawrence; until he knew what his income would be, Rob could not even look for a farm. The tree-covered slopes that formed the Notch were still deep in snow; he and Carol split wood every day to keep the stove-

fires burning in their bedrooms at the Lynches'. Marjorie's birthday was marked by meager celebration, but she didn't seem to
mind. Then came the news that the $800 a year from the Frost
estate could continue another five years or so before the principal
was exhausted. At least he wouldn't be in the poorhouse or jail for
that length of time, Rob observed philosophically in a letter to his
friend Sidney, on March 22nd.

He only hoped his children—or those who thought well of him—
would not judge him too harshly in five years for having written
poetry. Marj, for example, had told Mrs. Lynch she thought her
father was a good one to write poetry and to bring up children.
He suspected she was wrong, but as long as she believed what she
said, he was safe. The possibility that he was denying his children
a proper upbringing gnawed at him from time to time, but he
knew that for him there could be no other way. He ended with a
fatherly note to Sidney: "And a word more to you, my son. You
are to dispense with further talk of disparity between us. I have
never had such thoughts and I dislike having them thrust upon
me."

On the same date, March 22nd, 1915, he sent a biographical
account of himself, along with a copy of *A Boy's Will* to William
Stanley Braithwaite, poetry editor of the Boston *Transcript,* who
had requested both when they met at the Sedgwick dinner. In his
letter, Robert Frost analyzed, to some extent, his past life as it
related to his theories on the language and sound of poetry—perhaps to clarify his position in his own mind as much as Braithwaite's; he began by explaining the psychological basis of *A Boy's
Will;* then he went on to voice his interest in people—at first no
more than a technical interest in their speech, and later in their
emotions as revealed by their talk. Gossip, the actuality, the intimacy of it, gave meaning to their words. He believed that "the
sense of intimacy gives the thrill of sincerity."

Assured of a minimum income from his holdings and whatever
amount in royalties his books might bring, he still couldn't get
over the difference between his doubt-ridden dealings with Mrs.

Nutt and the feeling of confidence the Holts had given him by a single act of faith on their part. Even now Mrs. Nutt was causing trouble over the copyright, while the Holts were making plans to do whatever they could to help him over the financial hurdle. Meanwhile, Robert Frost set about finding a farm in Franconia. He started off on foot, circling the countryside in the next few weeks, tramping over snow or, later, sloughing in muddy roads in search of the right place. He felt once again "the importance of being versed in country things"; as he returned at dusk on one of the first nights, he experienced again the contemplative quality of "Evening in a Sugar Orchard," a feeling he expressed by writing a lyric with that title, capturing the scene as the tree branches caught the sparks from the sugar-house fire, turning them into momentary stars.

When the snow ran down the hills in springtime, melted by a mild vernal sun, Rob recalled for Carol one of his boyhood thrills —his original manner of responding to the joy of

A HILLSIDE THAW

To think to know the country and not know
The hillside on a day the sun lets go
Ten million silver lizards out of snow!

His unique figure was carried through the second stanza, which, like counterpoint, describes the opposite effect, and begins:

It takes the moon for this. The sun's a wizard
By all I tell; but so's the moon a witch.
From the high west she makes a gentle cast
And suddenly, without a jerk or twitch,
She has her spell on every single lizard.

Farm-hunting near Franconia took longer than the Frosts expected, because, as the poet wrote of their chosen state,

Just specimens is all New Hampshire has,
One each of everything as in a show-case
Which naturally she doesn't care to sell.

Not even New Hampshire farms are much for sale.

When he finally found a place, he almost had to take it by force. The farm next to it was for sale, but the poet preferred this one. The farmer, undoubtedly the owner, was outdoors raking up after winter, when Rob approached him, introduced himself, and announced boldly: "I'm going to put you off this farm. I want it." A born New Englander, the farmer showed little emotion; he scarcely looked up from his raking to ask, "Where do you expect to put me? in the road?" Rob was ready for him; the farmer could move to the next piece of property. The man eyed him sharply: "Why won't that farm do for you?" he demanded. Rob could only say that he liked this better, and after some further crossfire between them, the man, whose name was Herbert, said he would consider it.

In almost the same words, Rob related the scene to Elinor when he came back, his scouting at an end. (Later he included the entire colloquy in the satire, "New Hampshire.") The William Herbert farm lay on the west slope of Sugar Hill two miles from Franconia, looking out on the Lafayette range, its mountains "curled up in a coil," and the Pemigewasset River. The site was just the sort of "interval" Rob had been wanting for the creation of the third volume—Elinor's book; for this one was to be written to her. And he would get the Herbert place yet, she would see! If Elinor shook her head, it was with a fond smile at her incorrigible, remarkably youthful, mercurial, many-faceted, deeply gifted mate; but she couldn't help wondering if he wasn't being too optimistic.

However, in due New Hampshire course, word traveled that Willis Herbert was moving to a red farmhouse down the road a piece: he'd bought it to accommodate some "queer duck" who'd agreed to buy his place for $1,000—no down payment. But while the title was being cleared and some improvements made, farmer Herbert found out that Robert Frost was a well-known poet. Toward the end of April he showed up at the Lynches' to talk things over: since Mr. Frost was "somebody" (he'd heard), couldn't he pay a hundred dollars more? Rob consented: $1,100 final. Until the improvements were completed, the family couldn't move in, but Rob had already picked out an upstairs bedroom over the porch for use as his study; the front window had a majestic view of three mountains—Lafayette, Liberty, and Cannon—"cut into the sky." He and the children would climb those mountains several times during the summer.

In the meantime, the newly famous poet was invited to read some of his work before the Phi Beta Kappa Society at Tufts College on May 5th. The day before marked the fatal sinking of the *Lusitania*, setting the country on the brink of war; but Rob Frost, on his way to Malden, was almost as scared of facing his first "town-and-gown" audience. He was to stay at Sylvester Baxter's, and when he reached the professor's house, he was introduced to another guest speaker staying there—Louis Untermeyer. Between these two brilliant minds flashed an immediate exchange of wit, humor, and poetic insight. It was as if they had always been friends—and the bond betwen them was to last—so that by the time Rob had to read, he was much less scared. He had chosen three of his best poems as yet unpublished: "Birches," "The Road Not Taken," and "The Sound of Trees"; and he spoke the lines "in talking tones, following the curve and play of feeling, as people with some reserve speak when they have their hearts in what they say" (as his young friend Sidney once wrote). His distinctive style of delivery, utterly devoid of elocutionary tricks, yet moving in its naturalness and genuine emotion, was overwhelmingly successful, adding renown as a reader of poetry to his growing fame as a writer of new blank verse.

The time was ripe, Baxter advised him, to beard the editorial lion, Sedgwick, in his den on Beacon Hill; he (Baxter) would even arrange the appointment. So Rob Frost, with the applause of the honor society ringing in his ears and the three poems bulging out his pocket, suddenly found himself being ushered into the inner sanctum on Park Street. According to his account, told with gentle irony, Sedgwick began, with professional benevolence:

"We are going to be your true friends. We are going to hold you up to your best."

Rob eyed him skeptically and sat down in the chair Sedgwick indicated, offering no comment. The urbane editor then went on to discuss an essay which Frost had sent him, an article on the poet by the British critic Edward Garnett. To the poet's surprise, Sedgwick said that he liked the piece and was considering it for an early issue. Then he asked, "Have you any poems with you?"

It was too good to be true, but Rob was not going to leap at the chance to be published in the *Atlantic*. In a tone of mock-injury, he said he was not the kind of poet who goes around with a pocketful of poems. However, he continued, he just happened to have three right there, as he had been reading them at Tufts College.

Sedgwick reached out eagerly. "Let me have them," he said.

But Rob with wicked delight took the poems out of his pocket and raised them high in the air. "Are you sure you want them?" he parried.

The editor swallowed hard before he could say "Yes," and then Rob brought the poems down into his hands with the remark that he seemed to be playing in luck, since Sedgwick was taking his poems as well as the essay.

At the mention of the Garnett piece, the editor thrust at him, "I haven't decided to use it." The air in the office was fraught with hostility, the poisonous fumes of professional friendship. Both men were smiling, but there was a razor edge to their good humor.

"You shouldn't have told me about it," Frost said, referring to the essay. "You'll almost have to use it, for if you don't, it will do me more good than if you do. I'll tell the whole United States on you."

They both laughed—a hard laugh. In the end, Sedgwick agreed to use both the poems and the essay in the same issue. It was a great stroke in Frost's favor, and was to make "Birches" one of his best-known poems. (He always felt, however, that Sedgwick never liked him afterward.) As soon as the interview was over, he hurried back to New Hampshire to take the good tidings to Elinor, and help the family settle in the new farmhouse.

Chapter 11

FRANCONIAN OLYMPUS

Now all was peace again for the Frost family constellation—not the same sort of serenity Rob and Elinor had experienced in the move to Derry fifteen years before, or the same isolation they had deliberately insured themselves then. The boisterous confusion of their growing, semi-adolescent band increased the carnival atmosphere of moving day, and the fact that they themselves were older now made a difference, for one thing. After the youngsters had tumbled into bed that evening, the two who were as one in the plans for country living combined with poetry-making, talked quietly, reminiscently, yet with their eyes on the future, much like the married couple of the dramatic dialogue "In the Home Stretch," which the poet shortly wrote for his third volume. He showed the pair toward the end of moving from town to country at long last, unspoken phrases of love underlying their subtle observations—the wife as she stands above the kitchen sink, looking out of the window at a weedy patch not far from woods; the husband, as he gently questions her on what she sees.

> "It's all so much
> What we have always wanted, . . ."

> "Dumped down in paradise we are and happy."

And all of them were happy with it. No matter if the house had not all the modern conveniences like bathtub and telephone. In spring they had Hyla Brook to bathe their feet in (named after the tree toads that "shouted in the mist" during May); and when the flowers bloomed, Rob found his own kind of communication service to Elinor, which he described playfully in "The Telephone." From a trumpet of petals, he heard a voice say "come," though he was far from the house; he was sure it was sent through the flower on the window sill at home.—So he came.

Their neighbors down the road, the former owners, the Herberts, must often have wishel—had they known of it—that the Frost private "telephone" had an extension to take care of all the calls they received from people giving messages to be relayed to Robert Frost. He was already so much of a figure in the literary world that even if he had wished for the isolation they had known in Derry—and he did not—it would have been impossible. Some of their new neighbors were poets and writers—Ernest Poole's property and the Frosts' backed into each other; and Raymond Holden, a young poet who lived nearby, often dropped in for advice. Intellectuals whom Rob had met in Boston showed up in Bethlehem hotels, Justice Von Moschisker among them, and tried to get in touch with him. Joseph Warren Beach came, bringing his family. Jean Starr and Louis Untermeyer, both poets of stature, and important links in the poetry circles that were drawing Frost in as an established name, visited informally when they were in the vicinity—like old friends from the start. Professors from everywhere sought him out: Cornelius P. Weygandt from the University of Pennsylvania, Harold Goddard Rugg from Dartmouth, the college he had fled; and others. Sidney Cox called (at the Herberts) to ask if he could bring up a "singularly able young Ph.D.," who wanted to investigate "some new things in literature."

The country people around Franconia, who had known the Frosts intimately in past years when they were staying at the Lynches' in summer, were rather mystified and annoyed by the comings and goings of city folk up at the old Herbert place. As for the former owners, harassed by phone messages, they had to swallow the cutting maxim issued by Willis Herbert's father: "Next time you sell a farm, son, find out beforehand if it's goin' to be used as a farm or a park."

The social activity, however, did not interfere with poetry-making and compiling—or selecting—the pieces which were to form the nucleus for book three. The project went forward as planned, especially after Rob received a heart-warming letter from Alfred Harcourt, who was genuinely interested in the welfare of the poet—his "simon-pure poet," as he referred to Frost in editorial circles. The letter contained a check for $200, and outlined the arrangements he had made to take care of Frost's finances. (The company would pay what amounted to 10 per cent on sales of *North of Boston* and *A Boy's Will*, taking its chances with Mrs. Nutt; unless she stopped them, the honorarium would continue. The British firm was still making trouble over the rights. Report of sales would reach Frost on the 25th of each October and April.) Alfred added a few sentences on his own to reassure his "discovery" of a bright future in publishing poetry. From now on, hay fever would be the poet's worst trouble!

Such sentiments gave Rob the necessary impetus to push ahead with the mechanics of preparing a book.

For this volume he took out of hiding two poems—two poems written long ago, the first when he and Elinor were engaged, waiting for the time when their being "more than one as yet" would be over; this was "Meeting and Passing," which brought tender, yet bitter-sweet memories to both of them. The other was the branded "Bond and Free," which he liberated now with a feeling of exultation: Harcourt, he knew, would not reject the impassioned yet controlled lyric, written for Elinor.

The July issue of the *Atlantic Monthly* carried the three poems that Rob Frost had plumped down into Sedgwick's hands, and he decided to use all of them in the coming collection; "The Road Not Taken" and "The Sound of the Trees" like a prologue and epilogue would be placed, in italics, outside the body of the book, the first at the beginning, the second at the end. All of these had been written in England, and the third, "Birches," was set in between "Bond and Free" and the beautiful sonnet "Putting in the Seed." (Two other poems written in England, "A Patch of Old Snow" and "The Cow in Apple Time," would also be included. The latter, a delicious view of a demoralized cow, inspired by the bronze animals on the Albert Memorial, was nevertheless inherently all of a piece with the rest of the New Hampshire scene.)

As Sedgwick had promised, the same issue of the *Atlantic* printed the review of *North of Boston* by the noted English critic, Edward Garnett: "The question first to ask seems to me whether a given author is a fresh creative force, an original voice in literature," he stated at the outset of the long critique. "Such an authentic original force speaks to me from *North of Boston*. Surely a genuine New England voice, whatever be its literary debt to old-world English ancestry. Originality, the point is there." His highly valued opinion, coupled with such penetrating comments as likening "The Housekeeper" to a Theocritus' idyll, "The Ladies of Syracuse" ("cast in much the same gossiping style") gave the poet the impetus to keep his muse eloquent, emphasizing the force of his originality. Keeping the conversational tone of the lines, he experimented with form and meter—trying to see how much freedom he could allow himself within set patterns. In telling the tragic tale of the fearful, fragile young "Hill Wife," who succumbs to a mild, Ophelia-like madness because "It was too lonely for her there And too wild," he employed ballad verse in five separate lyrics, two of them single stanzas and three in short, four-line "ballad" stanzas. The last lyric, "The Impulse," portrayed the pathetic wife, like Ophelia, singing to herself as madness overtakes her, "and then she ran and hid In the fern." Troubled, her husband searched everywhere, but he never found her.

He borrowed from Catullus the eleven-syllable line (hendecasyllabic accent) in the first line of "An Encounter," in which the poet, "Once on the kind of day called 'weather breeder,'" comes upon a "resurrected tree" as he wanders through a swamp of cedar. He used the accent six times in the twenty-four-line poem, the other eighteen containing the decasyllabic accent of the last two lines, " 'Sometimes I wander out of beaten ways Half looking for the orchid Calypso.' " Much of the deep pleasure Robert Frost found in writing poetry was in "playing" with form, slipping in classic-line accent where one would least expect it.

He also farmed—in the same lackadaisical manner as before—and his method, or lack of it, found its way into a short poem, "A Time to Talk." In ten telling lines, he sketched himself, working in the potato patch: when a friend calls to him from the road, he says, he never stands and looks around lingeringly on all the hills he hasn't hoed, or shouts from where he is—not he. Unlike his industrious neighbors, he feels there is a time to talk; and, poking the handle end of the hoe into the soft soil, he leaves it, "Blade-end up and five feet tall," and makes his way across the furrows to the stone wall "For a friendly visit." His mention of the stone wall was significant; he was always counterposing man's tendencies to set up walls and then surmount them—or see them fall apart—with friendship. He here suggested the same opposing concepts he had analyzed in "Mending Wall"—a lighthearted reference to the long poem.

He wrote of Hyla Brook, in whose singing, rushing water the children had waded in spring while the tree toads shouted overhead: "By June our brook's run out of song and speed," the opening line of a sonnet variation on a Shakespearean theme. After exhibiting the now dried-up stream, its bed "a faded paper sheet Of dead leaves stuck together by the heat—" he observes that only those with long memories will still recognize it as a brook; and, like Shakespeare, he concludes, (in modern idiom): "We love the things we love for what they are."

And in the summer heat, the vocal call that came from the wood evoked the poet's intonation, "The Oven Bird," again a sonnet; and, like the bird song, almost a chant of mourning for the flowering of spring, the summer days already done; unlike other birds, the oven bird "knows in singing not to sing" (a wisdom the poet also shows). His question is "what to make of a diminished thing."

At about this time—August 14, 1915—one thing that had not diminished, but rather, ballooned, was Robert Frost's growing fame: Harcourt had just announced the fact that, as he had predicted, *North of Boston* was a best seller! Rob found the news "hard to know how to take," as he remarked in a letter to Braithwaite, who was compiling an anthology and had requested a few poems from Frost. The poet was almost embarrassed in confessing that his book had become a best-seller, and he could scarcely believe the fact even as he wrote. Of the request for poems, he told Braithwaite he would be "honored enough if you will use two, honored beyond dreams if you will use three."

The acclaim being showered upon Frost in his own country was too much for Ezra Pound to take. The ex-patriate poet had written a letter bristling with ungenerous jealousy to the editor of the Boston *Transcript* demanding, in a snide, negative, indirect way, that he, Pound, be recognized, too, for what he had accomplished in England. He also pointed out all he had done to boom Frost, but his acid tone negated the gesture. Rob, who had not seen Pound's petty attack, commented to Braithwaite, "What new terms of abuse has he found for your review? Why would you review him? He needs letting alone. The English have ceased to give him space in their papers."

Perhaps it was he who was being ungenerous now, but he could not countenance Ezra's high-handed arrogance, and saw no reason to make a pretense of feeling otherwise about it. On the other hand, Amy Lowell's extravagant, regal officiousness rather amused him, and he could communicate with her on friendly terms, tongue in cheek: "The great thing is that you and some of the rest of us have landed with both feet on all the little chipping poetry of a while ago. We have busted 'em up as with cavalry. We have, we have, we have. Yes I like your book and all I lay up against you is that you will not allow me a sense of humor. . . ."

The following month, William Dean Howells, perhaps the leading critical authority in Frost's native land, in reviewing the first two volumes (in the "Editor's Easy Chair" column for the September issue of *Harper's*), made some interesting observations on an unusual facet of Robert Frost's genius, mentioned by no other critic so far: "His manly power is manliest in penetrating to the heart of womanhood in that womanliest phase of it, the New England phase. Dirge, or idyll, or tragedy, or comedy, or burlesque, it is always the skill of the artist born and artist trained which is at play, or call it work, for our delight . . . here is the old poetry as young as ever; and new only in extending the bounds of sympathy through the recorded to the unrecorded knowledge of humanity . . . with a touch as sure and a courage as loyal as if the poet dealt with it merely for the joy of it." (That the poet really *did* deal with his subject matter in large measure "for the joy of it" seemed not to have occurred to the dean of American letters, but Robert Frost was not going to quarrel with a review of such high caliber.)

Late in the summer of 1915, Sidney Cox made the promised visit to Franconia with the young professor. Robert had been writing to Sidney some of his ideas in regard to literature and the teaching of it in American schools and colleges. "Sight and insight, give us those," he said among other things. He outlined his views until very late one night, adding, "Some of what I say is true. Run it all through a De Laval separator. I am up to my eyes in milk and such-like farm produce. Hence this Georgic figure. And I'm too tired to be awake writing."

Now the talk flowed freely after Rob had welcomed the professor without effusiveness, but with his customary casual hospitality, on Sidney's introduction, meeting him, accepting him fully as a person, which set the young doctor of philosophy completely at ease. The poet, his hair tousled by the summer breeze, wearing his usual open-collared, homemade shirt, creaseless pants, and comfortable old leather bluchers, showed the two young men around the new farm, all three of them talking as they walked.

They were still talking when they returned, through dinner with the family, and after dinner, when they settled in the living room, Frost slouched down in his morris chair, his position as comfortable as the old shoes he wore. Sidney, his early, ever-faithful disciple, was more of an observer than a participant in the conversations; he knew from Plymouth days that when his friend Robert sat quietly listening, his head cocked on one side, his deep, penetrating eyes on the speaker, he was about to let fly a dart, a piercing arrow that would leave the other's theory in pieces. Or when he slid even farther down in his morris chair and stretched his legs in front of him, he was about to launch some theory of his own at some length. They had proceeded from a discussion of Ibsen and Shakespeare, to earlier American poets, to patriotism; Robert took the occasion to distinguish between sound sentiment and sentimentality; he had made the point that man could not dismiss his emotions altogether, and that the feelings that gave him power and led to wisdom were those feelings he could not help having, when Elinor, who had just finished the dishes, interrupted him, her low, sweet voice a little sad rather than reproachful.

"Rob," she said with quiet firmness, "it's after nine o'clock, and you *must* go milk. It's not good for her to wait so long."

Rob went. When he came back, he lit the round-wicked, kerosene lamp, turning it up slowly, and suggested a little poetry reading. The others welcomed the idea and Elinor sat down in the rocking-chair to listen. Though the poet read in talking tones, his friend Sidney noticed that in poems like "The Hound of Heaven," with many moving passages, "every flick and flicker of emotion was made audible." He went on to some of the works of their British friends—Gibson and Abercrombie and one poem that Edward Thomas had sent him from camp (where he was trying his hand at poems every minute he was not in training). Both Rob and Elinor told anecdotes about the Dymock poets and the golden hours they had spent among them.

The talk turned to other subjects; after a while Elinor excused herself and went up to bed. The men continued to exchange ideas until the hour was very late, and the professor declared he had had a long day, and had better be getting back to the Forest Hills House in the village, where he was staying. Somewhat shamefacedly, he admitted that he was fearful of finding his way down the dark lonely road bordered with trees. He was obviously not versed in country things; so Robert and Sidney walked down the two-mile stretch with him, breathing in the night air, smelling the fir balsams and second-crop raspberries as they felt their way along the dust-laden road. As soon as the professor was safely within the sparse circle of Franconia lights, they left him, parting with a word or two about plans for the next day.

He joined them the next morning for a swim in the lake over on the other side of the hill. On the way back up, Rob, full of exuberance, burst into the ballad "Blow the Man Down," his voice echoing in the hills. After lunch, he suggested that the visitor take a nap in the tent out in the yard. (That was the tent, he had told them earlier, mentioned in his poem "A Servant to Servants"; he had been camping in it at the edge of the lake one summer when the farmer's wife, coming down to idle away a few moments in friendly gossip, told him her family history.)

The professor stayed two days more, most of the time alone with the poet, reading, discussing; never arguing, for Robert Frost rarely argued a question with anyone. (He and Elinor might have occasional heated discussions over domestic problems—or sometimes politics, since he was a Cleveland-Democrat like his parents, and she was a dyed-in-the-wool Republican, like hers—but they almost never came to an out-and-out dispute.) In the evening after dinner, Sidney, Elinor and one or more of the children—usually Lesley and Carol—joined them. The talk took many turns. To the professor's surprise, Rob began to praise Ernest Hocking's *Meaning of God in Human Experience,* and Elinor, who was more of a listener than talker, spoke up to say that she believed in immortality.

"So do I," Rob seconded. "I believe it with an almost physical certainty."

The scholar, who had thought him a skeptic—surely he was agnostic—was quite astonished; he wondered if the Frosts had found any proof.

Rob, with a low chuckle, declared he had no proof to offer. He

said logical systems of thought were nonsense as applied to immortality, and went on from there. Before he had finished, surely
before the three-day visit was ended, the young Ph.D. and budding
critic had learned that the poet was above all an original thinker
—that, as his friend Sidney Cox was to say: "He's for more inclu-
siveness than philosophers achieve; he's for eliminating what we
plainly can't incorporate in practice. This inconsistency—this refusal to pretend to be logical and complete—is the fierce radical
trait that makes Robert Frost."

In the fall, Rob made several short trips down Boston way to
read his poetry; he had never liked to be long away from Elinor,
and now he was especially reluctant to leave her, for she was expecting another child in the spring. The American Drama Society
had invited him to attend a performance of "Home Burial" and
"The Death of the Hired Man" in November, and he felt he
should accept. Later he gave a private reading before a distinguished company in Cambridge. Professor Palmer—his would-be
patron—who was at the gathering, greeted him with the good news
that Harvard had selected him as their next Phi Beta Kappa poet
(for June 1916). Other public appearances were pending; but before he could decide whether to take on any more engagements
just then, he received alarming news from Franconia and rushed
home to take care of Elinor, who had suffered a miscarriage. Lesley
was hardly old enough to manage the household, so the poet became chief cook as well as nurse.

Soon "The Onset" of winter was upon them:

> Always the same, when on a fated night
> At last the gathered snow lets down as white
> As may be in dark woods, and with a song
> It shall not make again all winter long
> Of hissing on the yet uncovered ground.

as the poet later wrote. The young members of the family began
compiling their Christmas books. Elinor was strong enough to sit
up in bed and start a little sewing and write a Christmas letter to

their old friend Susan Ward. Her poet-husband could make use of the extra time for further work on the third volume. And, with the children, he contrived a Christmas card, based on an incident that occurred just then,

> When between whirls of snow not come to lie
> And whirls of foliage not yet laid, there drove
> A stranger to our yard. . . .

The stranger proved to be a buyer of Christmas trees who asked if Mr. Frost would be interested in selling his fir trees—

> The young fir balsams like a place
> Where houses all are churches and have spires.

Startled at the mere thought and not really intending to sell them, Rob Frost, with his usual curiosity, had to find out how much the man would give him for his trees. He was thunderstruck to hear the buyer offer a mere thirty dollars for a thousand trees! The poem, which was subtitled, "A Christmas Circular Letter" dramatized the episode with Frostian dexterity, and ended with a wish that he might lay a tree in each letter, "In wishing you herewith a Merry Christmas." Lesley drew a sketch of the fir-covered slope deep in snow, with a new moon in the sky above for each card; below it, Rob copied his poem in his bold, flowing script, adding a personal note at the bottom. One of these read: "From Robert Frost and the children. And Mrs. Frost wishes to be remembered though she had no part in this nonsense."

"Nonsense" notwithstanding, the poem contained a good deal of sense as well as poesy, so the poet-farmer decided to open his forthcoming volume with "Christmas Trees" (directly following the frontispiece, "The Road Not Taken"). Now, as before in Derry, he spent the late hours near the stove, working by lamplight in the still winter night. The lines formed a descriptive passage in the blank verse lyric that he was writing, a piece of poetic realism which symbolized the parallel between age in man and in the world of nature, eventually called "An Old Man's Winter Night." He composed the unrhymed but rhythmic lines in strict iambic pentameter, using simple but eloquent words, setting the mood with the introductory triad:

> All out-of-doors looked darkly in at him
> Through the thin frost, almost in separate stars,
> That gathers on the pane in empty rooms.

He took particular pains to achieve the effect he wanted by means of sound and meter as well as meaning; and he succeeded in creating a distillation of poetic expression that has rarely been duplicated. He was to say in 1925 that "An Old Man's Winter Night" was equaled in form only by "The Mountain" and "Stopping by Woods on a Snowy Evening," and already, as it "unfolded by surprise" he knew that this was one of the poems in which without question he had reached his goal.

During the day—after New Year's, when Elinor was up and around again—the poet liked nothing better than to bundle up in warm wraps and boots for a winter walk on snowy roads, letting the subconscious flow of pre-thought crystallize into poetic idea as he crunched the snow underfoot. If his fingers and toes grew numb with cold anywhere near a farmhouse, he would stop and ask, "Do I smell coffee?" Like as not he did, and while he warmed himself over a steaming mug, either the farmer or his wife—or both of them—regaled him with gossip of the day, or some tale of the canny hill folk that he could store up for future use. On one of these impromptu coffee hours around a farmhouse kitchen table, after a heavy snowstorm the night before, he was given a graphic account of a remarkable minister who had stopped there at midnight during almost a man-killer blizzard. He was on his way back from preaching, and wanted to rest his horses for half an hour; he would not stay the night, and in spite of pleas and warnings, braved the storm in order to get home to his wife before morning.

In Robert Frost's perceptive interpretation, the story during the next weeks became a long dramatic "talk-poem"—the longest he had written so far, and, he felt, a high point in vocal creativity. In it he showed, by means of subtle interplay of conversation, the elements of faith, daring, opposition, and love which make up a marriage—inner human elements as contrasted to the elements of the outer world, in this case the howling blizzard. Giving the piece the single-word title "Snow," he put it at the close of the new volume (directly before the back piece, "The Sound of the Trees"; but first he sent it to Harriet Monroe, for possible publication in *Poetry*).

In the early evening, he read to—or with—the family, a copy of *Six French Poets*, translated by Amy Lowell, published in December, which she had sent as a Christmas present. He and Lesley read part of it together (Paul Fort's *Henry III*)—he with his head tipped one way, following Miss Lowell's English aloud, Lesley with her head tipped the other way, following the French in silence, the book being opened at both places at once. And even under those unfavorable circumstances, he told Amy in a thank-you letter, he brought tears of excitement to his daughter's eyes.

Later, when everyone else had gone to bed, he settled down to his writing at his desk-board laid across the arms of the morris chair. To keep his feet from freezing on the cold floor, he built a platform under the chair, close to the stove. In this way, and wearing a woolly smoking jackct, hc managed to keep warm enough to bring forth the songs inside him that kept demanding voice.

Toward the end of January, he took his packet of manuscript poetry and went down to New York for a day or two with Alfred Harcourt. While the young editor was going through his pages, Rob looked around for something to read, and noticed a copy of *Publishers' Weekly*. He had never seen the magazine before, and began idly glancing through it. Suddenly he came upon several columns devoted to *North of Boston* and *A Boy's Will*, highly favorable paragraphs, written from the point of view of the distributor—one Frederic Melcher (then an Indiana book salesman). Rob was so pleased that he asked Alfred to tell Melcher, and Harcourt was happy to oblige. (He felt as if two friends had met in his home, and it was not long afterward that a lasting friendship began between Robert Frost and Frederic Melcher.) The editor's admiration for Frost, both as friend and poet, increased the more he came to know him. Alfred was in a glow after the day they spent together; he found the new manuscript finer in form and spirit than *North of Boston,* if such were possible. And he was pleasantly surprised at the rate the poems were coming: he had been afraid the poet's inspiration would lag in his home country. And Harcourt was more than ever convinced that he had found "the simon-pure article, a real American poet."

By March the poet was "barding around" again, as he called the poetry-readings and lectures he gave in schools and colleges. Setting a fee of seventy-five dollars (which he sometimes had to lower to fifty), he accepted engagements at Hanover, Lawrence, Boston, Wellesley, Lewiston, and New York. Thirteen of the new poems had been accepted by various magazines for publication—almost as many in a few months as in the twenty years before recognition finally came! It was a novel, delightful experience for Elinor and him, after years of rejection slips, to find checks in their rural-route post box. (And they needed financial aid to pay the doctor bills for Elinor's illness and the constant colds Carol was having; Rob worried about his son's health, though he did not show his concern the way Elinor did.)

It soon became noised around the neighborhood of Franconia that Mr. Frost's comings and goings were accounted for in the fact that he was a poet—one who could perform. He began to receive unwelcome attentions, as he wrote Amy Lowell about the middle of May. For example, he was asked to read poetry at the movies one night, mostly to give the people time to get into their seats before the main part of the show began, it seemed. He was advertised on the bill like an act in a chautauqua: "Prayer by the Rev. Soambro. Poems by R.F. Pictures Life of Christ, 5,000 feet." Moreover, the poet was advertised first and invited afterward. Needless to say, he did not accept.

Even more unbelievable was a call he received one morning from a neighbor who got into the house on the pretext of wanting to sell him some seeds. The minute the man sat down, he began with,

"How are the books coming on, Mr. Frost?" Without waiting for an answer, he said, "Poetry it is exclusively I believe it is with you?" Then (very respectfully), "What do you ask apiece for them?" When Rob answered, "Seventy-five cents and one dollar and twenty-five cents," the neighbor informed him that Ernest Poole got one dollar and fifty. In closing the letter to Amy, Rob remarked, "All I ask is your sympathy."

He went on to ask where he could find her in the middle of June. He was referring to his forthcoming trip to Boston for his reading on Phi Beta Kappa day at Harvard. He was still working on the poems he hoped to recite on that occasion. Two of them concerned the war, drawing closer with each passing day, mounting in horror as new weapons were devised and put to use. In the longest of these poems, called "The Bonfire," the poet, apparently far removed from thoughts of war, revealed that he was among the first to perceive the far-reaching consequences of war from underseas and the skies. The first scene shows him craftily daring his children to come with him to the top of the hill at night, and with him scare themselves by setting fire to all the brush they had piled in the afternoon. They will build a huge bonfire, like the bonfire he built when he was a lad, one that scared him half to death in its all-consuming fury (the second scene). And when the children ask if a bonfire scares him, what will it do to them, he answers calmly that it will scare them. But if they are going to shrink from a bonfire, what would they say to war, he counters, in the third scene. And when they say that war is not for children, it's for men, he tells them of the destruction of lives on ships at sea and in small towns at night, through an opening in the clouds. *War is for everyone,* he tells them; for children as well as men. They can best cope with it by building a bonfire on the hill with him; together they can laugh and be afraid.

Another war poem was the unique interpretation, "Range-Finding," a sonnet as striking, as fatalistic in tone as the bullet it begins with:

The battle rent a cobweb diamond-strung

And cut a flower beside a ground bird's nest
Before it stained a single human breast.

He sent a copy of the sonnet to his friend Edward Thomas, now at the front, who answered that the poem was an amazingly accurate picture of no man's land, which stretched like a grim aisle of death in the theater of war between the enemy trenches. Ironically, that valiant spirit had been writing—both while in training in the Artists' Rifles Corps and in the thick of battle—poems that had nothing to do with the titanic struggle engulfing the world, but dealt with the struggle of the soul, the contemplative world of philosophic thought. His work was being rejected by the very magazines for which he had done reviewing. A few of these were miraculously relayed to Robert, whose heart bled for his friend, now going through, under much more desperate circumstances, what Rob had gone through for so many years. Since he had been responsible for Thomas's turn to poetry, he felt responsible for publication of the poems, and was trying to find a place for them.

As he read "The Bonfire" before the distinguished audience in Sanders Theater at Harvard that June day in 1916, he was troubled by the whole problem. And on his own horizon, another fear loomed, clouding his usual serene, sanguine countenance. Elinor and Carol had accompanied him to Boston for consultation with a specialist regarding the chest colds that persisted in hindering the boy's health; and the doctor's diagnosis of the dread tuberculosis struck terror to Rob's heart as he remembered his father's last days of agony, his mother's worry over his own tendency to the disease. Looking down at Elinor's anguished face in the front row of the theater just before he started to read, he resolved sternly that Carol must follow the doctor's orders and so avert tragedy. Small wonder that his new critic-friend, Louis Untermeyer, described him afterwards as having "a stubborn scholar's face, masking the irrepressible poet's." His poems were well received, however, particularly one he had just completed, "The Ax-Helve," which had not yet had a chance to ripen in his notebook. Ellery Sedgwick came up to shake his hand, complimenting him on the poem later to be declared a masterpiece. (Sedgwick wanted to publish it at once, but the poet was not ready to part with it as yet; he was hoarding some of his new work for a future volume.)

By following a strict routine of rest and outdoor living, Carol began to improve, and by midsummer the anxiety began to disappear from his parents' eyes. It was hay-fever time, when Rob could not stand to wear anything but an open-collared shirt and jeans, but he received notables from New York and Boston with incomparable ease; and all who came joined in the simple picnics by the White River falls, where the talk flowed freely as the rapids, and spirits rose with intellectual challenge. Jean Starr and Louis Untermeyer were two frequent visitors at these impromptu picnics; others were Morris Tilley of the University of Michigan, who summered in New England with his family; and Sidney Cox (an increasingly devoted disciple, almost like an elder son to the poet). Adolescent Irma had just discovered Jane Austen, and sat with a book by the eighteenth-century novelist always in hand, ready to take on all comers. Her father was just as prone to spar with his contemporaries, and usually proved more than a match for the flashing wit and intellectual banter of Louis Untermeyer. At last literary America was becoming aware of the extraordinary conversational powers of the poet in its midst—the gift the British had discovered so quickly, described by Gibson in "The Golden Room":

> We talked and laughed, but for the most part listened
> While Robert Frost kept on and on and on
> In his slow New England fashion for our delight,
> Holding us with shrewd turns and racy quips,
> And the rare twinkle of his grave blue eyes.
>   . . . we sat and talked—
> Now a quick flash from Abercrombie, now
> A murmured dry half-heard aside from Thomas,
> Now a clear laughing word from Brooke, and then
> Again Frost's rich and ripe philosophy
> That had the body and tang of good draught-cider
> And poured as clear a stream.

Tourist-like, they took snapshots—Elinor with the children, smiling fondly at them, glints of sunlight shining on her coronet of braids; Rob, standing on a hillside, sunburnt, lithe, looking at forty-two like the young poet-farmer of Derry; in another shot, perched on a rail fence beside Carol (a frail edition of his father), with a view of "all creation" for background, the poet was thoughtful, even brooding; he was still concerned about Carol—a quiet, introspective, moody boy, unwilling to emerge from the protective shadow of his father's imposing figure.

Yet, quite possibly the poet's sudden remoteness was due to his "dauntless wings of thought" that had sent his mind soaring to other spheres. The poems kept coming, out of nowhere, out of everywhere, every experience, no matter how seemingly casual. An accidental hike along five miles of mountain road with a man who carried "a swinging bag for load" led to the advent of "The Gum Gatherer" in the annals of American poetry. This analogy of the artist's "pleasant life To set your breast to the bark of trees . . . To loose the resin and take it down And bring it to market when you please," was published with pride in the early-faithful *Independent*, printed in the October, 1916, issue, with "The Telephone."

When it came out, Rob and Elinor, with Lesley, were visiting the Untermeyers in their West Side apartment near the Hudson in New York, and he told his hosts the story of his first editors and publishers, and how, for many years, the Wards and M. DeWolfe Howe, of the *Youth's Companion,* were the only ones who believed in him; he was in a reminiscent mood, because the copy of the *Independent* carried the announcement of the death of William Hayes Ward, Susan's brother, who had sought to give the poet fatherly advice. Rob, though he resented it at first, had long since ceased to be bothered by anyone's advice. Amused, he took it, and did as he pleased.

At this point, Jean cut in to ask: "Robert, how is it that, though you had those twenty unrecognized years, years that must have tested you fiercely and caused both you and Elinor much hardship —how is it that I've never heard you become bitter?"

He looked at her quizzically for a moment, thinking it out, his lower lip pushed forward, the shade of a twinkle in his eye.

"Well," he drawled finally, "with respect to poetry I have always felt like a man entrusted to carry a jar of precious ointment on his head: I didn't want to spill any of it; then, you know, one can never tell how the race will turn out till the end; then—" he glanced at Elinor, "then, I'm a lucky man; I've always been able to give full measure."

It was a "succinct account of himself," an utterly original "summing up," and Jean Starr Untermeyer loved him for it.

When he got home, Rob wrote to Miss Susan Ward, telling her that he and Elinor regretted not visiting her before "your circle broke," referring to her brother's death only indirectly. He told her also that he had been busy earning "rather more of a living than I ever made before—you will be glad to hear that!" He promised to visit her "this winter when I am south-along. I shall hope to find you well and ready for a poem or two of not too new a kind."

The third volume, which the poet called *Mountain Interval*, encompassing both the life and the place that brought the book into being, came off the press in November, 1916. Opposite the title page, all three volumes were listed (with prices) below the heading,

> By Robert Frost
> "An authentic, original voice in literature."
> —*The Atlantic Monthly.*

The inscription to Elinor was more personal, more revealing of the past than the one in *North of Boston* had been. It read:

TO YOU

Who Least Need Reminding

that before this interval of the south branch under the black mountains, there was another interval, the Upper at Plymouth,

> where we walked in spring beyond the covered bridge; but that
> the first interval of all was the old farm, our brook interval, so
> called by the man we had it from in sale.

Elinor was moved almost to tears, both by the dedication and
the poems in her book—a book of country things, of lyrics and sonnets interspersed with dramatic pieces, a book rich in form and
content, yet distilled as the clear mountain air. A book with touches
of that "sense of intimacy that gives the thrill of sincerity" as her
poet husband had put it. This volume was one she would always
cherish, perhaps more than any. One afternoon, some time later,
when Mrs. George Whicher, wife of the Amherst professor, was
visiting the Frosts with her husband, she found herself alone with
Elinor in the kitchen helping to make sandwiches, and took the
opportunity to voice her admiration for *Mountain Interval* at some
length. Her hostess listened in silent appreciation.

"Don't you think it's beautiful yourself?" the professor's wife
ended.

Elinor dropped the knife she was using and clasped her hands.

"Beautiful," she said fervently, with a catch in her low voice. It
was one of the rare moments when she expressed her rapture in
her husband's art, which, in her own way, she had helped to nour-
ish and perfect.

An early copy of *Mountain Interval* was sent to Edward Thomas;
and shortly afterward came the glad news from the poet-critic, on
leave in England, that he had just signed a contract with Selwyn
and Blount for a volume of poetry to be published under his own
name. He was dedicating the book to Robert Frost and was sending
him a manuscript copy of the poems for approval. It was a time
for rejoicing all around; and none of them dared think that he
might never see publication of his first, and only, book of poems.

Mountain Interval received instant critical acclaim, and among
other honors, brought a request for a reading at Amherst College
on December 16, at the invitation of President Alexander Meiklejohn and Stark Young of the English department.

After the reading, President Meiklejohn, nonconformist and an experimentalist in education, offered the poet an interim appointment for the second term (to replace a faculty member who was leaving to enter the legislature); no matter if he had no degrees behind his name. This unusual college president made Robert Frost a professor, at a salary of $1,500 for the term, and granted him the privilege of "barding around" to augment his income. The agreement would become effective right after Christmas.

It was with mixed feelings that Rob and Elinor discussed the offer of the vibrant Meiklejohn. To accept meant loss of privacy to create poetry, but they had discovered that even a best-seller in poetry did not bring much material success. Then, too, he had wanted a college post,—or thought he did, before they came to live in Franconia—and the teaching salary was tempting.

"Just one term," Rob pointed out to Elinor, mentioning again that this was an "interim" appointment. "We can stand that."

In reality, the move marked the end of their brief, unbroken Olympian way of life; from then on, the poet's consort with his Muse was to be periodic—a summertime idyll.

Chapter 12

NO ICHABOD CRANE WAS HE

Once the decision to accept the teaching post at Amherst had been made, the Frosts had no time to change their minds. Robert was to take over his predecessor's courses shortly after the first of the year, and would have to be settled in the college town before then. Luckily, he was able to find a small faculty house to sublet furnished for the term. The bungalow (shades of the Beaconsfield experience!) was downhill from the campus, on Dana Street—professors' row—protected by a canopy of shade trees, each house prefaced by an ample yard.

Late in the afternoon of a bleak, overcast December day, the whole family drove up in front of the house in a bulging, battered old Maxwell they had bought secondhand for the moving. Mrs. Otto Manthey-Zorn, wife of the German professor, watched in some amazement from her parlor window in the house next door as youngsters and pets, boxes and baggage, chickens in crates came tumbling out into the cold, damp yard, like a gypsy caravan unloading. Yet, as they trooped laden into the chill, dark bungalow, the professor's wife thought the newcomers somehow looked appealingly lost, and she ran over to see if she could be of any help.

Elinor had discovered to her dismay that there were no blankets in the "furnished" place, and Rob was in shivers as he tried to fire up the furnace. She confided to her future friend and neighbor that he caught cold easily and she was always afraid of pneumonia. Her classic face was full of tender anxiety.

Touched, Mrs. Manthey-Zorn hurried back across the yards and tore the blankets off her own beds, so the Frosts could keep warm. Her husband could sleep under his overcoat for one night, she insisted in answer to Elinor's protests. He would be over in the morning to help Mr. Frost get the furnace going bright. It was the beginning of a long close friendship between the two couples.

Before the year 1916 had quite ended, Robert, now Professor Frost, went to consult with Professor Churchill, whose place he was taking, about the three courses he was supposed to teach: Shakespeare; pre-Shakespearean drama; and English poetry based on Palgrave's *Golden Treasury*. Churchill, a proud adherent of conventional pedagogy, stated that he had built his whole course, the first term, on a single seventeenth-century poem, Andrew Marvell's "A Garden."

"Must be a well-trampled garden," Frost observed slyly.

The retiring professor replied acidly that he expected a teacher must, *on principle,* spoil a certain amount of great poetry in order to get it across to the students.

The newly appointed professor made no comment; only the glint in his narrowed blue eyes gave a hint of his thorough disagreement with the other's theory. Robert Frost's ideas on teaching had not changed, but rather, broadened, since those first years on the faculty at Pinkerton's. "Sight and insight, give us those," he had written to Sidney. He was to amplify this premise in a few words: "Then you might add one more, if you were generous about the pun: *ex*cite." The feeling of excitement and pleasure was the one requisite he was going to demand for his courses; stimulation, but no boredom on either the students' side or his, if he could help it. If necessary, he would shock them into having ideas of their own rather than have them repeat parrotlike his interpretation of a given poem. But how could he possibly expect an academician like Churchill to see his point of view? He kept silent.

The boys in his classes realized at once that Robert Frost was a different sort of teacher from any that Amherst students had experienced before. His manner was completely casual, for one thing. The way he ambled into class and slouched in his chair, or sat on the desk, swinging his legs as he might on a rail fence, tickled the boys, and gave them a feeling of kinship with their new professor. They sensed his unusual qualities (if they did not grasp them) when he appeared, four minutes late, for class the very first day, and began speaking informally, like a friend.

College, he told them, was to give them a second chance to learn to read—to gather some ideas from what they read. "I want you putting two and two together," he said, "and I don't care a hoorah for anything else. That's my interest." The test of education should be, he said, did it develop and equip the ability to go it on your own? "This is the time you can lose yourself," he said. "You've got to do some losing of yourself to find yourself." He expressed the hope that they would feel and show enthusiasm for something. That they would have "the weakness, the strength, to be swept away, to be carried away by something more than beer and games, and so on." But he added, "I'd rather it would be beer and games than nothing, I think. I like people who can't help thinking and talking about things to the highest reaches."

One thing he disliked, he let them know right off, was marking papers. He especially didn't like to mark for the things beyond accuracy and correctness. . . . "If I am going to give a mark, the hard part is where adventure begins." He asked provocative questions: "What is poetry? Why is it written?" "Why do we have classes, anyway?" Who knew when he was fooling and when he was serious?

Almost immediately he made an indelible impression, as a senior student, E. Merrill Root, of the class of '17, was to write. "I remember that shock of wavy wild hair shaking down triangularly over the broad forehead; the ample audacious nose; the large, sensitive lips, usually puckered into a whimsical, half-whistling position; the eyes blue-gray, aloof yet alive, that seemed to sleep in eternity."

His aim in teaching—since he was forced to teach—was to inspire students to find out for themselves the treasure in books, but never to force them. He took much the same attitude toward his children's education; they could enroll in Amherst's public schools, if they wished—it was up to them. The two younger girls sought out their proper grades unhesitatingly. Lesley was a senior in high school, and was supposed to have stayed in Franconia to finish her last year, but she preferred to join the family in the house on Dana Street, and was soon making a brilliant record in classics at Amherst High, a shining light and joy to her parents. Carol, a lanky stripling, fair-haired and blue-eyed (so like his father, yet so eclipsed by him), dominated by his older sister, doggedly refused to become a scholar, and his parents did not push him.

In general, the family quickly adjusted to academic life, and if Rob had moments of inner rebellion (revealed only to Elinor, and not always even to her) against the routine hours which took away his leisure to write poetry, if he had flashes of creative genius that pulled him apart from his fellow faculty members, he compensated for it by getting to know his students, sounding the depths of the young minds, enlarging his human horizons. He learned to bide his time till summer, and was perhaps the stronger for it. Common sense kept him from complaining; he had to teach, in order to make ends meet, and even then it was a struggle. *Mountain Interval*, in spite of its artistic success, was having such small sales that at the suggestion of Alfred Harcourt, Holt and Company worked out a subsidy of $100 a month for the poet.

From the first, Frost wanted no part of the politicians and administrators on campus. He refused to go to faculty meetings, or play along with one faction as against another. Aside from their neighbors, the Manthey-Zorns, the Frosts made only a few close friends among the faculty members—the George Whichers; later George Roy Elliott, and one or two others. Whicher had not yet started his monumental study of Emily Dickinson, but from his point of view, his perceptive interpretation of poetry, it was soon evident to Robert Frost that he was exceptional among the English faculty. On night walks together, the two men railled at the petty quarrels for power that raged in the department.

Frost advised his friend not to get caught in campus politics, as they watched the "great Overdog" in the sky. He urged him not to rest on appointments alone; there was another horizon and something beyond.

It was the something beyond that he looked for in students, just as he looked for it in himself and his friends. Here, as at Pinkerton's, he encouraged the boys to become better acquainted with their professor, to confide in him. Courses should be a means of introduction to give the students a claim on him, he explained, so that they might come to him at any time outside of class periods.

It was not long before those students who recognized the rare personality in their midst, who were carried away by something more than beer and games, started coming to him, at first stopping in his little office upstairs in the Fine Arts Building after class; and then, at his suggestion, dropping by at his house on Dana Street in the evening. Not too early, he told them. After supper he liked to read, to mark a few papers—if he bothered to look at them—and, if the spirit so moved him, to devise a few lines of poetry; the last, however, usually occurred in the late watches of the night, if at all during the initial and uncertain terms of college teaching.

One lonely boy turned up nearly every night at the Frosts' during the early months of 1917. He was not a particularly good student, he had little or no talent for writing, but he liked to talk, to talk about anything and everything; his enthusiasm was disarming, and he obviously needed an audience (most boys did not care to listen to him), just as he needed the companionship and comfort of being in a home instead of a dormitory. Elinor was always quietly cordial to the boys who came to see Rob, making them feel at home until he turned up. Carol and the girls accepted them as they accepted their poet-father's individualistic pattern for living. Carol or Lesley (if she wasn't too busy with Latin translations) would take on the lonely "regular" for a game of checkers till their father came in from his den. Then they would talk and, more often than not, wind up at the Greek's in the village for a midnight hamburg.

So did Rob Frost become friends with his students, and gain an insight into their minds and abilities. He soon decided never to "flunk" anybody, yet he rarely gave high marks. It was his idea that "students ought to be marked on the *closeness* to a poet, to which they come in reading him. Sometimes a chance remark will tell that."

He took little interest in extracurricular activities (except poetry readings). He had been appointed, through Louis Untermeyer, an advisor in poetry on the staff of *Seven Arts,* a brilliant journal, begun in the frenzy of approaching war, to keep the arts alive. Psychologist James Oppenheim was editor in chief, in association with Waldo Frank, fiction editor, whose initial discovery was Sherwood Anderson. In charge of criticism and essays was Van Wyck Brooks, whose *America's Coming of Age* had just been published; Robert Edmond Jones had charge of the theater column, and enlisted Eugene O'Neill (reforging an old-time family tie for Robert Frost), just as Louis Untermeyer, who was poetry editor and critic, had brought Robert in as advisor. "Bonfire" had been published in the November 1916, the first issue of *Seven Arts,* and now, in February, his only prose play, *A Way Out,* appeared. In between, he had read a few manuscript poems, but his heart was not in the enterprise, which, as he already saw, was bound to turn into a sociological and antiwar vehicle.

Robert Frost, while oppressed by the closeness of American entry into the war, and anxious over the fate of his friend Edward Thomas, three of whose poems he placed in the February *Poetry,* had too much of true patriotism in his make-up to support active antiwar views. He was distressed over the frantic opposition his sister Jeanie was exhibiting toward the country's entrance into the conflict. At the age of thirty-five, his sister had gone to Ann Arbor while the Frosts were in England, had completed her education with a college degree, and won a position on the faculty. But now she returned to New England and seemed ready to throw it all to the winds to become a militant—a violent—pacifist; she had much of their mother's religious fervor, carried to the point of the fanatic, and she would not see that she was banging her head against a stone wall.

Honors that Frost considered dubious came to him, among them his election to the post of Vice-President of the New England Poetry Club. He wanted no part of such societies, and had no intention of attending those any more than faculty meetings.

Poetry readings, however, were another matter; they were an important means to an end, to the aim of song that was never out of sight. The shift in the scene of modern poetry from England to America now bid fair to move from the east (where Amy Lowell considered herself the reigning chief) to the middle west (where Harriet Monroe, through *Poetry,* and Harriet Moody, in her salon, were looked upon as the royal potentates of the arts); Chicago boasted three celebrities—Carl Sandburg, Vachel Lindsay, and Edgar Lee Masters—more than enough to make the city a contender for the poetry capital of the country. Robert Frost, through Harcourt, who asked his opinion, had had "something to do with" the publication of Carl Sandburg's *Chicago Poems* by Holt and Company, and he was eager to hear the man with the mournful voice accompanied by the twang of his guitar. The boom of Vachel Lindsay's vocal chants had reverberated to New England also, and led Rob to write Harriet Monroe, proposing a reading there for $150. "And take my chances on picking up a little more," he added. "The money would mean much—we won't say it wouldn't—but the great thing would be to see you and Vachel Lindsay." He could not hope to compete with either poet in a "platform show," as he called it, but he was willing to have a go at midwestern audiences. The indomitable Harriet arranged readings in March at Chicago University and one or two other schools. Frost was to stay at the home of the magnificent Harriet Moody, who had priority on visiting poets, from Masefield to Tagore, from Padraic Colum to

Ridgely Torrence—all of whom he met at one time or another in her famous salon.

The author of *North of Boston* had heard something of the opulence of the Groveland Avenue residences, built around the turn of the century; but he was unprepared for the bizarre luxury that befell him from the time that he stepped from the train, and was met by his hostess in person, "an impressive woman of middle age, her face that of a wearied Buddha" (as she was described in *A House in Chicago* by Olivia Torrence), with her "imperial car," and liveried chauffeur. He hardly had time to open his suitcase before he was summoned to Harriet's unique salon, the main feature of which was an enormous swing, black velvet, that hung from the ceiling like a swaying throne for her majestic presence; the space beside her was usually reserved for the favorite of the moment. The poet was bowed in at the door by a Hindu butler—"Milary"—in a dignified frockcoat, who addressed him as "Papa" (his title for all male guests) and led the way to present him formally to "Mamma" (as he called the lady) and her assembled guests. Frost, half-amused, half-fearful, tired—he much preferred being alone before a reading—hesitated, almost turned to flee, but finally followed.

Inside, the large room was set up with small tables at which the other guests were assembling for dinner. (Mrs. Moody was a professional caterer, a gourmet artist, who sampled the sauces concocted in her kitchens and treated her guests to the finest of foods; there was hardly a moment, from tea hour till after midnight, when tempting viands of some sort were not being set before varying groups of people.) When the poet had greeted his hostess—the second seat was occupied by a young composer; the rest of the swing by a bevy of girls—he was assigned to a separate table arrayed with a formidable line of forks and spoons, and served a succession of rich dishes. He had found that he felt much better if he did not eat before a reading—a cup of tea and one raw egg (sucked through a pinhole in the shell) was just enough to give him energy, not enough to make him loggy. He sat there fidgeting, scarcely touching the food, staring baffled at the silverware till the meal was over.

Then it was time to go to the reading and he had had no chance to convene with himself, to assemble his thoughts as he usually did for a couple of hours—no wonder he looked "all scrouged up," as one of the young girls said afterwards! They all gathered around Harriet now, in a swarm, one carrying her purse, another her coat, another her glasses. "She never moved without her swarm," he told the family in relating his adventures. In spite of his apprehensions, the reading was highly successful, and led to other engagements in nearby cities.

Horace Gregory, at this time in his teens, heard him in Milwaukee and was spellbound through the performance. He wrote afterwards, ". . . in the first flush of becoming famous, Frost had a discreetly mannered yet boyish personality . . . as he read aloud his dramatic narratives from *North of Boston*, his voice, often dropping to a whisper, had lyrical qualities that modulated rather than stressed whatever histrionics his lines required. . . . In the years when many poets mounted the platform to read their writings aloud, Frost was a welcome exception to the rule of strained and overly dramatic performances. . . . His voice allowed his poems to speak for themselves."

As soon as the performance was over, the poet relaxed, and on that first evening, found he could do justice to the midnight supper Harriet provided. As the honored guest, he was invited to sit beside her in the velvet swing a few times, and although she kept being called to the telephone (once he heard her command, "Operator, give me Tagore, Bombay, India"), he managed to break through her impassive, Buddhalike exterior by making her laugh with his "playful extravagance in familiar talk." By the time he left, a feeling close to friendship had developed, and Frost realized that William Vaughn Moody's widow was a lonely woman trying to make up for her loss by promoting the arts in general and her husband's work in particular.

It was a pleasure to come back to Elinor and the children and their simple household in Amherst. Easter arrived early that year, bringing memories of the early spring three years before, when the sea of daffodils waved before their delighted eyes, greeting them in Dymock. Rob had half-hoped for a letter from Edward on his return, but there was none. He had written a poem, "Not to Keep," based on his friend's leave and the pang he knew it must have cost Helen to let her poet-husband be pulled back to battle. "The same Grim giving to do over for them both. . . . They had given him back to her, but not to keep."

The poem had been published in the January issue of the *Yale Review,* and Rob sent a copy to the front, but he did not know whether Edward had received it. He felt something ominous in his hearing no word. . . . Then came the tragic news: Edward had been killed at Vimy Ridge on Easter Monday—April 9, 1917. In her note, his wife mentioned that when he left for Flanders Field, walking away over the hill for the last time, Edward carried in his knapsack Shakespeare's *Sonnets* and the early copy of *Mountain Interval* that Robert had sent. It was almost too much to bear, and seemed to make it more heartbreaking that Edward's poems, already in the press, could not have been published before he fell.

The whole family was sorrowed by the sad news, but Elinor knew that Rob's grief was greater than any of theirs. She could not reach the barren peak of his loss beyond a certain point, any more than he had been able to reach hers, completely, in the past, and she did not try. Now in truth he "was acquainted with the night"; and it was not until April 27 that he was able to write to Edward's wife—the letter of a poet and a profound one: here was the quiver of his heart laid bare.

The fallen poet himself had spoken of talks at Leddington—and of their walks in friendship—in a poem published just before his death, "The Sun Used to Shine," which now seemed almost prophetic:

> The sun used to shine while we two walked
> Slowly together, paused and started
> Again, and sometimes mused, sometimes talked. . . .

We turned from men or poetry
To rumors of the war remote. . . .
. . . The war came back to mind with the moonrise. . . . Everything
To faintness like those rumors fades.

How that line stood out! Then the last eight lines might be considered an elegy:

> Under the moonlight—like those walks
> Now—like us two that took them and
> The fallen apples, all the talks
> And silences—like memory's sand.
> When the tide covers it late or soon,
> And the other men, through other flowers
> In those fields under the same moon,
> Go talking and have easy hours.

It was undeniable that they had both felt premonitions of Edward's fate, though neither one would mention the fear when he enlisted or at any time afterward. Yet Edward, in writing those lines, must have been as certain of his fate as Rupert Brooke who wrote, a few months before he was felled just two years earlier (April 23, 1915):

> If I should die, think only this of me:
> That there's some corner of a foreign field
> That is forever England.

Robert Frost's grief for Edward Thomas was to produce more than one poem in memory of his closest friend, but for months it was too poignant; no lines would come. Then, before a reading at Smith College, while he was resting in the home of President Neilson, leafing through the pages of Edward's book, half-drowsing, the verses came to him, and he composed five stanzas "To E.T.," relating this moment when he "slumbered" with the poems on his breast, to see if in a dream he would have the chance he missed in life, of calling his friend "a soldier-poet" of his race.

He did not offer the work for publication right away—he

couldn't. It did not appear until April, 1920, in the *Yale Review,* and as late as July, 1919, he wrote to George Whicher from Franconia, giving his reasons for hesitating about it. The fact that the two men had been closest friends, one that Robert had realized before Edward died, made his death almost too personal to talk about in the *Yale Review* "in the hearing of William Lyon Phelps even at two years' distance." However, Frost felt that as long as he was sure of his motives (practical, non-sentimental, far removed from his impulses in writing it), there could be no harm in printing one little poem. In any case, he had reached a point where he was willing to risk it. He added, "Some part of an ideal is sacrificed to some god in every deed done and the old formal sacrifice of one child out of so many to Moloch was no more than symbolic recognition of the fact. . . ."

From the date of Edward's death, more than ten years would pass before the masterful sonnet, "A Soldier," took shape—a fitting monument to the friend fallen in battle. The passage of time gave Robert Frost the objectivity to translate his grief into art, to offer a spirit-world, half-glimpsed through his mysticism—the immortality he (the "skeptic") so deeply believed in. Using a figure that never faltered, he compared the soldier (his friend Edward) to a "fallen lance that lies as hurled." A lance forever uplifted, for

> the obstacle that checked
> And tripped the body, shot the spirit on
> Further than target ever showed or shone.

At the moment, during the whole spring of 1917, the cloud of mourning darkened the poet's mind and left him small patience with being a professor. He still had not made up his mind to stay at Amherst when the college term ended, but since he was offered a salary of $2,500 for another year, he accepted—he could not afford to turn it down. The summer in Franconia went by like the wind; he hardly had time to get in tune with his inner self before he was looking for another sub-let. This time he found one in the village next to Amherst, wooded West Pelham; living there would mean a walk of several miles to campus every day, but that was no obstacle. Rob could—and did—often stop in at the Manthey-Zorns' before he made the trot up the hill, sometimes, if he was not too late, in company with his old neighbor. And many a morning—or late afternoon when classes were over—the German professor would have to convince the poet that it would be rash to resign his teaching post in such uncertain times: now that the United States was in the war, poetry was having a struggle to survive; but Robert would get upset with the actions of the Meiklejohn administration and threaten to throw caution to the winds every few weeks.

Logically, teaching was the solution for the Frost family and both Rob and Elinor knew it, no matter how much they might wish to live in the country all the time. The Whichers and the Manthey-Zorns remained their good friends, a comfort in hours of stress. In October, the volume of Edward Thomas's *Collected Poems* arrived, the mere sight of which was touching and sad for all of them.

In October, also, the poet's professional pride was ruffled by the essay on his work which appeared in Amy Lowell's latest book, *Tendencies in Modern American Poetry*. Actually, Frost fared better than some of the other poets who were the subjects of her studies—Robinson, Sandburg, Masters, and two Imagists, J. G. Fletcher and H. D.—but he was annoyed and irritated by such pat statements as her claim that his was an example of "the only true bucolic poetry being written in America to-day." (The term "bucolic" made him scowl. "I'd almost as lief she'd called me a nature poet!" he said to Elinor. And if there was one thing he could not abide, it was being called a nature poet.) The piece went on, "A few hundred miles was to contain all his poetic world, but these few hundred miles were to be deepened indefinitely by the delving of his own spade." Toward the end of the article the critic accused him of having "no *ear*" for New Englanders' "peculiar tongue"—of not "hearing" the Yankee dialect that James Russell

Lowell, author Amy herself, and Alice Brown had heard. Rob knew that this barb was aimed at his refusal to write dialect-poetry, as she had suggested. He was after the *tone* of speech, far more subtle and penetrating than dialect, and he knew he had succeeded in capturing it, whether the indomitable Amy realized it or not. But for her to claim that he had no ear—he, who concentrated on the sound of the spoken word, of conversation—it was too much!

He told her in private, "Trouble with you, Amy—you don't go to your back door enough."

He could have referred her to the poem of his published the month before (September) in the *Atlantic Monthly*—"The Ax-Helve," one of the few works in which he used dialect, but not New England "tongue," if there were such a language. In the trenchant and significant scene, it was the old French-Canadian neighbor in Derry—"Baptiste"—who spoke his own brand of broken English, yet it was a dialect one frequently found in New England, a spill-over from across the border. When Baptiste condemns the helve "made by machine" by observing, "You give her one good crack, she's snap raght off. Den where's your hax-ead flying t'rough de hair?", and in the next breath, invites his neighbor to "Come on my house and I put you one in What's las' awhile—good hick'ry what's grow crooked. De second growt' I cut myself—tough, tough!" he makes it plain that he has a knowledge of ax-helves beyond the ordinary—as clearly as if he had spoken correct English; perhaps more clearly. And when he selects a helve from the "quiverful" he kept in the kitchen, sits down and starts to carve the curve like a violin-maker ("Baptiste knew how to make a short job long For love of it, and yet not waste time either.") his artistry fulfills the promise of his words. Like the artist—like the poet himself—the man takes pride in the finished product of his handiwork: "Baptiste drew back and squinted at it, pleased; 'See how she's cock her head!'"

Whether Miss Lowell would change her dictum was doubtful; she was not likely to retract it publicly, but Rob was so provoked by the image of him as a regional poet (which she had presented) that he could not resist retaliating in his own inimicable language, joking in dead earnest about his parental background, his peripatetic life. He pointed out that he had lived ten years in the west, thirty years in the east, three years in England and not less than six months in San Francisco, New York, Boston, Cambridge, Lawrence and London. He had lived in Maine, New Hampshire, Vermont and Massachusetts. He had spent twenty-five years in cities, nine in villages, nine on farms. He had seen the south on foot and attended Dartmouth as well as Harvard for two years. He listed all the jobs he had had, ending, "teacher in every kind of school, public and private, including psychological normal school and college." With high comedy, he enumerated such items as "Prize for running at Caledonia Club picnic; 2 prizes for assumed parts at masquerade balls; medal for goodness in high school; detur for scholarship at Harvard; money for verse. Knew Henry George well and saw much at one time (by way of contrast) of a noted boss. Presbeterian, Unitarian, Swedenborgian, Nothing. All the vices but disloyalty and chewing gum or tobacco."

As if to vindicate his protest of devastating humor, the National Institute of Arts and Letters, late in December, awarded Robert Frost the Russell Loines Prize for the longest, most conversational of his talk-poems, "Snow," resonant with the speech-tones of New England.

"No ear"—indeed! He chuckled as he accepted the honor.

Chapter 13

PROFESSOR VERSUS POET

Teaching in wartime was a difficult task. How to keep students' minds on their work with the battle cries of Château-Thierry ringing in their ears? How to convince them that art was a vital and lasting ingredient of life, and that war had the urgency of a crucial hour, but no more, in the history of mankind? With Amherst a part-training center, with young men in and out of uniform, how to prevent them from taking up 90 per cent of the class-hour to harass each other with the war issues? Robert Frost himself was an ardent defender of the Allied cause, but he tried not to think of either war or political issues all the time. Yet he could not stop his own daughter—Lesley—from leaving Wellesley, where she studied during 1917, to join the war effort. She wanted to be a flier, but there her father put his foot down; so she became a war worker in a propeller factory in Marblehead, Massachusetts.

One way that the poet-professor solved the problem of dealing with his students was not to push too strongly—let the army and navy do that. He continued to be nonchalant—to lie back in his chair, to be always a few minutes late, to cut class whenever he could. He indulged his eccentricities, achieved a reputation for being anti-intellectual, yet found new methods of inspiring interest and holding it, at the same time cutting his own work down to a minimum. He repeated his invitation to meet the boys informally at his house, and they were glad to have a refuge from the rigors of militarism. His moods were mercurial; he could be serious or gently humorous, even comic if he chose—his caricatures of certain colleagues were deliciously accurate. He had the humanist's love of gossip and never tried to hide it.

One of the faithfuls this year was E. A. Richards, who later wrote a reminiscent article of the poet-professor, which he called "A Reality Among Ghosts":

"I met Mr. Frost in 1918. Amherst was then part military camp, part college, and not very much of either, although we all did our best to go two ways at once . . . we had no place in particular to head for, no place to go but where we were sent. . . . We were not *sure,* as young men ought to be. . . .

"During those months it was good to be even remotely in acquaintance with Mr. Frost . . . here was a man more deeply sentient, more solidly intellectual, with those qualities in finer and more equable balance than we had heretofore known, moving and living with us . . . and he lent us a sense of value and longevity in our thinking.

"We were glad to go to his house at ten or eleven at night and sit somewhat uneasily in his sitting room until he came in from some depth of the dwelling and sprawled out on a lounge. He read from this poet and that, throwing the book aside when he had reached what seemed to him the furthest reach of luminous expression in some particular poem. And then he would say what occurred to him in relation to that poem, going from there to the general considerations of poetry.

"He never, or rarely, talked about his own work. . . . I dropped in one afternoon. I was welcomed by Mrs. Frost, one of the few completely beautiful women I have known. I walked into the vacant parlor and looked down at the half-finished manuscript of 'The Runaway,' which in later years I was to see and hear scores of people charmed by. And at those later times I thought to myself, 'Well, I saw the runaway when he was only half born.'

". . . I must say the hardest job was to get him to say whether any of my stuff was good or bad. He did say at length, and the verdict . . . was hidden under such a half-kind, half-deadly phrase that the impact did not strike me until some hours later. Then it almost ruined me. . . ."

The poem that Richards saw "half-born" had been requested by the student publication, the *Amherst Monthly*, for the June issue, and the broad streak of mischief in Robert Frost could not resist the metaphor embodying the rash spirit of an untried boy (or perhaps of the poet himself) in the frisky, frightened antics of a runaway colt, completing it with the complaint that whoever left him out so late "Ought to be told to come and take him in."

The poem, complex in meter, contained a phrase that the professor-poet had picked up from one of his students—"Sakes, It's only weather."—which he used, like Baptiste's broken English in "The Ax-Helve," for its timbre, the sound of speech, and not as any particular dialect. He said of "The Runaway" that he added the moral for the pleasure of the aggrieved tone of voice. When the piece was completed—it was not written "right off"—he felt he had achieved what he wanted most but did not do often enough with the sound of words; and with certain words, he created unforgettable phrases: "whited eyes"; "shudders his coat"; of these he remarked that this was what he liked to write. Once he made those lines, he was lost.

One of the schemes the nonconformist Professor Frost devised to capture and hold the interest of the students (and the poet in himself) was to program a series of storytelling hours by the boys themselves. He divided a large lecture class of fifty into five or six groups, which met at different hours. The boys were to tell a story of their own choosing from books they had read—Balzac, or anything they wanted to pick, he told them. In telling the story, they were not merely to relate the plot, but to show the class why the story "called" to them or what single feature of it especially appealed to them. In this way, he learned a good deal more about individual students than a weekly examination ("spot" tests, some of the professors gave, just to see if the required reading had been done) or a daily theme would have shown him. When every student had told a story, he chose the best from each group, and these students were asked to retell their stories before the whole class of fifty.

"That whiled away at least a month and a half," he admitted with a roguish smile in outlining his methods to an interviewer; "and I didn't have to grade any papers!"

Another device he employed to get out of the latter was to have the students write just a few paragraphs, or perhaps a sentence or two, a few times—two or three or five—in a term, when something occurred to them as a result of their reading. The papers were to contain some original thought, not a critical writing of the work that they had picked up somewhere. He wouldn't grade the papers but would read them, and if he liked what he read, he would turn them over to write on the back some idea that had occurred to him from their ideas. It was by this means that he finally avoided assigning and reading mountains of papers once and for all; moreover, both the professor and his pupils benefited by the exchange of ideas.

Not all the young men who enrolled in Robert Frost's classes at Amherst during those early years were so taken with the teaching or the creative work of the poet. There were always certain eager minds that enjoyed writing reams of facts and little else, giving back on "exams" all a professor had said during the term, and these were disappointed in not having the chance to do so with Robert Frost. For one final examination at Amherst, he came in and wrote on the blackboard: "Do something," and went to his office on the next floor. Most of the students were baffled. Some got up and left as soon as he was in his office. Others climbed the stairs after a few minutes, knocked on his door, and told him how much they had got out of the course. Others crammed two bluebooks full of all they could recall of what they thought he said. Only a few

pulled themselves together and wrote a thoughtful paragraph, or
gave a vivid account of some incident that illustrated the most
memorable philosophic discovery they had made in the course of
study. With the last, he felt he had succeeded. Then there were a
number of conservatives on campus who found the poet's realism
revolting. They objected strongly to the coarse subject matter of
"A Hundred Collars," the menial duties listed in "A Servant to
Servants." They could not understand the poet's statement that he
took out a poetic license to use the word beauty three times and
he had not yet used it once. Equally disturbing was his listing the
kinds of beauty, all the way down to "vile beauty."

Nevertheless, he was already becoming "a prophet on his own
campus," as Elliott later called him, and the figure he cut in literary
circles lent a new glow to the slim Amherst faculty roster of luminaries. All through 1918, Robert Frost was sought out by the leaders of the surging movement of modern poetry, and since it was
a challenge to keep the home fires burning in contemporary literature as in everything else during the war, he let himself be sucked
in by the wave of enthusiasm. At the same time, he struggled to
keep from being swept away from his own stream of consciousness
—the inner flow of every man. He was to describe this quality,
bestowed upon all, first in "West-Running Brook" and then with
greater eloquence in the soaring love sonnet, "The Master Speed."

Yet he did become involved to some extent with his colleagues,
enough to be a pleasure, not compulsive or burdensome. Spurred
on by the explosive Louis Untermeyer, the argumentative Amy
Lowell, and the poets he had met in the middle west, he attended
one or two meetings of the Poetry Society, and at Untermeyer's
invitation went to New York for a poetry conference. One memorable, merry evening they spent together with Sara Teasdale and
Vachel Lindsay. The fragile, sibylline Sara, whose alternating leaps
of fantasy and dire predictions as to her own fate had them enthralled (most of all Lindsay, who worshiped her), somehow led
to the subject of John L. Sullivan, the famous, or infamous, boxer
of Boston whose death had headlined the news that day. Vachel

seriously suggested that they all write poems dealing with the fabulous career of the pugilist, in his place in the hereafter. The others
could not believe he meant it until he produced "The Strong Boy
of Boston," eventually included in his *Collected Poems.* The rascal
in Rob Frost could not help joshing the improbable notion in a
broad burlesque, definitely not for publication in any of his collections, but heartily enjoyed by his friends and colleagues: "John
L. Sullivan Enters Heaven" (to be sung to the tune of "Heaven
Overaches You and Me").

So did the poet lighten the misery of wartime stress, the lingering sorrow over Edward Thomas's untimely death, and his growing
concern for his sister Jeanie, whose fanatical opposition to the war
threatened her sanity (as if the war itself were not insanity enough).

Early in 1919, his one-act play *A Way Out,* published two years
before in the *Seven Arts,* was produced under his direction by the
Amherst Masquers, a college theater group; Roland Wood, who
was among the boys that frequented the Frost home, had been
taken with the stunning force of the double homicide at the end
as the poet finished reading the script one night, comparing it to
his murder poem, "The Vanishing Red." As prime mover of the
production, Roland played one of the principal parts in the double-
identity play of two psychopaths possessed by fear; and he secured
the performance date at the Northampton Academy of Music on
February 24.

The auditorium was packed with enthusiastic students, many
from Smith College; the performance was so successful that the
author had to be rescued by President Neilson from a mob of girls
who had recently produced a play and were bedeviling him for the
hidden meaning behind the conflict and violence of his one-act.

He had no intention of telling them or anyone else what the
short play purported to say. Nor was he any more communicative
on the subject when *A Way Out* was published ten years later by
the Harbor Press, at the instigation of Roland Wood, who went
into publishing after graduation. Robert Frost wrote the introduc-

tion his former student requested, but he cagily refrained from any discussion of the plot or motivation, let alone the meaning of his play. He began by observing that everything written is as good as it is dramatic. It did not need to declare itself in form, but it is drama or nothing. He then spoke of dramatic composition in general terms, and ended by saying that he had always come as near the dramatic as he could this side of actually writing a play. "Here for once I have written a play without (as I should like to believe) having gone very far from where I have spent my life." But it was not so.

Poetry was his sphere, and though he tried playwriting twice again, in *The Guardeen* and *The Art Factory,* he did not feel at home outside the realm of meter and metaphor, the measured lines, rhymed or no.

The Armistice had brought an end to shooting, but the war did not seem over until the Peace Conference was held and the terms were settled at Versailles in May, 1919. Then businessmen in America began taking stock of the postwar world and saw that many changes were to come to the book market as to all others. Alfred Harcourt, whose vision was far-reaching, resigned from Henry Holt and Company. He had been dissatisfied with the firm since the elder Mr. Holt had retired; his sons and the others in authority were conservative, lacking in judgment, Harcourt felt, and unwilling to take any risks—the kind he had taken when he bought Bertrand Russell's *Proposed Roads to Freedom* and which the company still did not like; when he accepted a novel by a *Saturday Evening Post* writer named Sinclair Lewis; and when he found *North of Boston.* Besides Robert Frost, he had brought to the Holt trade list Carl Sandburg, Louis Untermeyer (whom he set "anthologizing"), and the Benéts, all of the new movement in poetry, and all of whom were going to be on the list of his own firm, set up with two colleagues as Harcourt, Brace and Howe. Alfred fully expected the name of his happiest discovery—and friend—Robert Frost, to be there; and so did the poet, in the first glow of enthusiasm. He knew the young editor had dreamed of heading a firm of his own for some time. He wrote from Franconia on the 4th of July, saying that it all read like a fairy story, and that he hoped to have a book on one of the earliest lists.

Both of them, however, reckoned without the Holts, who declined to release *A Boy's Will* and *North of Boston* to their erstwhile editor, and the poet did not want to see his work divided among publishing houses. Faced with a decision to make, he and Elinor talked it over from every viewpoint before Robert sent any word. His writing was not like the novelist's or the playwright's; he "knew he had but one book in his system": the three volumes that Holt had published so far were merely the first three portions of it. And from a practical standpoint, the Holts had provided a subsidy for him, had given him "little raises without his asking"; he felt a loyalty toward them he could not deny.

In the end, he decided to stay with the original firm, the one that had established him in his native land. But before he had quite made up his mind—or at any rate before he had a chance to write —the Holt office notified him that Lincoln MacVeagh was to succeed Alfred Harcourt, and the publishers wanted the poet to meet the new editor. Rather than waste any of his precious Franconia summer, his writing time, Rob invited the young man to come there.

MacVeagh, who had been only a member of the College Department before the war, had met Robert Frost in 1916, at a luncheon given by Roland Holt in the poet's honor when he first returned from England. The college editor was much taken with Frost's distinctive personal quality then, but had no idea that he would come to know and appreciate it much more fully in a few years. At that time he was greatly impressed with Alfred Harcourt's enthusiasm over the success of *North of Boston,* and Roland Holt's inept attempts to be the benign patron of the arts—he referred privately to Frost as "our bi'gosh poet," an unhappy phrase which caused a small tempest when the poet himself got wind of it.

After two years in the army, MacVeagh rejoined the Holts, just as Harcourt was making the break with the company; and since he had shown both ability and insight in the College Department, he was assigned to take Alfred's place as head of the Trade Department. His first job was to try to keep Frost in the fold, so when he received the invitation to come to Franconia, he lost no time in accepting.

With their easy hospitality, the Frosts made him feel at home, so that he forgot this was a business trip. Mr. Bristol (treasurer at Holt) had left whatever was to be said to the poet entirely to the judgment of the young envoy. MacVeagh, helping Rob with his haphazard chores during the day and "outwatching the Bear" with him at night, when they talked philosophy instead of business (like the characters in "The Star-Splitter") could not seem to find the proper moment to bring up the matter of contract, subsidy, and so forth. Like Sidney Cox, he was swept at once into the mainstream of the poet's thought, swept along by the flow of ideas. He sensed that Robert Frost did not care to discuss business and "was hardly a person to relish pressure," so he decided to make the visit a social one, enjoying the pleasant days to the full. Frost would probably make up his own mind anyway, without urging from anyone.

Needless to say, young Lincoln MacVeagh was wiser than he knew. If Robert Frost had any reservations about remaining a Holt author, it was the fact that he could not be sure his new editor would be as understanding as Alfred. MacVeagh, who had majored in the classics at Harvard and was as fascinated by the firmament as Frost, was, if anything, closer to the poet in spirit than Harcourt. (When Robert finally wrote to the former editor, he wished him "Godspeed," and made it plain that they would always be friends.)

While he and Lincoln were star-gazing and talking philosophy, delving for truth at the same time they were watching the heavens, the germ of an idea had sprung up in the poet's mind; and after his new editor left, he began to give it substance, to play with form, juggling words in the meter of Catullus he had briefly used in the poem "An Encounter." The hendecasyllabic line seemed best suited to the mystical aspect of the work he was evolving, and he concentrated on the measured arrangement of words till he forgot everything else and Elinor would have to remind him.

Yet he could write about his ardent labors casually, humorously to George Whicher, joking about having fun with "Hen Dekker syllables" as if he had nothing more profitable to do. They weren't farming much either, that summer, and Elinor wouldn't let them hatch too many chickens for fear they would be neglected (in favor of the above-mentioned syllables.)

The poem was completed before the end of summer, a rich and lasting harvest from his months in the country. The work he had touched on so lightly turned out to be one of his most profound poetic statements: "For Once, Then, Something."

Using the conventional metaphor of the well, he depicts himself seeking to delve into the depths of thought, but for the most part he sees no more than a narcissistic reflection; once, however, he discerns "beyond the picture, through the picture, a something white." When his vision is shaken by a drop of water from a fern, the poem takes an unconventional turn. What was that whiteness, he wonders—"Truth? A pebble of quartz?" There is no answer. He only knows he sighted "for once, then, something."

With such an achievement in hand, it was harder than ever to return to the routine of teaching; and it was especially hard to go back to Amherst this time, since they had moved into an apartment —Miss Carrie Marsh's top floor—early in 1919. It was on Main Street, between the Masonic Lodge and the Town Hall, between the unsavory sounds of the mystic rites on one side and the mouthings of city officials on the other. More than once, George Whicher saw Rob Frost shoot his head out of the window in protest against the noise, but it did little good. However, they had leased the place for another year, so back they went. Even with the noisy accompaniment, the poet was able to do a little writing. When matters became impossible, he could always relieve his outraged sensibilities by dropping in on W. R. Brown, an insurance man he had made friends with at his first reading in Amherst. They had discovered a common interest in Thoreau—"as a passion"—a bond, besides Brown's love of poetry, that kept them lifelong friends.

As Christmas rolled round and the end of the year drew near, the poet in Robert Frost suddenly took the ascendancy over the professor or, more accurately, rebelled against academic life, and he made one of his lightning decisions—this one, to resign from Amherst. He would teach till the beginning of the spring term, March, 1920; then they would go up to Franconia so he could give at least a year, uninterrupted, to poetry. (He would take a sabbatical, though only half of his "week" of years would be over in March: three and a half years at Amherst. He would take a year of rest on his own authority. Actually, he was resigning from Amherst in large part because he could not reconcile the injustice of some of Meiklejohn's policies with the man's courage and foresight, which he admired. In his conflicting feelings about the president, Rob Frost appeared in his own eyes two-faced, and he could not continue to teach in a school suffering from "Meiklejaundice," as he labeled it.)

He once told Morris Tilley, the friend who taught at Michigan and summered in New England near the Frosts, that he supposed he had been guided in life so far by instinct to protect what he was or wanted to be. . . . He lost friends by leaving Harvard. He did not regret leaving, however, for he could not stay. He could not have explained, even to himself, why he couldn't stay. He just had to go. His instincts had guided him well from the time he left Dartmouth, and he trusted them now in resigning from his post at Amherst. In the end, he did not wait till spring, but made the break before New Year's Eve. Tilley had asked him to consider coming to Michigan at some time; and, after the "poetry year" was over, he might investigate the possibilities of the midwestern university.

Before they had quite settled in Franconia again during January, he was called to his sister's bedside; she had become much worse. On April 12th, he wrote George Whicher the story of Jeanie's tragic fate, telling it with the gentleness and understanding and the objectivity of a poet who was also a realist.

He explained that his sister had tried being everything from pacifist, pro-German and internationalist to draft-obstructor and seditionist in her protest against war, all to no avail. He did not hide the fact that she had gone clearly insane, had not known him; nothing but sheer insanity would do her feelings justice. Her brother did not blame her. In fact, he admired the courage "that is unwilling not to suffer everything that everyone is suffering everywhere." She had gone the way of the sensibilitist to the bitter end, he admitted; whatever hope there was for her seemed small. In a single sentence the view which was undoubtedly the core of Robert Frost's amazing ability to adjust, to balance the opposing forces of good and evil, came to light in this letter. "It is a coarse and brutal world," he granted, "unendurably coarse and brutal, for anyone who hasn't the least dash of coarseness or brutality in his own nature to enjoy it with."

The small hope there might have been for Jeanie soon faded just as her being did; her brother could not hold back the fatal hour when her protests would be silenced forever.

He turned to his art; it was as if some Voice had directed him to choose this as his poetry year.

Chapter 14

"I WILL SING YOU ONE-O"

It had been bitter cold when the Frosts retreated to Franconia, cold enough to make your teeth rattle, but dazzlingly white and serenely still, the sort of quiet the poet needed to regain his equipoise, as Morris Tilley called it. The farmhouse in winter was just the place to hole-up in with a few favorite books—including Shakespeare and the *Odyssey;* and the snowy slopes of Lafayette, the powdered evergreens, brought the peace he wanted just now for new poems. Perhaps he was making a subtle reference to his recent academic harassment in the double quatrain he soon wrote, "Dust of Snow."

Was it purely accidental, as he later claimed, that the tree from which a crow shook down on him the dust of snow just happened to be a hemlock? At any rate, the incident brought a change of mood and saved some part of a day he had rued. He used to scoff heartily at the idea that the mere mention of hemlock implied poison; but like so many of his poems, this short piece could be taken literally or figuratively.

Elinor and the children were used to the sudden changes the impulsive head of the household was likely to make; Marjorie in particular loved the high atmosphere of Franconia, the long white stretches of hillside for sledding, and she was already beginning to write porcelain-pure pieces about the snowland it became in the wintertime. None of them minded the cold especially; they lived in the kitchen, and when they went out, bundled up against the icy air. One day when the windows were glazed over, Elinor wrote Harriet and George Whicher that the thermometer stood at minus twenty, but before she sealed the envelope, Rob included "A Correction," which he dashed off—a little eight-line jingle to the effect that their guess of minus twenty (which had seemed "plenty") proved only half correct, according to the outdoor thermometer, which read minus forty (as they saw when they made a "sortie"). His bit of doggerel delighted the Whichers, who promptly framed it and hung it on the wall in George's study, where it stayed for many years. (Frost did not consider such "fooling" poetry or did not find it worthy of inclusion in any of his volumes or his complete poems. But in 1945, his friend David McCord asked George Whicher if he could publish it in an anthology of British and American light verse he was compiling—a spicy offering of wit and humor, which, after sifting and salting, he called *What Cheer*.)

Such lighthearted moments were frequent in Frost's mercurial makeup. But in the watches of the night, as the poet in Franconia pondered the sad state of his sister (hers was among the fatalities of war that one never heard about); the loss of his dear friend Edward; the wrangling among nations caused by the wranglings among men, he recalled a wakeful night in Amherst when he heard the tower clock followed by the steeple striking one. Now he let his mind soar to "the furthest bodies To which man sends his Speculation, Beyond which God is" to interpret the "One!" sounded by tower of learning and church steeple alike in terms of divine harmony far above the dissonance of men. The "solemn peals" sounded the song of the universe. And so he saw that "The utmost star . . . has not ranged." Although man might "drag down man and nation nation," the stars remained constant, visible, and reassuring to the heart of humankind since creation.

The verse of double-accented short lines, when read aloud, had almost the sound of a chant, though it had little repetition and the rhyme scheme was irregular. The theme of universal significance, of the stars in their heavenly courses, which he would develop and vary in his fourth volume, was set in "I Will Sing You One-O" like an opening hymn.

He was able to give rein to his ideas for new poems and rework (slightly, for he never did much tampering) a piece he had picked out in Amherst, above the din of Masonic rites; it dealt with the poet-farmer's advice to a young orchard—"Good-bye and Keep Cold"—as winter comes on, and was declared "pomologically correct" by the Massachusetts Agricultural College. "No orchard's the worse for the wintriest storm; But one thing about it, it mustn't get warm." In conclusion, the farmer half wishes he might be able to hover over his tender young fruit trees, but he feels that something must "be left to God."

Occasionally Rob Frost would ask himself, with perhaps a tremor of doubt, whether he might be a "nature poet," as some people still called him; but he would answer himself vehemently. "I'm no nature poet! All but a few poems have a person in them." Rereading Wordsworth in the quiet of a winter night, it occurred to him that in the line, "Bound each to each by natural piety," the nineteenth-century poet may have meant *nature* piety—"piosity"—as exemplified by "My heart leaps up when I behold a rainbow in the sky." Such expression was in line with what Rob later called "sunset raving" in one of his lectures—"Ohs" and "Ahs" and no more. Well, he was not a nature poet in that sense; he had no affinity for those poets who made a fetish of being nature lovers. He would neither be afraid of nature nor besotted with it. He was at home with nature, which he brought in as a backdrop for the actions and emotions of the characters in his poems.

When he wrote in "Looking for a Sunset Bird in Winter" a description of the fading gold in a February sky as he was "shoeing home" over white stretches, and mentions that he thought he saw a bird, he was neither nature lover nor bird watcher as such, but only insofar as the things he cited led to an expression of his philos-

ophy or portrayed the person in the poem, like the whimsical
farmer who gives orchards gentle advice.

Such familiar subjects were the fabric of poetry to Robert Frost.
It was around this time (1921) that he said: "The farmer on his
Sunday holiday is apt to stray out just to scratch the back of his pig
or to salt the cattle. It is a little ceremony—a kind of poetic ceremony—tender-like. You know after a severe winter a farmer will
go out to his trees and proceed to pick off a few blackened buds,
and there is a little poetry in that, more or less—a practical thing
to be sure—but another little ceremony into which enter the elements of poetry."

Once he had struck his stride, Rob continued to write apace
in this year of retreat. About ten poems were published in reviews,
quarterlies and other magazines (including the *London Mercury,*
which printed *Dust of Snow* in December) during 1920, paving the
way for the new volume. A number of already published works
were included in anthologies: one of the first books Alfred Harcourt brought out was *A Miscellany of American Poetry*, edited by
the eleven poets it included, Frost among them; he had selected six
of his current compositions. Also, Braithwaite was compiling another anthology, and asked for "To E.T." and some of the *Harper's*
poems, Louis Untermeyer had taken up Harcourt's suggestion to
"anthologize," and was collecting his first edition of *Modern American Poetry,* with biographical sketches (a highly successful enterprise which he kept revising through the years), and of course
wanted his friend Robert represented. The sound of poetry was
humming everywhere during the summer of 1920. George
Whicher, who composed a few verses now and then, "forded the
Mohawk" to come up and "compare progress" with the poet on
the hillside farm.

Other friends came, too, as they had in the previous summers—
the Untermeyers, Sidney Cox, Lincoln MacVeagh—a string of
luminaries in the literary and academic world, of which Robert
Frost, willy-nilly, was now an important part. He was glad to see
them, always happy for the opportunity for good talk, but he no-

ticed that his old friends among the hill folk, some whom he had known since the first summer at the Lynches' in 1907, resented the influx of intellectuals and sophisticates who were always driving up to see the poet. Old man Herbert's remark about using the place for a park was too much a reality to be a joke any more. Rob regretted their feeling, but could do little to change it. And unfortunately, he only made matters worse when he agreed to read poetry at a benefit held at a summer mansion, providing that the affair was open to native Franconia farmers, friends in whose kitchens he had dawdled over many a cup of coffee. Some of them were there, all right, but as servants. It was confusing for the Frost children, and for their parents as well. Rob began to think of moving—perhaps to the entrancing stone house he and Elinor had admired in South Shaftsbury, Vermont. They would always have a special affection for Franconia (where Rob would continue to come in hay-fever months); and Marjorie, who loved it most, begged them not to move. But "one morning in September," Rob said, telling the story, "I just piled them all in the old car and by night we had a new roof over our heads."

The Stone House in South Shaftsbury was in many ways more practical for the Frosts. Not far from Amherst—yet far enough to be removed from its contagious intellectual fevers; close to Bennington College and a friend they had made through the Harcourts, Dorothy Canfield Fisher; and within easy access of New York by train, for exchanging professional and friendly visits. The house itself was more picturesque than the frame farmhouse in Franconia; and there were a few acres here for farming, too—as much of it as Rob Frost would ever do, now that he was to be reckoned with as a poet among poets of the first rank. As he said in "The Lockless Door" (the sixth poem in the *Miscellany*):

> So at a knock
> I emptied my cage
> To hide in the world
> And alter with age.

He went straight ahead (though in zigzag fashion) with his compositions on the cosmic theme he had introduced in "I Will Sing You One-O." In what he shortly called "a crooked straightness—an absolutely abandoned zig-zag that goes straight to the mark," he shot forward with "A Star in a Stone-Boat." Dedicated to Lincoln MacVeagh, often his co-watcher of constellations, the poem spoke of a workman who unwittingly builds a fallen star into a stone wall, seeing nothing remarkable about the huge coal, which he loads into a stone-boat and drags home at a snail's pace (this mighty meteor that had sailed through space at lightning speed). He puts it to a lowly use in building a stone wall; and the poet feels that he must "forever go/To right the wrong that this should have been so." (Here again is a variation of the theme stated in "Mending Wall.") A modern Diogenes, he searches continuously, using the stars (i.e., light) as a symbol of truth. He never lifts his eye from following walls

> Except at night to places in the sky
> Where showers of charted meteors let fly.

His quest is queer compared to that of most men, but he must go on, and he concludes that the prize it promises is "the one world, complete in any size" that he may have a chance "to compass, fool or wise."

At this time "The Census-Taker" was written, and "The Star-Splitter," a mixture of skepticism and reverence, which opens in zigzag fashion with the audacious lines picturing Orion coming up sideways, throwing a leg up over the "fence of mountains" and rising on his hands to look in on the poet. It tells the story of one Brad McLaughlin, a hugger-mugger farmer and amateur astronomer, who mingles reckless talk of the stars with hapless hoeing and weeding. Failing at his confused farming, he burns his house down so that with the fire insurance proceeds he can buy a telescope, which is christened the Star-Splitter. In order to have leisure for star-gazing, he gets a job as a railroad clerk. The poet remarks among other things that the telescope "ought to do some good if splitting stars 'Sa thing to be compared with splitting wood."

The contraction " 'Sa" was an example of Robert Frost's use of the vernacular, also an earlier line: " 'What do you want with one of those blame things?' ", which he gives philosophic import by observing that nothing is more blameless than a telescope, or less " 'A weapon in our human fight. . . .' "

The poem ends on a querulous note, often to be repeated by the poet till the end of his life: "We've looked and looked, but after all where are we?"

As fast as the poems were finished, Rob sent them out to magazines, no longer afraid that they would be misunderstood (or not understood at all, not even considered) and returned with the dread brand of rejection. Just before Christmas, he wrote joyously to Harriet Monroe, who had requested something from him: "I am cleaned out for the moment. But I am having some more at a great rate." One of these was the first of the famous duo of witch poems, "The Pauper Witch of Grafton" in collections always printed with more powerful and shocking "The Witch of Coös." ("Double trouble's always the witch's motto anyway.") The pauper witch (and perhaps the adjective suggests that she is the lesser of the two) was a town character in Wentworth or Warren, whose tale was told in an old town history Rob found in the local library. Here again he slipped in expressions like, "He wa'nt but fifteen"; "All is, if I'd a-known"; and the last line, later cited as a classic Frostian use of the idiom: "I might have, but it doesn't seem as if." No one but Robert Frost would dare to end a poem with a conjunction—the way a person's thought might dribble off in conversation. Here was the difference between the genuine New England vernacular and the concocted, so-called dialect of Amy Lowell.

He kept on writing—of everything, anything that sounded some chord inside him. One night he and Elinor were talking of their children's names (Carol's teachers more than once asked if his name shouldn't be "Carl," and Lesley's name, from Burns' "bonnie

Lesley," was often bestowed on boys—which perhaps accounted for her athletic ability, her aggressive vitality); out of their musing, came the poem "Maple," a romantic tale of a girl named after a maple tree (but whose teacher thought it must be "Mabel") by her mother, who died in childbirth. What meaning there may have been in the dead mother's whim the poet never revealed, but the name brings the girl her mate in marriage; and though they both seek to discover the name's real meaning, if any, they never find it. The poet says, "Its strangeness lay/ In having too much meaning." And then he lists his own children's names in a row: "Other names, As Lesley, Carol, Irma, Marjorie, Signified nothing." But the last line of the poem reads, "Name children some names and see what you do." (After the poem was published, an order of nuns wrote to ask if the girl was called "Maple" because she was so sweet!)

Toward the end of January, he began to think seriously about an offer he had received, through Morris Tilley, from President Marion L. Burton, of the University of Michigan, to come to Ann Arbor as a Fellow in the Creative Arts for the year beginning in September, 1921-22. Rob and Elinor had one of their idle parleys on the subject, but had come to no decision when he wrote to Harriet Moody from South Shaftsbury on January 20 (1921) to tell that he and Elinor would be in New York about the 20th of February, and would like to talk to her before deciding whether or not to take the step into Michigan. They both took the attitude that they would be right whichever they decided. ("That's why we find it impossible to treat anything as momentous.") If she opposed the step too much, he declared, they would think it was because she did not want them that close to Chicago, or because she thought there were enough poets already "within the first postal zone from Chicago." Then he proceeded to twit her about looking up to poets outside of America. "Have a little national pride," he admonished. On the other hand, he thought it was provincial to brag about America; they would talk about provincialism when they met.

He was rather miffed because the expansive dowager and patron appeared to give preference to foreign poets. On one of his first visits to her salon, he had found his British friend Wilfrid Gibson, and although they had a happy reunion, he wondered that Mrs. Moody should go to the expense and risk of bringing poets across during the war when the Atlantic was highly dangerous. Later, when he and Gibson both read for the Browning Society in Philadelphia, they compared checks, and Rob discovered that his fee was exactly half of his British colleague's.

He was not one to haggle over price, and he bore his friend Wilfrid no grudge, but he could not help taking a few gibes at Mrs. Moody and anyone else who made a fuss over imported poets. Michigan was offering him $5,000 for practically the same thing he was doing in South Shaftsbury—he would be poet in residence, as the post was later called; and he really didn't need Mrs. Moody's advice to know the venture was worth a try.

Chapter 15

MICHIGAN'S "IDLE FELLOW"

In its advance story on the appointment of Robert Frost, the *Michigan Alumnus,* after a few remarks on President Burton's innovation in providing space for the creative spirit in literature and art at a university dedicated in large measure to science, stated that "Mr. Frost will do no teaching nor will he be expected to accomplish anything definite unless he has something authentic to say." Whether the university and the poet would agree on the definition of authentic remained to be seen; but at least it was the avowed aim of the institution to give him time and opportunity— with the stipend, freedom from economic pressure—to pursue his "talk" song as he pleased. Although their summertime neighbor and friend would not admit it, the Frosts could see Morris Tilley's fine hand in all of these arrangements.

He and Roy Cowden, head of the English Department, were on hand to make the poet feel at home, after he had been officially welcomed by President Burton and Dean Bursley, who had found a comfortable place for the Frosts. Only Lesley had accompanied her father; the rest would soon be along—at Mrs. d'Ooge's, widow of the former head of the Classics Department. Morris Tilley smiled at Robert's obvious relief when he saw the pleasant old yellow frame house, set back in a green lawn on wide Washtenaw Avenue, bordered by a line of urn-shaped elms, arching overhead— very much like Dana Street, where they had twice lived in Amherst. (That this was often called Fraternity Row, Morris did not tell his friend; he would find it out soon enough.) Just what sort of town Rob had expected to see in the middle west, he could not have said, but he was agreeably surprised at the number of very green, quiet, old-fashioned streets, full of fine trees, that he found here. The name itself, originally Ann's Arbor, connotated trees, and the Arboretum, the pride of the Botany Department for its varieties of trees, provided a haunt for a poet in search of an hour of solitude. These facts he soon picked up in his explorations while Lesley, who had tried a year at Barnard and given up college to go to work for the Publishers Association, now went about getting enrolled as a Junior at Michigan. Roy Cowden, originally a farm boy from upstate New York, and something of Frost's own disposition with his slow smile and simple, straightforward manner, suggested that the poet order a pair of walking shoes, custom-made by a local shoemaker, an expert craftsman; and before long, the two were taking country walks through the surrounding hills, where Frost was pleased to find plain white farmhouses like theirs in Franconia.

The campus buildings, too, were more like those at Dartmouth or Amherst than he had expected. As he went through the Engineering Arch with Tilley and Cowden, who took him around the first day, and they came onto the two crosswalks that cut diagonally across campus like an immense "X" (familiarly called "The Diag" by students), he felt reassured at the sight of the old gray stone and red brick buildings—covered thickly enough by English ivy to have been there for some time; with the exception of the neoclassic Angell Hall, they were mostly of Civil War or Victorian vintage, homely, familiar, traditional college architecture. And the poet made friends with the faculty he met inside, particularly Campbell Bonner, Professor of Greek, who, like Frost, was interested in archaeology.

After Elinor and the others came, the poet-in-residence might be happened on in the grocery store any day, looking around vaguely, as he was when the journalism professor John L. Brum noticed him one morning. He was trying to remember, he said, the three things his wife had told him to buy for lunch; but so far he had spotted only two.

So he said they might as well go for a walk.

As they ambled along the winding streets, they spoke of the many ways that well-intentioned women can frustrate men; it was remarkable. Frost told his fellow sufferer that only the week before some clubwomen had inveigled him into giving a lecture to one of their literary societies. As he stood on the platform, he suddenly "heard a strange voice bellowing a lot of nonsense." The hall was large, filled with ladies eagerly listening, and after a minute, Rob realized that it was his own voice shouting to be heard in the back row, and he was ashamed of himself. "You simply can't bellow anything worth listening to!" he finished in protest against the women who invited him, and then innocently asked him to speak louder.

Characteristically, he called himself "Michigan's Idle Fellow," but he had never been busier. Inside of the first three months at Mrs. d'Ooge's he had written one of his most dramatic pieces in blank verse, acrid with the sharp tang of New England talk, chilling in its macabre tale, told mostly by the old hag of its title, "The Witch of Coös." Here was a work that would be termed (by the critic Randall Jarrell) the finest poem of its kind since Chaucer; it arose out of some scattered experiences and a dream the poet had. Yet he gave small sign of the poem brewing in his brain like a witch's broth when he met informally with students and listened with an attentive ear while young hopefuls read manscripts submitted to the college literary publication *The Inlander* (unfortunately called, during the first Frost residency, *The Whimsies,* but changed back the following year to its original and permanent title, perhaps at his suggestion).

The staff and chief contributors to the magazine, rarely more than twenty, selected and supervised by Roy Cowden, met at his home, where Rob Frost, greeted by Mrs. Cowden as kind hostess, joined the group after they were gathered in the living room. The students always set a big wicker chair under the reading lamp for him, but he never took it; he chose to sit in a dim corner, far away from the center of attraction. Early in the term he gave them some cogent advice, later quoted in a *New York Times* article: "Don't write for A's," he said, and explained, "Athletics are more terribly real than anything else in education because they are for keeps, for blood, and that is the way I want you to write. Studies are done just for practice. Write only when you have something to say." This perhaps was the hardest lesson he could have given the young writers to learn, but they were eager to hear more, and sat enthralled in the Cowdens' living room (some on the floor when the seating space was used up) for as long as the poet—*their* Fellow— would consent to stay.

Besides establishing himself as the guiding spirit among the literary lights of the university student body, Rob continued to pile up poems to build a new book. "The Witch of Coös was published in the January issue of *Poetry,* and in sending it to Harriet Monroe, he included the fact that Coös is the next county above Franconia in the White Mountains. Wild country, it was fertile territory for a poet with an ear ready to listen to lurid tales told him by old settlers when he stopped for water or a night's lodging. He was considering calling the new book *The Upper Right Hand Corner* because of its thorough New England flavor, yet he felt strongly that the basis of his poetry, of any poetry, must be its universality. And he was thinking of looking around Detroit or Chicago for possible fresh fields. It might be true, as his friend Van Wyck Brooks claimed, that the future in art lay with the east, but that was no reason why he, Robert Frost, shouldn't survey the rest of the landscape with an impartial eye. There were any number of sections that might prove likely.

Part of his looking around was a trip to Chicago for poetry-reading and the purpose of lining up some of his colleagues for a series of readings in Ann Arbor, a project he suggested (to be paid for by the students themselves), and had promised to organize. He and Elinor were going to stay at Harriet Moody's in Chicago, but at the last minute he wrote to say that he was bringing Lesley instead, and he hoped the lady could arrange to keep her there for a while. Lesley had grown tired of the University already, although she had received excellent marks and liked most of her teachers. Her father was afraid her restlessness was due to his line of talk, which wasn't "calculated to make her like any institution." He ended, "You know how I'm always at it against colleges, in a vain attempt to reconcile myself with them."

Here was the contradictory core of the poet, the two-headed dragon of genius inside him that threatened or seemed to send him in two directions at once; yet in the end he could somehow correlate his warring impulses and go "straight to the mark."

When they arrived in Chicago, Mrs. Moody lost no time in asking Lesley to remain several months in her midwestern mecca for poets, an invitation quickly accepted by the poet's daughter. The other Harriet, spunky little Miss Monroe, gave a dinner for Robert Frost, inviting a galaxy of poets to surround her star guest. Afterwards, the two "argued about poetic rhythms till three o'clock in the morning, against a background of cheers and jeers from three or four other poets who lingered as umpires, until at last Mrs. Moody called up my apartment and asked me to remind my guest of honor (her house guest) that she was waiting up for him," the editor of *Poetry* acidly described the incident in her autobiography.

Rob found the statuesque Harriet seated on her velvet swing, waiting impatiently for the poet who lost track of time, her face a little less than Buddha-like. Two or three devoted satellites had kept vigil with her; on the second seat in the swing was small, wiry Padraic Colum, who had arrived in town too late for Miss Monroe's dinner; and Frost immediately nailed him for the poetry series in Ann Arbor. Before he left Chicago, he enlisted Carl Sandburg (with his guitar) and Vachel Lindsay to give readings at the

University; and on his return to Ann Arbor, he wrote to Amy Lowell and Louis Untermeyer, inviting them to represent the east among American poets.

The festival, held in the spring (1922), opened with Amy Lowell, who arrived toting her own lighting equipment—a large reading lamp, which she bade the poet plug in for her, against the janitor's rules. In the blackout that followed, twenty-five hundred people sat enjoying the ad lib exchange between the two poets till the fuse was replaced.

From the darkness of the house, a voice suddenly pleaded from the audience: "Please smoke your cigar, Miss Lowell!"

"Why don't you smoke?" Frost urged her in a stage whisper. "They'd like to see you do it."

"Don't I know it? Come on out behind the barn," she whispered back.

The series was held during five successive weeks, and Carl Sandburg, who came to read in the third week, stayed with the Frosts. He went to his room soon after supper, and somebody asked, "What's Carl doing? Priming for his lecture?"

"No"—Rob sounded pure Yankee—"he's standing by his mirror fixing his hair so it will look as if a comb never touched it."

While Padraic Colum was there, his pixie sense of humor and spitfire temper evoked Rob Frost's responsive imp, and the two had many a merry argument on the relative merits of Yeats and Synge. (Yeats was to win the Nobel prize for literature in 1923— one of the few honors withheld from Robert Frost during his lifetime.)

Louis Untermeyer's visit with the Frosts was a happy occasion for all concerned, but especially for the two men, who enjoyed each other's company to the full. Untermeyer, whose lecture sparkled with wit and crackled with ideas, was extremely popular with both students and faculty; after he returned to New York, people kept calling the Frosts, who were kept busy answering questions and giving out his address.

The season closed with the resounding boom of Vachel Lindsay's vibrant, husky-toned voice pounding out the rhythms of "The Congo," "The Kallyope Yell," and "General Booth Enters Heaven." The huge, robust yet gentle fellow was a favorite of Rob Frost, who insisted on staying in the background, letting Vachel take over completely, listening to the performance with great relish. It was an effort for Frost to enjoy Carl Sandburg's renditions, because he was never sure he approved of the guitar accompaniment that Carl had made so essential to his poetry reading. And sometimes the soupy inflection of poets annoyed him. "Slopping over isn't poetry," he remarked to Morris Tilley. But Vachel was Vachel and one couldn't help admiring him, loving him.

Frost had not scheduled himself for the series, nor did he give poetry readings at any time during his first year in Ann Arbor. Whether this had anything to do with the mild cordiality of the invitation he received to return the following year, he could not be sure; at any rate, no mention of salary was made; and in June, the University, after awarding him its Honorary M.A., allowed him to go home without making definite arrangements. The honor was rather slim, he thought, and the uncertainty over finances was irritating.

Just before leaving the college town, he made a speech in front of a large Chamber of Commerce audience of Ann Arbor businessmen, and in it he gave vent to his ideas on commercialism in general—selling; his sense of values, literary and otherwise; it was a provocative—and provoked—address, and he put his heart into its delivery, especially when he spoke of New Hampshire, the state that had nothing to sell, the state he had loved so; his words, his sentences ran mellifluously, just short of poetry.

And when he got back to South Shaftsbury, the great, wise, witty poem itself, "New Hampshire," came pouring out. He now had one of the happiest experiences of his creative life: in a single night, at his writing board, he produced the long, brilliant Horatian satire, setting down in blank verse the ideas he had voiced in Ann Arbor. On and on he wrote, until "the morning stars sang together" as he completed the last line and went out into the dawn, to breathe the fresh, soft air, to view the early light in the east; then, turning back indoors, he composed, "in one stroke of the pen," like a contrapuntal note, the clear, calm, and probably the most perfect lyric in the entire Frost canon—"Stopping by Woods on a Snowy Evening."

Then he went to bed and slept the good sleep of gratification. The kind of "gratification you can't get any other way," he once said; that was "the primary thing" in writing poetry, "to gratify some feeling that nobody else has gratified for you. . . . You gradually find out what the particular craving of your own is—that the other poets haven't satisfied, and you slowly eliminate them until there is nothing left but the pure you." The pure Robert Frost shone from widely different facets in both of these poems.

When he spoke, in his Horatian satire of New Hampshire, about the lack of products in commercial quantity—"one each of everything," even a bit of gold—he made two exceptions. Mountains was one of them and literature the other—poetry in particular. Considering the market, there were more poems produced than any other thing! In his satire, Frost praised both New Hampshire and Vermont—"the two best states in the Union"—with his own unique evaluation and style. He speaks of the people he writes about, "the little men," as Emerson called them in relation to "the lofty land"; of the criticism another poet makes of them (undoubtedly Amy Lowell). He calls himself "a sensibilitist," and comments with irony, "Being the creature of literature I am, I shall not lack for pain to keep me awake." But he refutes the implication of provincialism—and here he was getting back at Amy—in lines mentioning countries round the world, and points out that he did not aim his "novels" at New Hampshire just because he wrote them there. Much more important, he was asserting the universality of his poetry in general, not only of his characters, but of his locale and ideas.

The other poem, the lyric, was to be the most widely quoted, overinterpreted Frost poem of all; and yet, when he set down the exact rhythms of "Stopping by Woods on a Snowy Evening" (one

...ght say it was written in three-quarter time: iambic quatrameter lines, four quatrains, three with the interlocking rhyme-scheme a,a,b,a; the fourth using "a" throughout, the last line being a repetition of the next-to-last), he certainly had not planned any of it. He said, speaking of commitments in the creative process, "There's an indulgent smile I get for the recklessness of the unnecessary commitment I made when I came to the first line in the second stanza of "Stopping by Woods on a Snowy Evening." It was at that point that he started the interlocking rhyme-scheme ("My little horse must think it queer"). "I was riding too high to care what trouble I incurred. And it was all right so long as I didn't suffer deflection."

He was riding high on his Pegasus in that emerald dawn, as he had ridden high when he wrote "To Earthward" in England (also in the new book); and before that in Derry, and long before that in Lawrence; and afterwards, often and often, he would be riding high. Late in life he told one of his biographers that many other poems of his had been written in one stroke. Some had trouble in one spot, like, "The Gift Outright," and he might never get them right. He never liked interpretations of his poems "and rarely gave any." "Stopping by Woods . . ." he felt could be read for the sheer pleasure of the spoken song, or it could be combined with whatever meaning the reader received from it. Certainly from his earliest poems, the deep woods symbolized for Frost the lure of life's darkest mysteries, the temptation to be led into the maze of nature's insoluble secrets. A poem, like a painting, like any other work of art, should inspire its own interpretation, he held.

He had need to lose himself in nature for a little while, however, during that summer of 1922, and with his growing-up family planned a mountain-climbing tour over the two-hundred-mile "Long Trail" through the Vermont ranges. Elinor and Irma bowed out of the project, but Rob, bolstered by the enthuasism of Lesley, Carol, and Marjorie, who brought along her roommate at Bennington High, Lillian LaBatt, went ahead with the scheme. On a drizzly day in July, Rob, suffering from a sore foot, started off by himself, leaving the others to buy shoes someplace. He reached the first shelter in a dampened state, and found an elderly couple there, already set up, who eyed him suspiciously. But he refused to budge.

"I said I'd agreed to wait there for my children, who would come along at four o'clock. The couple didn't believe a word of it. But come the children did, streaming at exactly four around the bend. We were all hived up there in the rain." (Carol for one didn't mind; he had taken an immediate shine to Marjorie's room-mate.) As soon as the skies cleared, they hit the trail again; the poet hiked over one hundred miles with his sore foot; then he decided the young people could finish by themselves, and hobbled home at a slower pace via the White Moutains, crawling into his sleeping bag on the ground every night to contemplate the stars before he closed his eyes.

The dome of blue above him when he woke perhaps engendered a mood that brought forth a poem like "Fragmentary Blue" for the new volume when he reached home. He spent the rest of the summer at Stone House, writing occasionally, and sorting out poems for a volume of selections for his first three books, to be published in the spring of 1923, as a kind of prelude to number four, which would probably come out in the fall. He worked on both projects with Lincoln MacVeagh, who practically shuttled between New York and South Shaftsbury during August. As usual, Sidney Cox spent half his vacation with the Frosts. At the height of the hay fever season, Rob and Sidney went up to Franconia for a few days, and, when the sun beat down hard even there during their walks, they would stop at the drugstore in Littleton, talking all the while. Rob was very fond of ice cream, but it was the making of poetry that he ate, drank, and breathed most of the time; between their first and second dishes of ice cream one day he remarked that "there should always be people in poems, even in lyrics," and he launched into one of his pet theories as he sailed into the second dish of a favorite sweet.

Before returning to South Shaftsbury, they went to Bread Loaf

Mountain, where, during the summer before, the poet had helped to establish the Bread Loaf Writers' Conference at Middlebury, Vermont. Here young writers could develop and learn the art of their chosen profession (provided they had the initial talent) from the more experienced. Frost and Louis Untermeyer were among the founders of this summer school which was to furnish the pattern for writer's conferences in other parts of the country, and continue to flourish through the years.

Back at the Stone House, he found an official letter from Ann Arbor, telling him that the University had raised the $5,000 salary, so he could "stay around" in 1922-23; but by then it was too late. Poetry demanded commitments he must keep for his inner self's sake, and he had made public commitments for readings in various places. For the moment, he sent no reply to Michigan, but he knew what he must do as far as poetry was concerned. In September, he received unusual recognition in the anonymous publication of "A Critical Fable," a shimmering satire on the most eminent poets in the country, Frost among them. Although Amy Lowell was also included in the unsigned work, everyone soon realized she had written it; and while she took a few jabs at Frost's hill folk "who have so many ills 'Tis a business to count 'em, their subtle insanities. One half are sheer mad, and the other inanities," she included more than one tribute, as, for example:

> He's an unexplored mine you know contains ore;
> Or rather, he acts as a landscape may do
> Which says one thing to me and another to you,
> But which all agree is a very fine view. . . .

In these lines, Amy was publicly acknowledging Robert Frost's stature and his universal appeal, giving him a private chuckle, shared by Elinor and a few others who knew how Amy had tried to influence his writing.

At the same time, "The Witch of Coös" was awarded the Levinson Prize of two hundred dollars as the best poem of the year from *Poetry*. And on top of this came the good news that the firm of

David Nutt was dissolving, releasing the poet from the clutches of Mrs. Nutt at last. Through the efforts of Lincoln MacVeagh, British publication of his works would be renewed in 1923 by the house of William Heinemann.

In the midst of so much poetry business, Rob could not bring himself to return to Ann Arbor to stay. He and Elinor rushed out to Michigan for President Burton's reception in October; and while there, the poet made a flexible arrangement whereby he could be "formally of Michigan," but not in residence. He planned to spend much of his time in South Shaftsbury during the coming year, writing (as he put it with false modesty) "little verses." It was in the agreement he had made in Ann Arbor that he should be wherever he pleased in order to write. Theoretically, University administrators could see that he ought to be, but Rob had a strong suspicion that in practice they would be quite cross if he did not make up for the lack of his presence on campus by publishing a book, dedicating himself to poetry.

It was a year dedicated not only to poetry writing but to a broad extension of the poetry readings. In the winter, Rob traveled to the southwest as far as Fort Worth, Texas, and to New Orleans, where the "Yankee" poet won over his Confederate audiences in no time, and if he let drop the fact that he was christened Robert *Lee* Frost because of his father's sympathies, he had their blessing before he ever read a line.

He was called to the south by John Crowe Ransom, a young poet he had helped to discover for Henry Holt and Company. In teaching at Vanderbilt University in Nashville, Tennessee, Ransom had organized a growing poetry group called the Fugitives, who felt they would benefit by a conference with Robert Frost. Here he became good friends with Dr. Merrill Moore, the psychiatrist-poet, who eventually came to Boston to practice psychoanalysis, at the same time acquiring a good deal of fame for his sonnets. Here also, Rob Frost found an additional faculty member for the Bread Loaf school, in Donald Davidson, a poet in the English Department at Vanderbilt.

In early spring the New England poet headed north again, to be in Vermont before March 15, 1923, the publication date for his *Selected Poems,* which he dedicated to Edward Thomas. He had taken special care in both the choices and the grouping of poems for this volume—a labor of love and a memorial tribute to his lost friend. As the first selection of Frost's published work, the book was a literary landmark. Elinor, who acted as her poet-husband's judge (in matters of poetry), felt that there was much brought out by this volume that the public had not yet grasped in Rob's poetry, and Lincoln MacVeagh was inclined to agree with her. An early copy was sent to Helen Thomas.

Two months later, toward the end of May, Rob and Elinor went to Ann Arbor again, where he read his own poetry to a packed auditorium in Angell Hall—his only contribution as Michigan's "Idle Fellow" in 1923.

Chapter 16

PULITZER PRIZE POET

He did not know whether he would return to Ann Arbor or not. The appointment was only provisional, and there had been no talk of making it permanent. Moreover, although he had made many friends, and liked the students he dealt with, a poet who was as much of a "sensibilitist" as Robert Frost felt rather out of place in a great sprawling university that had a student body of twelve thousand, of which by far the largest number were engineers, scientists ("med students"), and "politicians"—students of the social sciences, for which Rob Frost had little use. He preferred a small college like Amherst, primarily an arts college; and if it had not been for his differences of opinion with Meiklejohn, he would never had gone to Michigan in the first place.

The trouble that was brewing when Frost left Amherst had continued to ferment, and in June, as the Frosts knew beforehand through their intimates on the faculty, the college took the extreme, harsh course of dismissing its President at commencement. It was sad and embarrassing; some of the seniors, outraged, and loyal to Meiklejohn, refused their sheepskins. Some professors resigned; others were dropped. The cry of Meiklejohn's supporters was that Amherst would not countenance any radical or liberal thought.

The acid explosions had reverberations in South Shaftsbury where Robert Frost was trying to complete the last-minute manuscript preparations for his new book. The Whichers, the Manthey-Zorns, and others kept him informed with campus and faculty bulletins, urging him to take a stand. He did so, but only after he had taken stock within himself, and then he planted himself firmly behind those who had supported the dismissal. He felt, as he had before, that Meiklejohn had been "too high-minded for any *modus vivendi*," and so had divided his house against itself. It was not a question of his being liberal or radical.

Acting President George Daniel Olds, on hearing Frost's position in the controversy—and this was the *raison d'être* behind the prodding—asked the poet to return to the faculty for the year 1923-24, first as Professor of English, and then, at the sudden death of the Philosophy professor, to take a course in Socratic thinking, based on "cases." He would share administrative duties with his old friend, Manthey-Zorn, who taught German philosophy. Frost's own course in the English Department was to be in "reading off the main stream," as he said.

Here again the conflict, the two-headed but benigned dragon in the poet—one facing his art, the other the world—pulled him both ways at once. There were talks with Elinor, with Sidney, with George Whicher and the Manthey-Zorns. In the end, he accepted largely because he felt a loyalty to the college that first made him a professor, and because he hoped he could restore something like serenity to the strife-torn campus.

He felt he owed some explanation to the people at Michigan; it was typical of "the sensibilitist" in him that he wanted them to understand his position, and he wrote to his good friend Tilley, explaining that the contract at Michigan on a year-to-year basis was too indefinite; the way Burton apparently conceived of the fellowship could not help making a man of Frost's age feel homeless. If he had been asked, for example, to give one seminar a week regularly, for as long as he wanted to stay at a salary of $5,000 a year, the poet might have snapped up the offer and settled down there with his family. Certainly he had liked the people, had made a wider circle of close friends in Ann Arbor than he ever had anywhere else.

With this off his conscience, the poet settled down to the mechanics connected with his fall publication—varied correspondence, correction of galley proofs, and all the rest of it. The unexpected, meteoric burst of creativity, "New Hampshire," thrust itself in first place, even to the title, outstripping, outshining the more subtle, tentative one, "The Upper Right-Hand Corner." Both the poet and his publishers felt that the more succinct, definite title of the place-name was stronger, so *New Hampshire* it was going to be; and it was dedicated, as he had promised, to Michigan and (to his private preference) Vermont. Lincoln MacVeagh, who had become his friend as well as editor, was resigning from Holt's to become the directing head at Dial Press, but not before he had seen *New Hampshire* through. After many conferences, for Rob was not sure he approved of illustrations for poems, they decided on a Limited Edition, illustrated with the woodcuts of J. J. Lankes, whose spare, delicate block-prints for "The Star-Splitter" had appeared when that poem was published in *Century Magazine* for September. Rob remembered how much he had admired the fine Limited Editions put out by Thomas Bird Mosher, how he had dreamed of seeing his own work published with such an eye for quality, and now the dream was a reality. He was pleased; but he was too old to feel the reverent delight that he might have known then—the soaring elation he had felt when those two little copies of *Twilight* were put into his hands. For all his warmth and enthusiasm, the poet, as he once said, "almost never experienced ecstasy."

At the last minute, just as the fall term at Amherst was about to begin, some of his faculty friends who had read the poem "New Hampshire" were afraid part of it might be construed as derisive comment on the whole Amherst controversial upheaval; in the passage, Frost had spoken of "a New York Alec" (who might very well give some readers the impression of being Alexander Meiklejohn—an innuendo the poet never affirmed or denied). The section under scrutiny began with an impudent rhyme, coupling the said New York Alec with the controversial school of the "pseudophallic." The poet was told to make a choice, he says, using a sprinkling of Shakespearean terms; but he chooses not to choose: "Me for the hills where I don't have to" . . . Being pressed, he parries, suggests: "How about being a good Greek, for instance?" Pressed again, he still says, in effect, "A plague o' both your houses," as he sketches the amusing self-portrait of a plain New Hampshire farmer that ends the piece. His final line, "At present I am living in Vermont," is a typically Frostian turn.

It would not take much perspicacity or imagination to find a parallel between the controversy in the poem and the one at Amherst, and the poet's resignation a few years earlier. But Frost would make no change in the name—how could he destroy a lovely rhyme like Alec and phallic?—except to use the lower-case "a" which appeared in the final version.

The book was not yet off the press when the poet-professor had to rent a house—this time they were back on Dana Street, number 10—and start his class in philosophy. As in his English course, he gave no lecture; he asked questions calculated to stir up young minds and set them seeking after truth of their own volition. "What is an idea?" to begin with, he wanted to know. "It is the essence of symposiums I'm after," he said once. "Heaps of ideas, and the subject matter of books purely incidental. Rooms full of students who want to talk and talk and spill out ideas and suggest things to me I never thought of. It is like the heaping up of all the children's hands, all the family's hands, on the parental knee, in the game we used to play by the fireside."

Sometimes he spoke, but never for long, and when he did, his voice was lazy yet alive, as if he was leaning on his hoe, swapping the latest news with a neighbor, dropping his "g's" occasionally like a plain dirt farmer. (There were those who thought he did it purposely, but he once remarked that he never realized what a dropper of g's he had become during his farm days until he heard a boy mimicking him when he first started teaching again at Plymouth. It took him some time to recover his g's, and he still found himself saying occasionally, "believin' " or "thinkin' "). They spent the whole first portion of the term defining an idea, an idealist. He might ask the boys how the idealist measures his standards, up from everything, or down? Or, in the case of the artist, somewhere in between? And then they would try to figure it out.

In his course of minor writers, he explained that the boys would become "acquainted with some of the fellows who didn't blow their trumpets so loudly but who nevertheless sounded a beautiful note." They would read Borrow, Cobbett, plays and things; but not in class. The boys were to do their reading at home, and read in class the things that most appealed to them—an incident; a bit of dramatic action; they could choose what they wished, read what they wished. Again he admonished them to wait to write till something spoke to them, and, to drive it home, he added: "The first thing you show will give you your year's mark. You can appeal from this." He always tried to escape the penalty of teaching by making the work more interesting for himself as well as those he taught.

He suggested that the students accumulate a library, tell him about anything they found, and to buy one hundred and fifty dollars' worth of books. Later he visited the boys' rooms, and gave them credit for the number and the quality of the books they had bought. Some of them were surprised at his approval of Damon Runyon stories, or Ring Lardner, or Will Rogers (whom he admired greatly, and called "the international court fool"). They were also surprised to hear that the poet, when asked to name ten books he would take to a desert isle, included, along with the *Odyssey* and two collections of poetry, Anthony Hope's *Prisoner of Zenda.*

"I don't want to analyze authors," he said. "I want to enjoy them, to know them. I want the boys in their classes to enjoy their books because of what's in them. Criticism is the province of age, not of youth. They'll get that soon enough. Let them build up a friendship with the writing world first. One can't compare until one knows."

In the house on Dana Street during that winter of 1923, the first wedding in the family took place: Carol, who had looked upon Marjorie's roommate Lillian and claimed her as his girl since the Long Trail hike the summer before, now claimed her as his bride, but first he had to overcome her father's opposition. The two had been so young when they were engaged—Lillian not quite eighteen —that Mr. LaBatt felt the romance would not last, especially when his daughter went off to college. But when she left in the first term, lonesome, unhappy; and, as the poet said, "Carol went to her mother's and got her," the most decisive move the boy had ever made, it was a sharp reminder of that desperate and unhappy time of Rob's own young love. Now he recalled the runaway weeks, those wild and lonely wanderings he had endured in the fall of 1894. As he relived the whole episode, the names of places he had been, the strange experiences he had had, came back with startling clarity.

It would be another thirty-five years before he put the Kitty Hawk events into a poem, tying them up with the great event that took place there some years after his walk along the beach, —the experimental flight of the Wright brothers that led to "a pageant like a thousand birds" in the sky. In 1923, as the pictures flashed before his memory's eye, including his own brash insistence on engagement and early marriage, he could not help giving Carol and Lillian his blessing. Elinor felt as Rob did, and both of them were fond of the girl Carol had chosen, whose gentleness and appealing tenderness toward their son endeared her to them as no amount of brilliance could have.

The young couple decided they wanted to raise apples (and later went in for sweet peas) just as Carol's father had done in Derry; nothing could have pleased the poet more, and he wanted the newly married pair to share the Stone House, where they would probably be by themselves in the winter. The acreage at Stone House had no real orchards, and he, Rob, would help with the setting out of young trees. Before too long, he and Elinor let the children take over this home, and found themselves another farm, The Gully, not many miles away.

Small wonder that a poet so deeply involved in family ties should fail to seem excited over the tremendous acclaim showered upon the latest offspring of his spirit. Volume four, *New Hampshire,* which appeared in the late fall of 1923 (seven years after *Mountain Interval*), was universally hailed by the critics for the art, the variety and uniform excellence of its poems. Here the dramatist and songster in Robert Frost combined to give this book a wider appeal than any so far. The first edition was divided into three parts: New Hampshire; Notes—the "talk" poems, fourteen in all, full of the tones of speech; and thirty poems under the music heading, Grace Notes—the lyrics, the songs of speech. Here were the titles that, before too many months had passed, read like a list of famous quotations: besides the title poem, the early critical readers found in these pages "A Star in a Stone-Boat"; "The Census-Taker"; "The Star-Splitter"; "The Ax-Helve"; "The Grindstone" (which harked back to Rob's first summer on a New England farm); "The Witch of Coös" (placed first under the heading "Two Witches"); "The Runaway"; "Stopping by Woods on a Snowy Evening"; "For Once, Then, Something"; "Good-by and Keep Cold"; "Two Look at Two"; "A Hillside Thaw"; "On a Tree Fallen Across the Road"; "The Lockless Door," to name the most frequently quoted. Here was the love poem written in England, "To Earthward," and the memorial to the poet's "closest friend," "To E.T." A number of lyrics had a reference to the poet as singer: "The Aim Was Song"; "I Will Sing You One-O"; "The Valley's Singing Day," a tender love-poem; "Our Singing Strength." A few very short pieces pointed to the core of the poet's thinking: "Fragmentary Blue"; "Nothing Gold Can Stay"; and the powerful nine-line "Fire and Ice," written in Amherst, and, in its concentration, calling to mind the Amherst songstress, Emily Dickinson.

One of the most moving of the dramas was the love poem "Two Look at Two," a work which, forty-three years after publication, was called (along with the later "Directive") a "supreme accomplishment in blank verse" by the critic William G. O'Donnell. When it came out, T. S. Eliot, as well as Pound, was already preaching the virtues of free verse; but Robert Frost paid no heed to any muse except his own. When he wrote tall tales like "Paul's Wife," also in this volume, and "Wild Grapes," a story he heard from the aged Susan Ward on his last visit to her—a poem he called "a girl's version of Birches," he could not have written them except in blank verse—iambic pentameter, for the most part. Soon after publication, critics were predicting the *New Hampshire* would receive the Pulitzer prize, a prophecy that brought the poet's skeptical smile; he would believe it when word came—and even then he would not believe it to the point of resting on his laurels.

Yet the critics foretold correctly. In the spring of 1924, Rob and Elinor went out to Ann Arbor, where the poet had scheduled a reading of his own work before a University audience. They stayed at the home of Dean and Mrs. Bursley, and while they were there, President Burton came over to sound out the poet's feeling about a possible return to Michigan on a permanent basis. If Frost was interested, he thought the financial arrangements could be made. The poet promised to think about it. He was already consigned to Amherst for 1924-25, and just now he had to get back for examinations, which he hated to give. He also had to be present at the opening of a little bookshop in Pittsfield, Massachusetts—the latest enterprise of his daughter Lesley, who had invited Marjorie to join her in the venture. The shop was to be called "The Open Book," and Frost was looking forward to it almost as much as the girls.

Shortly after the launching (which created quite a stir in the Berkshire community), word came to Robert Frost that he was to receive the Pulitzer Prize in Poetry for *New Hampshire,* a fitting climax to an eventful year. The presentation took place in early June at Columbia University, with Elinor and the family looking on proudly; the honor was a pinnacle of achievement, perhaps more than any other, since it was the first of four Pulitzer prizes he would receive; this moment would be stamped in his memory and Elinor's as none of those that came later could be. Directly afterward came the presentation of Honorary Doctorate in Letters by Yale University and Middlebury College, again the first of myriad academic honors that would be heaped upon the poet in the years ahead. It was as if these in June presentations of 1924, the reputation of Robert Frost was indelibly marked in the annals of American poetry, one that would not be erased but further impressed by future work.

Symbolically, the only poem of his to appear in 1924 was the succinct lyric "Lodged," identifying himself with nature. His poetry, like the rain and wind-driven flowers after a storm, was fatefully lodged in the sacred soil of immortal thought. He would use the metaphor again many times in regard to achievement.

As soon as the ceremonies were over, he hurried to South Shaftsbury to help Carol put in the seedling orchards. Lincoln MacVeagh came up from New York to lend a hand and report on his fortune at Dial Press among other topics touched upon while they watched the stars of the summer night. By the time the fall term began at Amherst, Rob and Elinor were grandparents; Carol and Lillian, parents of a son, William Prescott Frost, harking back two generations before him.

The poet was hoping to get through the teaching year at Amherst, and he wondered about the status of his Michigan appointment when President Burton died suddenly in October. He was perpetually complaining about the perpetual decisions he had to make in regard to teaching. His good friend George Whicher, in one of his essays on the poet, evaluated such moods in a few sentences: "Frost . . . would not be fully himself unless there were an educational project somewhere in the offing for him to cherish and humorously despair of, for he is a born teacher with a knack of charging dry subjects with intellectual excitement and a large patience for struggling learners. Teaching to him is a natural expression of his unfeigned interest in people."

And he got through this teaching year as he had the others—by widening his world of human interests without in any way trying to do so. Between Whicher and Manthey-Zorn, he was prevented from resigning more than once, all the while becoming more popular with his students. In March he would be fifty-one, but he—and everyone else—at that time was under the impression he had been born in 1875, so his literary friends and colleagues wanted to celebrate the occasion of his fiftieth birthday with a dinner in New York.

He was pleased, but he wrote to Frederic Melcher, "I won't say I don't like to be made of by the right sort of friends, if it is understood beforehand that I don't have to look or act my own age."

The dinner, attended by forty guests (in addition to the poet and his wife as guests of honor), took place in the pleasant atmosphere of the old Brevoort Hotel—an intimate gathering of distinguished minds. Rob, who looked that night like the "good Greek" out of New Hampshire he had designated himself (his classic features and sculptural brow as if cast in bronze), was determined that this should not be a stuffy, formal affair. These were all close friends and associates: Jean and Louis Untermeyer (with whom Rob and Elinor were staying); the Holts; the Harcourts; Willa Cather; Elinor Wylie; Sara Teasdale; Dorothy Canfield Fisher; James Chapin, the painter, and Arroldo DuChêne, the sculptor, both of whom had caught the spirit of the poet in their art; Fred Melcher, Wilbur Cross, and the Van Doren brothers; Carl was toastmaster, though it was Mark who was the closer friend of Frost.

He set the tone of the "after-dinner speeches" by reading a delightful one-page, one-act Irish verse play he had written for the occasion, "The Cow's in the Corn"; and the merriment that followed was high among the brilliant company. The only one of literary circle not present was Amy Lowell, who was at home in Brookline nursing her professional pride, which had suffered a severe blow at the hands of British critics, who had torn her two-volume biography of Keats to shreds in their reviews.

She was preparing to go to England to refute the charges in person, but before sailing was planning a much more glittering "cut-glass" dinner than Frost's in celebration of her own birthday, in Boston, on the fourth of April. When she invited Robert Frost, he had told her he "wouldn't go to hers unless she came to his," but she still expected him to be there and to make a toast at the dinner.

While Rob and Elinor were still at the Untermeyers' a day or so after the Brevoort celebration, Amy made one of her impulsive, imperious 1 A.M. telephone calls and commanded in Rob's ear, "You and Louis come here first, *and I'll tell you what you will each say at my dinner.*" That was all it took to make both men bow out immediately.

Elinor, who took care of such correspondence, wrote a tactful but firm note to Amy before they left the Untermeyer's:

My dear Amy—

I am writing to say what we ought to have said decidedly in the first place—that it's simply out of the question for Robert to speak at your dinner. He just isn't able to. He is tired now, and has three lectures ahead of him this week, with much traveling. He is sorry, and we hope very much that it won't greatly disarrange your plans.

And we hope very much, too, that the occasion will be a happy and satisfactory one for you. I am sure it will be.

With love to you and Ada—

Faithfully yours,

Elinor Frost

This was the last communication between the leader of the Imagist movement and the independent, individualistic poet she could neither command nor manipulate. On May 12, Amy Lowell suffered a fatal stroke, which took her life a few hours after she recognized her condition on seeing her face in her bedroom mirror. Uttering a cry of anguish for her good friend Ada Russell, she lost consciousness and never regained it. Rob and Elinor sent Mrs. Russell a telegram, and it was then that the "image" of "the immortal wound," a Frostian phrase soon to become well known, crystallized in the poet's mind. When he spoke to his students on "The Poetry of Amy Lowell," he found himself bringing forth the fruit of a concept that had been germinating for some time:

"It is absurd to think that the only way to tell if a poem is lasting is to wait and see if it lasts," he said to his students two days after Amy's funeral. "The right reader of a good poem can tell the moment it strikes him that he has taken an immortal wound—that he will never get over it. That is to say, permanence in poetry as in love is perceived instantly. It hasn't to await the test of time. The proof of a poem is not that we have never forgotten it, but that we knew at sight that we could never forget it. There was a barb to it and a toxin that we owned to at once. . . .

"The most exciting movement in nature is not progress, advance, but expansion and contraction, the opening and shutting of the eye, the hand, the heart, the mind. We throw our arms wide with a gesture of religion to the universe; we close them around a person. We explore and adventure for a while and then we draw in to consolidate our gains. The breathless swing is between subject matter and form."

His remarks that day included some of his finest utterances on the subject of poetry in general, whether or not they applied to Amy Lowell's work. She had, he said, "lodged poetry" with her generation that would stay. There was both truth and poetry in the few sentences he devoted to her contribution: "The water in our eyes from her poetry is not warm with any suspicion of tears; it is water flung cold, bright and many-colored from flowers gathered from her formal garden in the morning. Her Imagism lay chiefly in images to the eye. She flung flowers and everything else there. Her poetry was forever a clear resonant calling off of things seen."

His unsentimental yet deeply poetic observations were printed in the May 16 issue of the *Christian Science Monitor;* and the following week he went to Ann Arbor to deliver the *In Memoriam* address for Marion L. Burton. Before he left there, he agreed to come back to the University in the fall, at a salary of $6,000 a year; if he wished, the post would be permanent. He found a house to rent which he had remembered noticing on Pontiac Street, "the wrong side of the railroad tracks" (or in this case, the bridge over them and the Huron River) in Ann Arbor. It was a small, white clapboard house with fluted columns across the front—of great appeal to the "good Greek out of New Hampshire," who leased it for the coming year; the fact that it was far from campus and the intellectual aristocracy was of some but no deep concern, and in the end might prove an asset rather than a drawback to the poet who had leaped into much broader prominence with the Pulitzer prize award.

In September, when the Frosts took up their residence in what the newspaper account called, to Rob's amusement, a "Mid-west Greek Revival house," Irma was the only one of the children who came with them. And before another month was out, she was married to John P. Cone, an undergraduate in the School of Architecture, a talented student who fitted into the Frost family environment easily. At the end of the term, he took Irma to Kansas, where they lived with his parents on their farm. For the rest of their Ann Arbor stay, Rob and Elinor were alone for the first time in many years. It was like the poet, however, to want his family near him, so in the summer he bought a farm outside of Bennington for Irma and John, just close enough to South Shaftsbury to make them accessible.

He had been welcomed back to Ann Arbor with open arms, praised both by the Board of Regents and the Michigan press (including the Detroit and Dearborn papers) for his past work as Fellow in Letters—his title was still the same—and for his present achievements in poetry. For their part, the students clamored to get close to him, and no little jealousy was aroused by the privileges allowed to several of them, whose fathers were faculty friends of his. Sue Bonner, who was now a sophomore at the University and on the *Inlander* staff, was one of these. Full of charm and enthusiasm, she brought the description "a girl like a spring bulb" from the poet, who had not the heart to discourage her ardor. But in the little poem he gave to the *Inlander* for January publication, she thought she detected a note of exasperation, albeit good-natured, in the metaphor of "A Minor Bird," very possibly a reference to embryo poets who sang by his house all day, until he wished they would go away. However, he saves face—and his disposition—by admitting that "there must be something wrong in wanting to silence any song."

To any who might recall "The Runaway," written at Amherst, "A Minor Bird" was a dead giveaway, but "R.F.," as he was often called (and referred to himself) from about this time, would neither confirm nor deny the implication.

His class, if such it could be called, met in the library this time, and was so large it had to be divided into two sections. Since his fame had spread, students strove to qualify for the meetings, and some managed to "sneak in" somehow.

Before too many weeks had passed, Frost suggested abandoning regular classes in favor of gatherings at his home like those at the Cowdens' during his earlier Fellowship. The students could bring poems they had written, which would be read and discussed. Elinor presided at a small tea-table by the fire during the informal Poetry evenings, watching over her poet-husband like a protective, bright-eyed wren. Rob said little by way of criticism when he read the student efforts, as they sat around in the firelight. Sometimes he would read the lines aloud without offering any comment. Then again he might say, "This is a nice little poem," or, "It does just what it is trying to do." He let the students try to figure out the flaws themselves, perhaps putting in a word or two here and there.

All went well until the middle of winter, when Lesley sent news that Marjorie had to go to the hospital for an operation. Elinor dropped everything and rushed off to Pittsfield, leaving Rob deserted, jealous, half-sick with the flu (his regular winter siege). Feeling terribly alone, he built a great fire of black walnut logs for comfort, and lay on the couch in front of it for three days and nights, stretched out full length, writing down the lines of a delicate, playful, yet faintly sinister poem. Oblivious to all else, he staggered to his feet when the fire burned low, threw on another log, and crawled back into his cocoon of creativity. The poem that emerged was in direct contrast to the wintry "outer weather"; perhaps it was wishful thinking that made him write with an ethereal touch of "Spring Pools." And perhaps it was some protective instinct toward the fragile that made him warn the massive trees above the pools to think twice before using their powers of absorption to obliterate a beauty lowlier than theirs.

The fleeting loveliness of youth, the knowledge that all of life is transitory, lies in the last lines of the two-stanza poem.

It was just as well that the poet had picked a house on Pontiac Street, out of the mainstream of social life, for even so, he had a hard time to keep from being lionized more than he wanted to be. He was expected to play up his role of public bard; and, while he liked to further the cause of poetry, he did not want anything to interfere with the composition of further poems from his pen. Luckily, the man who had replaced Burton as president, Dr. Clarence Cook Little, was a research biologist, who continued to pursue his laboratory work outside of his administrative duties, so he had some understanding of the position of the poet who wanted to go on composing while he taught.

The new president, young, attractive, progressive, and vitally interested in his field, was immensely popular with the students because of his democratic approach, much like the poet's. At more than one college tea, Dr. Little was known to sit cross-legged on the floor with a ring of undergraduates around him, in a heated discussion on birth control. Early in the year, R.F., with his intuitive approach to personalities, felt that he had run into another exciting president, perhaps more dynamic than either Meiklejohn or Burton—a "youngster" who took slight interest in noble sentiments but was after some earth-shaking discovery. ("Some think he doesn't realize how troublesome the truth can be," the poet commented.) Later on, when Frost had come to know the biologist president better, he decided he liked him immensely, even if the man's motto was more mice than men.

Occasionally Robert Frost would talk to his group of budding poets about form, his reasons for preferring blank verse to free. He realized full well, he said, that the strictness of traditional form had "driven so many to free verse"; yet he enjoyed the game, the challenge of seeing how much freedom he could find within the forms, or what he used to call "moving easy in harness." One of the forms he had great fondness for was the sonnet, spurred on by the difficulties it imposed. The sonneteer had to face the problem "whether he will outlast or last out the fourteen lines—have to cramp or stretch to come out even."

He never gave traditional or long-winded outlines of the mechanics of poetry. He assumed that by the time students reached college level in creative writing, they knew enough about form not to require basic informtaion. He might add, by way of explanation, to refresh their memories, "A sonnet is supposed to go eight lines, then take a turn for better or worse and go six more." In his sonnets, he took certain liberties; sometimes he reversed the order to put the sextet before the octave; sometimes he subtracted or added a line. He let the subject decide whether a sonnet was to be Elizabethan, Italian, or his own variation.

A poem, he said, was fashioned of intuition and form; but the intuition had to come first, and the form grew out of it. He himself never knew how a poem might turn out. It was like taking hold of the hem of a garment, he said, without knowing the shape the garment is going to take. Then, sometimes automatically, sometimes miraculously, under the fingers of the artist, the fabric shapes up.

His definitions of poems and poetry were in themselves poetic, full of originality and charm. If he mentioned mischief in connection with the freshness of language and ideas, of capturing a feeling as it comes over a writer, a look of mischief would dance in his eyes. He emphasized the quality of freshness a poem must have to be successful—freshness of feeling as well as idea. He told his Michigan students not to hoard an idea; if they held on too long or idled over it more than necessary, it would be overdone by the time they were set to make a poem. He confessed that he often put ideas he was too "lazy" to write into his lectures, and suggested that his students used theirs for *Inlander* pieces.

His young listeners ate up his words. Yet, much as he was liked —nay, loved, or even adored—by his students in Ann Arbor, Robert Frost resigned from the University of Michigan in June (1926). He had been offered a permanent professorship in the English Department at Amherst, and, although the salary would be $1,000 less than he had received at Michigan this year, his teaching schedule would be much more flexible; he would have more time for poetry, for "barding around" if he chose. In Ann Arbor he was treated too much like a celebrity.

The challenge of life had not lessened since he had become a leading creative spirit in America. Perhaps there were those who thought he was wasting his time and effort in producing poetry, but to him there was no finer yield from any labor than poems. And there was no one to say where the harvest should stop!

Chapter 17

"DEVOTION"

For the next twelve years Robert Frost was, in effect, Poet in Residence at Amherst, although he bore the title of Professor in English, and taught classes with a degree of regularity; but no professor ever had so flexible a schedule, so broad a freedom as the college extended to the poet who had already "lodged" enough poetry for permanence in the halls of learning. Yet he continued to grow, to increase the volume of his "song," not so much in intensity as in depth and variety of subject matter.

Amherst required him to teach only three months of the year, and those not always the same, so that he could protect his health by spending the winters in the south. The cold weather had been taking an increasing toll on his physical fitness, and he wanted to avoid, if possible, the sieges of flu that sent him to bed for days at a time. He had plenty of time for poetry reading, lecturing, and he could even teach in other schools if the opportunity arose, as it inevitably would, with the broadening horizons of his work and name. For example, in 1931, 1933, and 1935, he taught during the academic year at the New School for Social Research in New York; and in 1936, at Harvard, when he gave the Charles Eliot Norton lectures. During the summer, he was usually on hand for the writers' conferences at Bread Loaf, and several times for those in Boulder, Colorado.

His publishers, too, "re-renewed" the relationship, which had grown rather frail when Lincoln MacVeagh left the firm, on the poet's return from Ann Arbor in 1926. His books were not selling well at the moment, and the Holt sons did not seem eager to continue the contract. Harcourt and one or two others tried to ensnare Robert Frost for their lists. But Elinor, who handled the business of her husband's poetry, including the correspondence, brought up the matter of a new subsidy; and the Holt firm sent up Richard H. Thornton, a new editor, to "think things over with *Thornton* the Frosts." Once again South Shaftsbury was the scene of walks and talks that led to another publishing friendship as well as an increased subsidy for the poet.

Because of Thornton's report, the Board of Directors granted the poet two hundred and fifty dollars a month for five years, subject to renewal. When the time came, there was no question of its not continuing, thanks to the good offices of Thornton, who, for the ten years he was with Holt, saw to it that the value of sustaining a poet was not underestimated by the publishers. In that time, his efforts were rewarded by the appearance of three Frost volumes: *West-Running Brook,* in 1928, which was to receive the highest praise for its lyrical qualities; *Collected Poems,* in 1930, which received the Pulitzer prize—the poet's second; his third was presented for the third book, *A Further Range,* in 1936, which also received the Book-of-the-Month Club award.

The subsidy continued through the financial crash in 1929, the Depression, and "The New Deil," as R.F. mischievously spelled it in his letters. Thornton wrote of the arrangements that Frost's royalties, permissions, etc., took care of the monthly payments every year before he left the company, except one, and that was fully compensated for by the large amount of royalties paid him the year of the Book Club award. After Thornton left, Holt increased the monthly payment, which continued for life. The publishers always gave Frost the full amount of moneys received for permission to reprint.

poverty

The poet who never minded poverty for himself, and still, in theory, advocated the value of poverty for young people ("I don't want to see poverty abolished; too much good has come of it!" he would say), would not allow his children to suffer the pangs of hunger. Carol, who was a fine gardener, was not much more successful at apple raising than his father had been; and then there was illness in the family—Marjorie's recent operation, and many later illnesses—the burden for most of which fell upon the Frosts' shoulders as solicitous and loving parents. And, for all his talk of the benefits of poverty, Rob Frost did not forget that it was through the stern and forbidding grandfather he had early resented that he had been able to settle on a farm at all—the grandfather who had twice staked him to a college education, which he ran away from, before buying him property.

If the poet appeared to drive a hard bargain at times, it was because he had just cause or need; and if he came to praise money at times, to enjoy the things it allowed him to do, while still advocating poverty, it was all a part of his contrariness, one of his pet idiosyncrasies, or, in a larger sense, his ability to "swing," as his disciple Sidney Cox would have said.

Sidney came often to the Stone House in South Shaftsbury at this time, not only in the summer but on a weekend in the late fall, when they would talk by the fire. The younger man wrote of an especially searching, memorable discourse with the poet: "His very posture was symbolic as he talked large and loose one night by the side of his huge stone fireplace at South Shaftsbury: slumped way down in his big chair, with spread legs stretching forth his comfortable old-fashioned shoes. His mind moved swift and far; his words came measured though in play. Now and then his broad, hairy fingers rubbed around the blunt tip of his nose, and now and then they deliberately mussed his graying hair.

"Metaphors," he said, try "to say matter in terms of spirit, or spirit in terms of matter—to make the final unity. . . . We stop just short there. But it is the height of poetry, the height of all thinking, that attempt to say matter in terms of spirit and spirit in terms of matter."

He could not seem to make it emphatic enough. He had been working during the summer in Franconia (in the house they still owned), looking out on Mt. Lafayette from his upstairs room over the porch, on the major dialogue and title poem for his next volume, *West-Running Brook*. Here, in the single, extenuated figure of the brook he and Elinor had walked beside in Derry—the brook that ran counter to itself—he was carrying out, or attempting to say matter in terms of spirit, and spirit in terms of matter, and he hoped, before he was through, to make the final unity. He was writing in blank verse, as he must continue to write, no matter what the trend in the late twenties and thirties—a trend that had started with Eliot's *The Waste Land* in 1922. Robert Frost, a modern poet in the truest sense of the word, had no desire to run with the *avant-garde*, who were coming into prominence with their poetic efforts in the sudden rash of *Little Magazines* that had broken into print during the decade.

"I'd as soon make love in lovers' lane as write for the *Little Magazines*," Rob declared in typical hyperbole.

However, it was true that since *The Waste Land*, the temper of the poetic renascence in America had altered; new names, like Edna St. Vincent Millay, Elinor Wylie, Marianne Moore, John Crowe Ransom, Robert Hillyer and others were coming to the fore with a different approach, foreign to Frost's very nature. Largely an extrovert (though he claimed to be neither "extro" nor "intro," but "just a plain Vert from Vermont"), Rob did not hold with the analytical process in poetry. His use of the psychological was implied rather than stated or discussed, as in his picture of the emotional conflict between the husband and wife in "Home Burial," or the insanity of the young woman in "The Hill Wife." Certainly he must have realized the importance of a work like *The Waste Land;* he was too much of a craftsman himself not to recognize its merits, no matter how much he might disagree with its methods. But he could not bring himself to join the trend, or even admit to its value. He was frank enough to admit to his jealousy of its increasing acceptance (not to say popularity) in the public eye, but he was not broad enough at this time to grant its essential worth, or the unquestionable stature of a figure like T. S. Eliot. Even his enemy-friend, E. A. Robinson, once his rival in the realm of New England poetry, had strayed far afield from "The Town Down the River" with his current best-seller, *Tristram*.

"What!" demanded Frost, meeting the crusty bachelor at the Place of Bitters, "Do I have to read *The Idylls of the King* all over again?"

"You have to," was the dour reply.

But Frost, who thought Robinson's finest poem was "Mr. Flood's Party"—"the guarded pathos is what makes it merciless"—was not interested in King Arthur's court. Though he used classical meters, he used them with a contemporary touch, and the stuff of his poetry was everyday life, the vital joys and tragedies—the limitations—of human beings in relation to nature. The sources of his craft might be Virgil, Horace or Catullus; from Dante he might take the terza rima; from Shakespeare the flavor of an Elizabethan phrase or two; but the plots and characters of his "novels" were rarely drawn from farther back than the twentieth century. Many of the poems in the new volume would come from the early part of it, and he unearthed a few poems that had been written in Derry years.

It was Elinor again who was to receive the dedication—she who was the guiding spirit of all his poetry, whose judgment he trusted more than his own. To her he gave each poem—complete and final. For her he strove in secret for perfection; if the slightest raveling or loose end hung from the thread of thought or pattern, she would catch him up on it; and the needle-sharpness of her criticism caused him more pain than he could bear. He had learned through the hurt he felt when she would not let a single flaw pass in a poem that he must wait until he achieved final form before presenting the gift of his inmost being.

The book would not come out until the fall of 1928, so there was time during the summer to take the trip to England and France that the poet and his wife had been wanting to make—to revisit the scene of that romantic and portentous summer of 1914, and the tragic site at Vimy where Edward Thomas fell. (Marjorie was the only one of the children who accompanied them; Lesley had recently married a man from Pittsfield, Dwight Francis.)

They found only a handful of the Georgians left, and those scattered by the scourge of war. Gibson, whom Frost had seen several times in Chicago and Philadelphia, was still a poet first and a critic second, but of the poets he wrote about in "The Golden Room," only he and Frost remained. Abercrombie had turned to teaching and poetic theory to the exclusion of creative work and was totally occupied with his post as Professor of English at Oxford—later lecturer and Fellow of Merton. Davies, who had found himself a wife, had continued to dish up airy poems by the dozens, and caused considerable diversion when he asked Rob: "You still interested in poetry, Frost? I'll give you a book with my autograph." The solicitor, John Haines, still looked after legal affairs of poets and carried on his botanizing, which he and Frost picked up again as if they had been out together the week before.

But most of all, Rob and Elinor had come to see the widow of Edward Thomas; Helen had written occasionally, but the poet wanted to hear from her directly how it had been with Edward when he knew his poems were to be published, when he walked away over the hill after his final leave. Alone now, the American poet trod the lanes, the flower-starred fields of Gloucestershire, meditating again on the loss of his British friend, the shameful, the needless waste of war. In 1925, he had written, in "The Peaceful Shepherd": "And see how men have warred. The Cross, the Crown, the Scales may all As well have been the Sword." The previous winter, his bitter sonnet, "Blood" (later called "The Flood") appeared in the *Nation* for February, 1928. Now, after these dark, contemplative hours of remembrance here and in France, Frost wrote the masterful sonnet and tribute to "A Soldier"—to Thomas, representing a sacrificed generation of men—"that fallen lance that lies as hurled."

And when he walked in the small treesy park called "Place du President Wilson," the poet was moved to change his estimate of the founder of the League of Nations, whom he had mocked for being "afraid." He saw now that Wilson had seen life "as vastly as anyone that ever lived." Perhaps his greatness lay in the greatness of the mistake he made; but that was also the whole world's mistake. Perhaps his failure lay in missing a mark that a later leader would pierce; but to Frost's mind it was much worse: Wilson had "missed a mark that wasn't there in nature or human nature," he concluded cynically in a letter to Manthey-Zorn.

In this darkly prophetic mood, the poet sailed for home with his wife and daughter. For the most part, their journey had been a melancholy pilgrimage to the shrine of the unsung war dead, and he could not help brooding on the blindness of human nature, ever groping in the dark, despite occasional flashes of insight. During their stay in England, he had had a visit from the Irish mystic, A.E., and they had pondered the enigma of the human race, the sadness of the war and postwar years. A.E. had murmured, "The Time is not right."

After his visit, his subtle statement of tragedy remained with Robert Frost, and eventually evoked the immortal "Acquainted with the Night," called by Randall Jarrell "a poem in Dante's own form and with some of Dante's own qualities." Published following the return from France, in the *Virginia Quarterly Review* for October, 1928, and included in his new volume, the poem, in a sense the dark counterpart of "I Will Sing You One-O," added to the already impressive stature of Robert Frost as an original poet. Here, in the simplest of language, he employed the classical rhyme-scheme of the Italian terza rima, Dante's interlocking triplets; but he ended the poem with fourteen lines, in a couplet (the last line a repetition of the opening line of the poem), suggesting the sonnet. The two forms were blended into one entirely his own;

and the Frost form was combined with content to achieve the unity for which he strove.

In contrast to the grim grayness of these poems, the new book (which included them), published in November, 1928, opened with the Mozartian strains of "Spring Pools"; "The Freedom of the Moon" (an exquisite analogy on the freedom of form, which begins: "I've tried the new moon tilted in the air Above a hazy tree-and-farmhouse cluster As you might try a jewel in your hair."); and the playful love poem, "The Rose Family" (obviously written "to E.M.F.," as the dedication read, and a gentle gibe at the great Gertrude); he took care to change the first word in the opening line, using *"The"* instead of *"A* rose is a rose," as Stein's lines begin. The other nine lines of Frost's poem either rhyme with "rose" or end with it, and the last two pay tribute to Elinor, who was "always a rose," he says.

The title-poem, "West-Running Brook," was placed well along in the book this time, but as if to strike the note of fidelity between the married pair in the blank verse dialogue, the eloquent quatrain "Devotion" appears in the early pages of the volume, expressing the philosophy of a lifetime in a single four-line stanza.

Significantly, "West-Running Brook" was the last of the dialogues of two wedded people still in love, or bound together by an understanding beyond the stage of being in love, born of the shared experiences of years of living together. As they speculate on the meaning of life suggested by the contrary course of the brook, the two personalities are revealed as individual and divergent, for all their being so closely welded.

In a passage toward the end, the poet, through the musings of Fred, the husband, offers "a clarification of life . . . a momentary stay against confusion" when he draws a parallel between the life of man and the life of the brook, the span of both as they relate to the sun. It is in "this backward motion toward the source" that he finds man's place in nature.

Of the lyrics in *West-Running Brook*—and there were many, including the portentous "Once by the Pacific," perhaps the most exuberant was "Canis Major," which might be called a celestial romp with "the great Overdog, that heavenly beast" who "gives a leap in the east" as he prances across the sky. One of the finest and most fully realized metaphors is "The Armful," in which the poet shows himself loaded down with parcels, one or another constantly slipping or dropping, and as he stoops to seize it, he loses a different one, until finally he has to "drop the armful in the road And try to stack them in a better load." No clearer picture could have been drawn of man, confused by multiple ideas and interests, trying to cope with everything at once, to create order, if not first then last.

One poem was added to this volume when it was included in the *Collected Poems* of 1930—a strange, cryptic, tender, ironic poem, "The Lovely Shall Be Choosers." It was Frost's only poem in free verse—"with a few iambics thrown in." Not all of it was written at the same time; the best portion had its source in Franconia, the poet sitting on the chair perched on the platform he had built to keep the cold winter draughts off his feet. Asked for the meaning, he said guardly, "It's a poem—well . . . it says a lot about . . . women." Then, after greater hesitation: "It's about my mother." He gave no details. With the flavor of a religious morality play, the poem leads off by calling out a command: "The Voice said, 'Hurl her down!'" and when the Voices ask, "How far down?", the mystic answer is, "'Seven levels of the world.'" A second command is, "'Do it by joys, and leave her always blameless.'" Although Frost did not like to hear poetry set to music—he felt that the notes detracted from the spoken song—he once asked a composer friend to set this verse to music after hearing the man play the piano with great feeling at his farm one night. The second "joy" that the lovely "She" of the poem "chooses" is that her grief shall be secret; and although there is "some *one*" with whom she almost finds communication, she never does. Thinking back on his mother's later life in Lawrence, Rob said sadly, in his old age: "She just sank out of sight, and I never knew she was suffering, never even realized I should have tried to keep the school alive; if I had, it might have kept her alive longer. . . ."

At around this time, the first books concerning the poet began to appear. In 1927, Gorham Munson, who had won his reluctant consent to invade his private life, had published the biography, *Robert Frost: A Study in Sensibility and Common Sense*. Sidney Cox, the poet's devoted disciple since 1911, had been teaching in Dartmouth's English Department since 1926, where he was sowing the seeds of Frostian philosophy; in 1929, his slender volume of his mentor's probings and insights appeared, entitled, *Robert Frost: Original "Ordinary Man."* And Frederic Melcher was preparing an authoritative bibliography to be published in the *Colophon*, to coincide with publication of Frost's *Collected Poems* in 1930. On February 9, 1929, the poet informed his editor-friend: "I have a small edition of one copy of an early book of mine that nobody but Elinor and I and the printer ever saw. You'll have to say if it counts in my bibliography." This was of course the treasured copy of *Twilight*, which Elinor had carefully preserved despite the insults it received from her professors at St. Lawrence, and which she had held on to through all the years of struggle and privation.

Characteristically, Rob Frost had made no effort to push his publishers for a volume of his collected work; rather, the reverse was true, but he had taken his own sweet time, and in 1930, when the *Collected Poems* finally appeared, it bound together all five volumes into a cohesive whole, representing a "unity," as Frost chose to consider his work. With "The Pasture" as a prelude, the song of the poet was echoed as a work of art in the arrangement of titles, the typography—a new Dutch type face, Lutetia—and the classic beauty of binding. The poet, who was fast becoming "the best-printed American writer," had collaborated closely with Joseph Blumenthal of the Spiral Press, in the physical makeup and production of the book.

"Crisp, severe, venturesome" were the words applied to the style of the printer, an expert in the graphic arts. The type was hand-set, and had to be proofed in small lots; and, as Frost had included all his poems but three (from *A Boy's Will*) and had added six new ones, the process took some time. Though Rob became impatient, and the two men badgered each other through the mail, they were friends as much as collaborators when publication was finally achieved. The poet invited the printer up to Vermont to partake of the typical Frostian hospitality, the "all-hours" talk, when he and Joe argued the relative merits of monotheism and Talmudic law as opposed to the trinity and the tenets of Christianity—the poet's intense, warmhearted, yet casual way of inducting an acquaintance he admired and respected into his circle of intimates.

Soon after its appearance, the *Collected Poems,* universally hailed by the critics as a milestone in the history of American poetry, was slated for the Pulitzer prize; and the author nominated a member of the American Academy of Arts and Letters (on November 13, 1930). Although he had been a member of the lower body (the National Institute of Arts and Letters) since 1916, there was some opposition to presenting Frost with this honor, mostly from Robert Underwood Johnson, who based his noisy objections on Frost's early rejections from magazines, but he was quickly voted down by the poet's sponsors, Paul Elmer More, Irving Babbitt and Wilbur Cross.

Always the supreme individualist, R.F. continued to swim upstream, making his own headway against the currents of thought sweeping the poets of the thirties along. He was no New-Dealer, no believer in personal (behavior) "complexes" as the cause for poetry of one sort or another. To him the idea was paramount. He considered it "soft" to search his past emotional pattern for the sentiments he expressed in a poem like "The Death of the Hired Man." Moreover, he found it presumptuous to be subjective about a work of art after the artist had managed to make it objective; probing could only "render ungraceful what he in pain of his life had faith he had made graceful."

In 1930, when many families were doubling up after the Wall Street crash and as the Depression set in, the Frosts moved into their own farmhouse, The Gully—a white frame house with a deep comfortable porch, perched on the peak of a hill; and a year later, they bought their own home in Amherst—an old Victorian mansion on Sunset Avenue. Built by the famous New York architect Stanford White, for the president of the agricultural college in Amherst, it was complete with Victorian furnishings and luxuries —Brussel carpets and a zinc bathtub set in wood. It was fitting in the light of his past struggle that Rob Frost should begin to savor financial security just as the rest of the country was rocked by the worst financial insecurity in its history. Between the two places Rob and Elinor could be by themselves if they chose, yet they were close to their children, and to the grandchildren that came on the scene. (Lesley now had two tiny girls, Lesley Lee and Elinor, but her marriage broke up soon after the second was born.) The poet, though burdened with family illnesses and the marital problems of his children, had the seclusion in both town and country for the poetry that "fountained up" in him. He let the poems "jet up out of him," but he kept them in manuscript for the next volume, not caring to offer his work to magazines, which were all featuring the analytical postwar poets, best epitomized by T. S. Eliot, the leading light of the late twenties and thirties.

Frost, who made no contributions to magazines from 1928 to 1934, a solitary poet continuing on his own course, was invited to meet his rival at a select dinner given for Eliot at the St. Botolph Club in Boston, on the night of November 16, 1932. Rob, having steamed his evening suit on a hanger over the zinc bathtub before he left Amherst, sallied forth to meet his foe, "his come-one-come-all chin saved from being forbidding by the quizzical cock of head and eye, now and then"—described by his disciple Sidney as a typical expression when he was about to draw the sword of his wit.

Some twenty distinguished minds, among them half a dozen poets, and a scattering of professors, publishers and editors, had been gathered together by Ferris Greenslet of Houghton Mifflin, who had arranged the whole affair for Mr. Robert G. Dodge, President of St. Botolph's, the host. Eliot, as guest of honor, was placed at his right; and following down the side of the table, Frost nodded to his poet friends—Theodore Morrison, David McCord, Robert Hillyer, John Brooks Wheelwright and a few others. He sat next to Professor John Livingston Lowes of Harvard.

The festivities started off with a reading by Mr. Dodge of two early poems of T. S. Eliot, "The Boston Evening Transcript," and "The Hippomotamus," a rather embarrassing choice for the somber, serious, and highly sophisticated Mr. Eliot, who looked slightly uncomfortable during the reading. Then it was proposed that both Eliot and Frost recite a new poem each had written recently. Eliot responded with formal gallantry: "I will if Frost will."

R.F. hung back. He was still experiencing a touch of the jealousy he felt when Eliot had replaced him in the questionable graces of Ezra Pound and when, as a result of Pound's zeal in booming him, Eliot's poetry began to appear in all the major literary magazines. He wished to beg off, he said, on the score that he had just published his *Collected Poems* and was "ready to loaf." But at the genuine disappointment around the table, he made another proposal: "Let Eliot read one and I'll write one." His idea applauded, he borrowed a few place cards and began to write out a poem that had been brimming up in his brain since his return from a summer's trip to California.

Not hearing a word of Eliot's poem, he concentrated on the lines he was setting down on the small cardboard squares. As usual when he was intent on a piece of writing, his upper lip grew longer and longer, and the page seemed to amuse him (according to a description by his friend Gordon Chalmers, then President of Kenyon College, who gave a hearsay account of the incident). Even the applause for Eliot could not disturb him; after it subsided, he kept on writing while the others chatted around him. When he finished, he picked up the cards and read off the poem—it was "A Record Stride."

As Eliot, with the others, listening to the nine four-line stanzas of "A Record Stride," which appeared four years later in *A Further Range,* he must have realized from the significance of the poem about an old pair of shoes "in a Vermont bedroom closet" that the idea for it had been yeasting in Frost's mind for some time.

What neither Eliot nor any of the others could know was that Frost had actually written his poem some time before and now was merely "pretending an inspiration" (as he confessed a few weeks later in a letter to Louis Untermeyer). Some devil in him, the rascal that always rose up when he saw people taking themselves seriously, prompted him to pretend he was writing out the poem spontaneously. He even went so far as to fumble toward the end, and claim to be faking the tail stanza! It was a huge practical joke, based perhaps on an unconscious desire to take the limelight away from Eliot. He never knew what made him do these things. He might have admitted his prank on the spot if anyone had questioned it, but several murmured with admiration that his performance was "quite a feat," remarkable, and the like. (They were so solemn about it, he couldn't very well tell them he had been lying.) Eliot said nothing; from his expression it was impossible to discern whether he had guessed the truth or not. The biggest joke of all may have been on Frost himself (for the devil in him sometimes defeated his intentions). Certainly Eliot was astute enough to know that he faced a formidable rival, one that might go to great lengths to defend his position.

But whatever each felt, the two major poets were soon at swords' points on the subject of a third—Robert Burns. Eliot announced flatly that Burns couldn't be considered a poet at all; in fact, he claimed, no poetry had *ever* been written north of the River Tweed, save in the sixteenth century, in William Dunbar's dour lament, with its stanza endings repeating the Latin refrain: *Timor mortis conturbat me.*

Rob Frost, whose Scotch blood was suffocating, murmured, "Eliot sounds like a Border name."

"We were Somerset Eliots"—a bit tartly.

Rob leaned forward slightly, looking up the table at his opponent. "Might we consider Burns a *song writer?*" He gave the thrust full irony.

"One might grant that modest claim." Eliot tried to keep contained, but it was touché, and he knew it as well as Frost from the ripple that went around the table.

The next day, the newspaper accounts of the evening carried the story that Robert Frost had risen from a sick-bed to defend Robert Burns; but it was the other way around. After his defense of Burns, when the strain of the meeting was over and he had bested his rival, Rob came down with the flu, as he had done from the time he began making public appearances. In the early Franconia days, Elinor, full of resentful anguish after seeing her husband to bed, used to grieve to the children: "Your father *must* give this up. His health is failing. It *can't* go on!" But it had, and now she was resigned to the fact that Rob was always laid low by a trip for readings or a state affair like this, particularly in the cold weather.

As for the poet, he was relishing his triumph as he lay a-bed, and soon found himself composing a poem, just in his head, for he had no paper and pencil at hand. He called it "Willful Homing," a picture of a man trying to find his house in a blizzard, but the storm "gets down his neck in an icy souse." That one rhyme—"house–souse"—made the whole thing worthwhile! he thought joyously between sneezes. There were three stanzas employing the metaphor of the blizzard to represent the hostile climate he had encountered at St. Botolph's Club before coming into his ascendancy over Eliot. (Subsequently the two poets became good friends, colleagues who respected each other; and in 1957, when Frost went to England to accept honorary degrees from Oxford, Eliot showed him the most generous attention. They saw more of each other during the final years of Frost's life. "We've drawn closer together in the assumption that some sort of serious belief—or unbelief—is what lifts a poet out of the ruck," Frost commented, adding, "The poet must have something large it would break his heart not to have come true.")

Illness—the dread tuberculosis—stalked Rob Frost's life like a haunting ghost of the past. Marjorie, the youngest child, closest to the poet, the one who had most inherited his gift—"sweet, cynical Marj" he called her—had also inherited the Frost tendency toward the lung disease; she had to give up a nursing career she had begun at Johns Hopkins, and the Frosts had sent her out to Boulder, Colorado, in the hope that she would regain her health. The Bartletts, who had moved to Colorado in 1917 because of John's asthma, lived only three blocks from the sanitarium, and would keep her from feeling lonely. At about the same time, Carol's wife Lillian, had contracted the disease, and had been established in Monrovia, California, with small Prescott. It was to find out how things were going with the two patients that Rob and Elinor had taken the western trip in the summer of 1932. As Marjorie in Boulder and Lillian in Monrovia were both making good progress, Rob, who had not been back to California since he left there in 1885, revisited some of the childhood spots he recalled. One of them was the Cliff House, where he had stood watching the sea with his father, and now stood with the grandson who bore his father's name. It was this he referred to in "A Record Stride" about the shoes wet by two oceans. The other one he wet the year before at Montauk, trying to save a hat for one of Lesley's little girls. He felt that putting one foot in each great ocean amounted to "a record stride or stretch."

It was while gazing out over the Pacific, fascinated by the sight of the surf breaking, not on the rocky coast at Cliff House but on the sandy shore farther south, that the idea for a poem—the sensation of an idea taking shape—took hold of him; and the result, shortly afterwards, was the ominously simple, almost monosyllabic, three-stress verse—one of the most profound and devastating of all his poems: "Neither Out Far nor in Deep." Its very simplicity of language is an indictment of man's limitations, his capacity to see and to understand. Here again, the poet used four quatrains, but with an alternating rhyme scheme, to form what Lionel Trilling called at one point "the most perfect poem of our time."

> They cannot look out far.
> They cannot look in deep.

> But when was that ever a bar
> To any watch they keep?

When he and Elinor returned to The Gully, and sat on the deep porch during the sun-warmed hours of Indian summer, the queer, piping whistle of the drumlin woodchucks that plagued the hills sounding faintly in their ears, the poet had time to think on the events of the past summer, to muse before his classes at Amherst began. Rob and Elinor, in their late fifties and early sixties, had no need of words for communion of spirit. Both enjoyed the peace and quiet of living in The Gully by themselves—it was almost like the early days in Derry—yet they were always glad to see the children and grandchildren, who came there frequently. And as children do, the younger Frosts still came to their parents when they were ill or in trouble. Though Rob did not believe in divorce, and tried to prevent it in the marriages of his two older daughters, he was not having much success. Lesley was already on her own, with her two small girls; and Irma, although her father had bought the young couple their farm and started her architect-husband on the road to a fine career, was about to separate, and would soon be divorced. For all his insight, his faith in love for good, for order in a chaotic world, for all the wisdom in his verse, the poet could not solve the emotional problems that beset his children's lives. He recognized that where the heart is concerned, each individual can only take care of his own life; like "A Drumlin Woodchuck" (which he called "my most Vermontly poem" written just then) he had dug his "own strategic retreat." He could reassure his own love that if he could confidently say he would be with her for another day or year, it was because he had been so "instinctively thorough" about his "crevice and burrow."

The news, then, that Marjorie, whose recovery in Boulder was rapid and complete, had fallen deeply in love with an archaeology student at Boulder, Willard Fraser—a modern young Lochinvar who wanted to marry her and carry her off to his home in Montana, far from the scene of her illness and trouble—was a message that brought her parents much happiness. Marjorie her-self, in a moving love poem, "I Always Knew," wrote:

> For out of all eternity—
>   My one immortal love—
> I knew that you would come to me,
> Like rock ascending from the sea,
> The redwood from the aspen tree,
>   The eagle from the dove.

And it was for this marriage that the poet was moved to compose a nuptial song—the surging sonnet "The Master Speed." It was to sweet-cynical Marj and her brave young bridegroom that he gave the strong tender advice that they, and all lovers who marry, must follow to learn of life forevermore.

But the two who had so joyfully, voluntarily begun their lives "together wing to wing and oar to oar" were cruelly cast asunder less than a year after their marriage. Early in April, 1934, Marjorie gave birth to a healthy baby girl, Robin Fraser, only to be stricken by septicemia shortly after childbirth. When blood transfusions did not improve her condition, she was rushed to the Mayo Clinic in Rochester, Minnesota, where the Frosts went to join their son-in-law in the vigil that lasted for weeks.

Starting April 12, in telegrams, in poignant notes to the Which-ers, Robert and Elinor told the heart-breaking story of their daughter's marvelous resistance in the teeth of intense pain; only her gallant fighting spirit kept her alive, and kept alive the hopes of those who watched over her. One serum after another was tried —all that medical science could offer at the time—yet she lost ground day by day.

Her young husband Willard and Elinor scarcely left her bed-side, as if their presence could stay the hand of death. In those dark hours, Robert, dejected, wrote George that their devotion, added to Marjorie's tenacious spirit—and God's mercy—might pull her through, but his hope was faint.

For a full day's watch, her father stayed beside her, hoping to reach her through her fever of 110 degrees, the highest ever recorded at the Mayo Clinic. By moving his hand back and forth between them as he might in counting, and repeating with overemphasis the words *You* and *Me,* he managed to get a dim response. A faint smile shone, and she uttered the words "All the same," frowned as if concentrating, and came forward with, "Always the same." Although delirious with fever, she kept on the lofty plane of intelligence and purity of mind she had always shown. The poet's heart was torn asunder by her spiritual strength in the midst of suffering. Then, on May 2nd, the day after she had spoken to him, he sent a final telegram, the more tragic for its stoical acceptance, to say that Elinor's love couldn't save her from loss, silently expressing his own deep sorrow in terms of his wife's inconsolable sadness over the death of their daughter.

They took the infant grandchild Robin home with them to The Gully so that Elinor might care for her and cherish Marjorie's child; but after a short while she returned the baby girl to Montana, where the Frosts felt she should rightfully be—with her father. Nothing could ever make up to Elinor for the loss of Marjorie; she could never forget the suffering, never accept her daughter's death for a single hour, as long as she lived. She did not hesitate to express her feeling to the intimate friends who came to see them.

Although his grief was as deep as hers, the poet's attitude toward death was much more fatalistic than his wife's. Long ago in Lawrence the lines had come to him "That life has for us on the wrack Nothing but what we somehow chose," though we lack the memory of our choosing; he could recall the exact spot, a few blocks from school, when he was walking to meet a friend, that those lines had come to him by themselves. Later he had put them into the poem "The Trial by Existence." Many times he had thought of them since—whatever life had in store: the good, the bad, the joyous, the sad—all of it was in the realm of human choice, conscious or unconscious. Recently he had expressed the same idea in a different way in "The Lovely Shall Be Choosers." Now he wrote in a lonely poem, "Desert Places," published in *A Further Range:* "They cannot scare me with their empty spaces Between stars—on stars where no human race is. I have it in me so much nearer home To scare myself with my own desert places."

They might each mourn Marjorie's death in a different way, but Rob and Elinor were agreed that the one thing they could do for her was to have her poetry printed. Elinor wrote to Joe Blumenthal, "Robert and I think the poems are lovely, and would very much like to have you make a book of them for us and for her friends." The small printing of the graceful volume, sent as a gift to family and friends, was a fitting memorial for the "sweet-cynical Marj" that was no more.

The deep winter of 1934-35, after a fall term of teaching at Amherst, was spent in Key West, Florida, with Carol, Lillian and ten-year-old Prescott established down the road. The first thing Rob Frost did in the semi-tropical "crown dependency" was to make himself a Yankee lapboard or knee-desk, not out of a closet shelf this time, but out of corrugated boxboard—"one of the chief creations of my mind," he called it. He was proud of his handy invention, which he could take along when he and Prescott explored the narrow strips of white sand beach stretching in the hot sunlight. If he found a likely spot, he could plunk himself down for an hour or two of poetry- or letter-writing. It was here the witty satire "Departmental" (or, "The End of My Ant Jerry"), poking fun at certain administrators at Amherset, with whom he had just tangled flashed into form as he watched the busy trail of ants hurrying everywhere in the hot climate.

Other poems came to him as he learned to live with grief—some to be included in the new volume; others, like "The Gift Outright," he would hold till the moment was ripe. By the summer of 1935, he was ready to teach again at summer schools in Bread Loaf and Boulder. But when he and Elinor came to the University of Colorado, the scene of Marjorie's recovery and happy romance was more than his wife could bear, and she broke down. She was not well enough to accompany him to Santa Fe, New Mexico, where he had promised to give a reading to the Writers' Editions, a group of poets and writers that included many old friends. He had to shorten his visit to get back to Elinor, but not before he had suggested an expedition to the Puyé cliffs, where the ancient Santa Claras had dug their caves into the curve of a canyon in prehistoric times. He *had* to see the cliffs, never mind the formal luncheon that was being given for him in Santa Fe! He could joke with the disappointed guests afterward; he could ask the painter John Sloan to "show him an Indian who would spit in his eye"; but deep inside of him, the site of an archaic civilization was already marked as the setting for an ageless song, "A Cliff Dwelling," in which he caught the vastness of the canyon country and the tragedy of a valiant, disappearing race.

From the west, the Frosts went to the Sugar Hill place in Franconia, where, during the hay-fever time, the poet was going to write a preface to Robinson's *King Jasper,* finished just before his death a few months earlier, to be published posthumously by Macmillan. But here neither Rob nor Elinor could stand to stay even for a few weeks in the place Marjorie had loved so well. So for the hay-fever season, they located, "between two burrs on the map," a group of farms, north of Saint Johnsbury, Vermont. In "A Serious Step Lightly Taken," the poet added the "deed" of words (thoughts on American history) to the deed of purchase. His passion for farmland made him drive a hard bargain in selling his own wares. The first draft of the preface to *King Jasper* discussed Robinson's work at some length, and came out with the flat statement that the author of "Tristram" had written nothing of note since "Mr. Flood's Party," which Frost considered Robinson's finest poem. When the editors at Macmillan objected that they could hardly print such an indictment in the preface of the last work which they were publishing, and asked for a revision, Rob Frost asked for a new contract. He needed the money for part of the down payment on the latest farm, and he argued till he got it. The Macmillan officers may have been vexed at the time; but the result was a perceptive piece of writing on poetry and poets—on the artist—in general rather than on Robinson, and has been quoted, cited as a contribution to prose writings in modern American literature long after *King Jasper* was forgotten. Just as he had written on "the immortal wound" a poem inflicts, at the time of Amy Lowell's passing, so Frost took this occasion to express his feeling about the artist, the "difference" that makes him one, and the significance of that difference.

Beginning in March, the year 1936 was an eventful one for Robert Frost. Coincidentally, it marked the three hundredth year for the Frost family in America, and the three hundredth birthday of Harvard University, which was to be celebrated in June; the poet had already received an invitation to assist in the gala festivities with a new work. Before he had quite made up his mind to accept, the offer came to occupy the Charles E. Norton chair, and he started looking around for a place to stay in Cambridge; by the time the Norton lectures were over, he would have to start writing the poem to be read before Phi Beta Kappa at the three hundredth anniversary. Sometimes he felt people were almost too good to him, but he made no bones about enjoying it all hugely. He might even end sentimental, like Dreiser, Mencken, Hemingway and Anderson, he joked to David McCord.

The lectures, which lasted from March 4 till April 15, were announced well in advance; under the heading "The Renewal of Words," they were entitled successively, "The Old Way to Be New"; "Vocal Imagination—the Merger of Form and Content"; "Does Wisdom Signify?"; "Poetry as Prowess (Feats of Words)"; "Before the Beginning of a Poem"; "After the End of a Poem."

The return to Harvard—the second college he had fled—in this post of honor represented a justification of a way of life to Robert Frost. The young married man who had been carried, broken and feverish, from these halls of learning, was now being called back to a place of distinction on the strength of his achievements in poetry and teaching, attained through experience rather than academic knowledge or conventional education.

This was his interpretation, at any rate, of the tremendous ovation he was given when he stepped on the platform of Harvard's new Lecture Hall on the 4th of March. He received a double intro-duction by Bernard deVoto and John Livingston Lowes, to which he listened with a little smile, half-amused, half-skeptical, playing about his lips. As usual, he spoke with only a few casual notes, if any. The overflow audience of professors, students, student-teach-ers, and poetry-lovers in general that crowded in on opening night increased as the course went on, so that lines began forming at four o'clock in the afternoon for a lecture that began at 8 P.M. The fact that he spoke to more than capacity crowds was a boon to all poets, but especially to the Cambridge poets who had been instrumental in bringing Frost to Harvard.

John Holmes, who covered the series for the Boston papers, pointed out that in each lecture, the poet, though he might seem to digress with marginal excursions, reached the exact conclusion he had aimed for—the "abandoning zigzag that goes straight to the mark" was here brought into play in the epigrams, the witticisms, the pungent sound advice to poets. Each lecture was an entity in itself, one that might stand as a brilliant essay in American writ-ing; but when Frost was asked (as are all Norton lecturers) to turn in his manuscript for publication by the Harvard Press, he once again proved nonconformist: there was no manuscript. He had merely intended his words to lodge a few ideas in the minds of his listeners—precepts that might form a base in their relation to poetry. Beyond this, his spoken words were not meant for posterity.

He hoped that those he had written in his latest poems might qualify—the sixth volume, published in May, *A Further Range*—but he was not overly confident. The new book, as its title indi-cated, represented a definite departure from regional subjects, or rather it included a much broader territory than New England, though the flavor was still there. More definite than the title was the dedication: "To E.F. for what it may mean to her that beyond the White Mountains were the Green; beyond both were the Rockies, the Sierras, and, in thought, the Andes and the Himalayas—range beyond range even into the realm of government and religion."

He wondered how the critics would regard his venture into—for *him*—untried areas like the realm of government. His eclogue, "Build Soil," for example, was his answer to the welfare state, his fear that the trend toward socialism would destroy the individuality of man. "Keep off each other and keep each other off," and the renewal of the soil formed the keynote of his almost dirge-like dialogue. As militant as he was against the basic reforms initiated by Franklin Roosevelt in the welfare state he tried to create, Frost could say to his students at Amherst in 1934: "If there is anything in the New Deal for me, it is an attempt to restore the balance between the country and the city." In "Build Soil" and "To a Thinker" (a satire on FDR so biting, so obvious, that even Elinor, a more rabid anti-New-Dealer than the poet, begged him not to print it) Rob Frost was expressing his feelings on a vital issue, and so strong was his vitality that he could not disregard in his work a basic factor of life; and so deep was his integrity as a poet that he had to include these poems in his new book (just as he *had* to write them), no matter what the criticis might say of him. (Toward the very end of his life, after his visit to Russia in 1962, the poet was to say, "On the questions of socialism and the welfare states, I go slow. I drag my feet. I have, however, about decided that socialism is the only way to handle the billions being born. I see that ahead, but I'll be dead.")

The entire first section of "A Further Range" was in some way connected with current events and politics. Under the heading "Taken Doubly," the poems are all listed with a subtitle which gives them a different, sometimes opposite, meaning from the title. The opening poem, "A Lone Striker," the poet's lyrical description of a mill, a factory worker ("Her deft hand showed with finger rings Among the harp-like spread of strings"), and his own one-man strike in 1892, bears the telling subtitle, "or, Without Prejudice to Industry." Under "Two Tramps in Mud Time"—one of his most felicitous dialogues—the subtitle reads, "or, A Full-

Time Interest"; "The White-Tailed Hornet, or, The Revision of Theories"; "A Drumlin Woodchuck, or Be Sure to Locate"; "The Gold Hesperidee, or, How to Take a Loss," are all, in this manner, given permission by the poet to be taken two ways.

The next section, "Taken Singly," contained a full measure of lyrics, some of his finest in both form and content, including the great, sinister, fatalistic sonnet "Design" and the powerful "Provide, Provide." Here was "The Master Speed," "Neither Out Far Nor In Deep," "A Leaf Treader," and "Unharvested." In a section called "Ten Mills" (a penny's worth of thoughts) the first Frostian epigrammatic couplets and quatrains appeared, one of them, "The Wrights' Biplane," marked his first mention of the flight at Kitty Hawk. In "The Outlands," a section dealing with the far-flung mountains, the poet placed his intimate memorial to Edward Thomas, "Iris by Night." The last poem in the volume, in a section by itself headed "Afterthought," bears a title almost eerie in its modernity: "A Missive Missile."

He had not been apprehensive without cause. The first criticisms of the book were negative; the poet was attacked for his conservatism in "Build Soil," for the prosiness of some of its passages, for his entry into the realm of politics, where his poetic gifts were lost. A number of eminent critics misinterpreted his lines, and took him to task for trying his hand in a new field. However, there were more than enough critics and devoted readers of Robert Frost who could see the true worth of his sixth volume to negate the negators; and two months after publication, came the Book-of-the Month Club adoption, followed by the announcement, in the late fall, that *A Further Range* would receive the Pulitzer prize in May of 1937. In June, he was to receive a Doctrate of Letters from Harvard.

The summer of 1937, like the clear, calm light just before the sudden darkness of a fading sunset sky, was one of peace and contentment for Robert and Elinor Frost, both now learning to live with their grief for Marjorie. They moved into the new midsummer farm, Concord Corners, well ahead of the hay-fever season,

and, as always, made the most of transferring to a different place
to live. As many times as they had moved, settling in was still an
adventure to them. Neither of them had lost the ability to enjoy
each other: they had enough within themselves "not to sink under
being man and wife," and were still young in heart in moments of
minor upheaval. A few weeks after they came to the mountain
farm, they had some unexpected company, and Elinor went into
the kitchen to see what she could scare up for supper. After a few
minutes Rob followed her, and the friend heard him say something like, "Woman, don't lose your head!"

"How can I help it when you're around?" came the retort.

Elinor, during that summer, was if anything more concerned
than Rob over the tone of a book which Richard Thornton of
Holt's was preparing, the first collection of the critical and biographical articles about the poet, to be entitled *Recognition of
Robert Frost.* They had both discussed the material with Thornton, but Elinor was to be the final judge, just as she was of her husband's poems, of the pieces the book should include. The Frosts
both wanted to be sure it would be something more than a publisher's "praise book," and that credit was given where credit was due.
In this connection, Robert wrote to Thornton that he was glad the
editor, who had included an account from Solicitor Haines in England, had not left out of the record those days at Little Iddens and
the Gallows. After all, Rob could never forget that the British first
called him a poet. Looking back from a distance of some twenty
years, he saw that he had had nearly a perfect life over there—"a
romance such as happens to few," he declared. He wanted to
emphasize the fact that he would always feel indebted to the British for recognizing him. He hoped there would be time to let
Elinor see the manuscript before it went to the printer.

It was a summer practically free from personal troubles connected with their children, free to enjoy the fruits of success. One
of these, not unmixed with wormwood, was the suggestion from a
group of Harvard associates, most of them Cambridge poets, that
he should run for the Alumni office of Overseer (a member of the

University's governing board). He would be elected—or rejected—
by a vote among the Alumni in the spring of 1938—"Trial by ballot," he termed it, and, although he was pleased by the offer, he
had grave doubts about the outcome.

He had not yet decided when the Frost family left for their
winter sojourn in the south, this time in Gainesville, Florida, accompanied by children and grandchildren. He was deeply affected
by all the attentions he was getting from Harvard. But he wondered if the height had not been reached the previous June when
he had received the honorary doctorate, and whether, in running
for Overseer, he was not running the risk of negating all the
honors that had been bestowed upon him beginning in 1936. He
would wager anything that the class he deserted back in 1899
would vote against him to a man!

Great as his misgivings were, he made up his mind to run the
risk of trial by ballot as he languished in bed trying to get over a
sneak attack of the flu in March. The house in Gainesville was a
duplex, large enough for Lesley and the two little girls, who were
in the downstairs apartment; upstairs, the poet could hear no
running footsteps when he was composing. Carol and Lillian, with
Prescott and small Robin Fraser, were set up in a single house
close by. Gainesville was far enough north to be chilly, and Rob
could not help wishing they had gone back to Key West or Coco-
nut Grove, where the climate was consistently warm. An easy prey
to sharp winds, he had been taken unawares with the flu during a
damp spell.

Elinor was worried about his low resistance. Though she had
not been too strong herself since Marjorie's death, she was taking
care of him as she always had done, quietly, gently nursing him
back to health, when, on the 20th of March, 1938, she was struck
down by a heart attack, dying even as she tended him.

Then all was darkness for the poet. His fever mounted again,
he was mortally ill, he felt, he even hoped; for he could not see
how he could pretend to live on without the one who had made
possible his life as poet.

Chapter 18

"THE URGE OF A SONG"

All during his bereavement, and for some time afterwards, a wildness of heart possessed Robert Frost. Even as he lay in sickness and
despair, threatened on all sides, it seemed to him, by the chaotic
blackness which he sensed just beyond the "pillared dark" in nature, a recklessness overtook him, and he responded with savage
swiftness to the slightest word.

Something that was said—no one would ever know what it was—
at the time Stanley King, president of Amherst, visited his bedside
in Florida caused an irreparable rift between the poet and the
college he had served so many years. In his sorrow, following Elinor's unforgettably sad, ceremonial funeral in Amherst, nothing
his friends tried to tell him could stop him from resigning his
professorship. And at the same time, as if he could not bear the
connection with the immediate past in any part, he sold the house
on Sunset Avenue.

His marriage to Elinor had lasted forty-three years, and would
not have ended except in the death of one or the other of this
extraordinary pair. It was the irony of fate (and one of the reasons
for the poet's recklessness) that Elinor should be taken just at the
height of his career, just as they were beginning to enjoy the har-

vest of honors that continued to be heaped on the poet's head. Through all the years of poverty, of public rejection, of illness, and the loss of two children, it had been because of the central figure in his life that he had been able to create poetry, to teach, to give lectures and readings. (After Marjorie's death, he had done a great deal of traveling for many public appearances, as if the sowing of the seeds of poetry in the minds of listeners somehow compensated for the loss.) Now he did not seem to care. Now he was indeed "Bereft," as he had written in his early poem, "Word I was in my life alone Word I had no one left but God"—and for a time he could not find God.

But it was borne in on him that he was not alone when in May, 1938, he received word of his election as Overseer of Harvard University by a larger vote than any alumnus had ever polled, much less a "renegade" alumnus. The figure was a reassurance of his achievements in the Norton lectures, and somehow gave him the fortitude to plan to live in Cambridge for the coming winter— an initial step in the long road back to health. At about the same time, Professor Arthur Stanley Pease, a former president of Frost's at Amherst and now at Harvard, came forward with the suggestion that the poet occupy a unique post in the Latin Department at the University. It was only two months since Elinor's death, however, and Robert could not bring himself to consider the confines of a scholarly teaching job without the impetus of his wife's presence. He was still far from healed; he dreaded to think of the desolate summer ahead, the empty houses he must face, the empty hours he must while away in the rooms they had shared.

One place he resolved not to live in again was The Gully, with its deep porch that held such poignant memories; he loaned it to his young poet friend John Holmes, who, with his growing family, needed a place for the summer. In June, Frost went to the Stone House in South Shaftsbury to stay at his son's for a while. From there, he was normal enough to write Richard Thornton that he was taking some interest again in whatever he did: en route, he had gone to three baseball games in Boston. He ended, "I enjoyed my break-up with Amherst while the somewhat mysterious row lasted. Now I am up here with Carol taking my memories as I must and can."

Every day, as if by a magnet, he was drawn over to The Gully, where the woodchucks' piping whistle still came to his sensitive ear. He would invariably, without a glance at the familiar house, dare John to beat him at pitching rocks into tin cans, until the vindictive echo resounded in the hills. And after supper every evening, he would return like some haunting and haunted soul, an endless stream of talk erupting from the volcano of his inner stress, talk that went on until the hour before dawn. Then he drifted back to the Stone House, sometimes to watch the sunrise before sleep took over.

Before the end of dog-days, as his hay fever became bothersome, he pushed on to his last house, Concord Corners, now deserted, a dreary ghost-house, that only a year ago had been so good for him and Elinor. Early in September he was able to send David McCord a detailed, objective account of himself, including the "inner and outer weather" at Concord Corners. When he said that he was "where the wind never ceases blowing," he knew that his fellow-poet would understand how matters stood within him. The fact that he could not mow the field waist-naked in the sun any more because of the knife-chill in the hilltop air was an outward manifestation. Soon he would be going to live in Boston, where he would attend the Overseers' meetings when he was not "all abroad lecturing the other colleges in Cimerian darkness." He was not going to stay up in Concord Corners, wallowing in a bath of memories for very long—"damned if I am, not for any hay fever!" he vowed.

His recklessness had reached the point where he had paid $250 for a first edition copy each of *North of Boston* and *A Boy's Will*, which he wanted to give to a friend. His attitude at the moment was "to hell with living on a sound financial basis!" But he had enough stability left, enough horse sense to realize that his "gallop would level off into the same old trot" as soon as he got back into harness. Knowing this, he indulged his grief by giving vent to the restlessness in his soul.

Seeking diversion, he went to sheep-dog trials, his favorite country sport; and at one of these, he found a handsome specimen of the huge black-and-white Border collies; he had seen many a sheep-dog in the years he had been going to trials, but he had never encountered so noble an animal as this one. He bought him as a safeguard against sheer aloneness, named him Gillie, and taught him to walk behind his right heel unless given permission to run. Between man and dog there was immediate communion—Gillie was both protector and companion to the poet, and went along to the small Beacon Hill apartment rented for Frost in Boston by Mrs. Theodore Morrison. The former Kathleen Johnston and a Bryn Mawr student of Frost in the twenties, Mrs. Morrison had married the Cambridge poet and lecturer in English at Harvard a few years earlier, and the Morrisons had opened their home to the Frosts at the time of the Norton lectures. Now "Kay" was to be the poet's secretary, to bring order out of the chaotic state of his papers, neglected since Elinor's death. His small, sunny apartment at 88 Mt. Vernon Street (without a tree at his window or a dooryard he could step out on at dawn if he chose) fit the farmer-poet more like a snug glove than an easy shoe; but it was close to the Morrisons, and he had Gillie for those long night walks till he was tired enough to sleep.

Yet the wildness of heart persisted; the word "wild" came into his poetry, his writing, when he began slowly in the fall to take up his life work again. In a poem entitled "November" and dated "1938"—and always printed with the date—he speaks of seeing "leaves go to glory. . . . In one wild day of rain." And he hears " ' 'Tis over' roaring." Like a cry of anguished realization that an era is gone forever, the poem, from its last line, "The waste of nations warring," and its placement in *The Witness Tree,* could refer to the fall of Austria as well as to the personal sorrow in the poet's life. At this time, William Sloane 3rd, who had succeeded Richard Thornton at Holt, came to Frost and gently persuaded him to write a preface to the second volume of *Collected Poems,* which was to be published in January (1939). Then it was that Robert Frost, still in mourning, wrote his extraordinary preface on "The Figure a Poem Makes." He finished the writing and signed it, "Boston, January 11, 1939." He went to Florida for a couple of months, but he had a wretched stay there and was glad when it was time to come back to Beacon Hill, where Mrs. Morrison could keep him lecturing and living on a schedule, talking as of yore. All the same, he was "very wild at heart sometimes," he admitted to Sidney Cox. "Not at all confused. Just wild—wild." The feeling was easily read between the lines of the Preface, and indeed, in the lines themselves. He did not know whether he could overcome it or not.

In the third paragraph alone (of the Preface) he used the words "wildness" or "wild" six times. It was as if some of the wildness in his heart was exorcised by connecting it with poetry. And by the same token, in the distilled, moving definition that follows, he relates "the figure a poem makes" to his love, to love as a force. This was probably the most objective-subjective piece of prose writing about poetry that a poet could write, and it may have resulted in a "momentary stay against confusion" for Robert Frost. The book itself, containing *A Further Range,* was another achievement. The poet was deeply touched by a telegram in Latin he received from young Sloane on publication, paraphrasing a line from Horace to read, "You have erected a monument more lasting than bronze." It was a fine omen, a demonstration of faith on the part of his publishers.

But the upheaval in him did not subside. In that "crazy-reckless Boston period," as he called it, his inner savagery knew no bounds. He managed to stay busy during the day, doing all manner of things to keep occupied. At night he would walk along Charles Street and round the Hill, with Gillie at his heel, throwing all the change under a quarter he had in his pockets into school yards; the quarters went into the water at the dockside. "If George Washington could shy coins across the Potomac, I figured I could throw my quarters into the Charles River," was his way of putting it. The silent companionship of Gillie was his sole comfort on many a night walk. There was a rare understanding between man and dog; the poet never had to raise his voice when he gave an order. If Sidney or some other friend was walking with them, R.F. might interrupt a sentence without changing his tone: "A poem must —Gillie, you may run," softly, the merest aside; and the flash of Gillie's tail would disappear in the darkness. And he would as quickly, silently return, if his name were mentioned in an offhand way during the conversation. There may have been moments when the poet might have been tempted to throw himself into the river if it had not been for Gillie.

Gillie could not protect him, however, from reckless dealings in real estate, from yielding to the temptations of collectors who persisted "in putting Christmas presents down his chimney." He began teaching again at Harvard in the fall of 1939 in a post created for him—the Ralph Waldo Emerson Fellowship in Poetry—through a group of devoted friends, Howard Mumford Jones, Archibald MacLeish, Robert Hillyer and David McCord. But the four thousand dollars they had raised for the position could not tide him over some of his heavy expenses, and he was an easy prey for rare book collectors who hungered after early editions of his work. Against his better judgment, he let one of the most persuasive of them talk him into parting with Elinor's treasured copy of *Twilight*. Just as he had torn up his own copy in a fit of anger long ago, so he now in a fit of recklessness, born of bitter feeling against fate, let the little book go out of his hands. Afterwards he regretted it, for ten years later, the man sold his entire collection, first offering the copy of *Twilight* back to Frost for $10,000. At that time, the poet conceded that the collector had made no promise not to sell, and that it was he, Frost, who had lost his head, as he did so often in the two-to-three-year period after Elinor died. He estimated that he must have thrown away close to $20,000. It wasn't all wasted, because some of it went into real estate; but a large share was sheer madness in handling his affairs. He no longer cared.

In the fall of 1940, as he began his second year of teaching and was getting accustomed to the way of life in Boston, fate delivered a third blow. Carol, who had been writing poetry without any more success than he had had in apple raising, became alarmingly despondent when Lillian had to go to the hospital for an operation. Frost, who loved Carol's wife as much as he did his own children, went up to South Shaftsbury to be with his son and young Prescott, now sixteen years old. Carol refused to see a psychiatrist. They talked a night through together, and when dawn came, the poet thought he had talked his son out of any rash deeds. He had to get back to Boston, and Carol, who saw him off on the train, remarked, "You always have the last word."

Two days later, Prescott called unexpectedly: Carol had shot himself.

When he put an end to his frustrated life, he and Prescott were alone in the Stone House. The sixteen-year-old grandson showed the maturity of a man; he had called the neighbors and the police, and then phoned his grandfather in Boston. The poet was proud of his courage and presence of mind. It was something to be grateful for in the blackness of another tragedy.

There was much pathos in Carol's pallid life. He had never found himself; he had always shied away from books as if they might harm him, and his parents had never pressed him to acquire a formal education. It was too late now for his father to wish they had. He could not tell whether the poetry Carol had been sending to magazines was of any value or not, but each rejection brought a further sense of defeat which finally became too great to bear.

"God's stress in whatever he's up to is our distress," the poet remarked stoically in telling the sad news to his friend and biographer, Elizabeth Sergeant. It was then that he began to read some of the prophetic books of the Bible, not for the "poetry" alone, but to find the meaning in the biblical naratives—the Book of Job, for example. What was the Creator trying to prove in the trials He heaped upon Job? And what sort of Heavenly Father could allow a daughter like Marjorie to die of septicemia in an age of ever-widening science? One of the precepts of Swedenborg that the poet's mother had relied on came from the Book of Micah: "What doth the Lord require of thee, but to do justly, and to love mercy, and to walk humbly with thy God?" and Robert Frost tried to follow it now. But the challenge to God's justice as he saw it in the Book of Job and in the three great losses in his own life during the past six years he had to reason out for himself.

Then, with the rare objectivity only a great poet possesses, he began to view his tragic losses impersonally, through the medium of poetry, to the gain of the world.

Some time late in 1940, Robert Frost at the age of sixty-six bought the Homer Noble Farm in Ripton, Vermont, covering almost three hundred acres of wooded hillside, clear-running brooks, and tree-crowned heights; with it came old cellar holes, three farmhouses and a log cabin. Early in 1941, he purchased a half double house at 35 Brewster Street in Cambridge; and with the two pieces of property, he more or less laid out the plan for the rest of his life —or, as it proved, nearly a quarter of a century. Some time after this, he bought land and a home in Florida, but in 1940, the first two places were acquired with an awareness of his needs after years of experience. His greatest need was for freedom—to come and go as he pleased, and to write, as and when he pleased. He might have asked Lesley to give up her career, and come with her two girls to live in one of the dwellings on the Ripton property. But he chose to live in the log cabin, just large enough for himself and Gillie, to do his own household chores, and cook some of his own meals. Here he could follow his old unconventional routine of late-to-bed, late-to-rise, and if it was the converse of the farmers, its effect on the poet was as beneficial as the opposite advice of the ancient adage. On his "Sabine farm," as he called it, he could take those long, rambling night walks with Gillie, and then come back to work or read; or, if a friend was with him, to carry on the all-hours talks, wise and witty, often religious or deeply philosophical. He could work with nature as much, or as little as he pleased; usually some part of every day was spent in woodcutting, or in the vegetable garden, planting, weeding, harvesting.

His ideal schedule was feasible only because his good friends, the Morrisons, lived with their two children in the original Homer Noble farmhouse on the land. Frost took most of his meals with them—he usually dug the potatoes for supper, a contribution he made to the end of his life. Mrs. Morrison was at hand if he needed secretarial help—in Cambridge, too, the Morrisons lived nearby— and the summer school at Bread Loaf was one of Ted Morrison's interests, so there was a pleasant community relationship between the two households, a social and working arrangement always in effect except for the few months the poet was in Florida.

The old farmhouse stood by the side of the road, about three hundred yards down a sloping, flower-starred meadow from the rustic log cabin. With his passion for leisure, for freedom from the outside world while he was writing, Frost rigged up a communication system with the front house so that he wouldn't be bothered by a telephone. The Yankee invention consisted of a clothesline equipped with a bell and stretched from farmhouse to log cabin. Gillie, ever watchful with eye and ear, was bellman to his master, and when the clothesline, pulled from below, gave a sharp peel, Gillie relayed the sound with a brisk bark; if the poet did not appear at once in the cabin doorway (or the clearing in the woods), a second bark usually succeeded. The contraption continued to serve its purpose until the early 1950's, when, after Gillie died, R.F. consented to having a phone put in, an extension line from the Morrisons'.

All during the forties and fifties the children and grandchildren came and went at vacation time; Frost, always solicitous for the welfare of his family, made one of the dwelling houses available for use by family or friends. Lesley's two daughters attended the Putney School, not too far from Ripton, and after graduation, went on to Radcliffe, just a few blocks from their grandfather's Cambridge house. Lesley, who forged a career for herself in the State Department and did a great deal of traveling, was always in touch with her father; Lillian and Prescott, and Robin Fraser from Montana came at various times to visit. Irma, who was divorced from her architect husband, became a chronic invalid, a source of concern to her father.

Among the intimate friends, the first to come to Ripton were the Whichers from Amherst, James Chapin the painter, and, of course, Sidney Cox, who was instrumental in bringing Frost to Dartmouth, and who was working on an expanded version of his earlier 1929 book. Lawrance Thompson of Princeton's Department of English, beginning his research on a biography of the poet, stayed in the fourth house for a time—the "U-Bar" (Euber) place over the ridge, as it was known—and, with his family, was a companionable addition to the life that the poet had evolved for himself at Ripton.

With Mrs. Morrison to take care of his correspondence, arrange for his public appearances and keep his calendar from being overloaded or mixed up, Robert Frost was able to face the world at large calmly; he could set out to teach, to accept some honorary degree, to read his poetry, to lecture (or preach a sermon, as he did more than once from the pulpit of Rabbi Reichart in Cincinnati) and to give radio broadcasts, with an ease he had never before possessed. His return to his Ripton base was equally calm; he no longer had to take to his bed for several days to recover from readings. It was as if the time away was merely an interlude in an otherwise unbroken pursuit of poetry. Whenever he came back to the farm, he was always able to take up the threads of his creative thought as if he had never been interrupted.

It was the *sense* of leisure that was important to the poet, and this he now had. Through the life he had set up, and his own powers of concentration, of objectivity, and of constant self-renewal, he brought into being four volumes in the space of ten years: *A Witness tree*, 1942; *A Masque of Reason*, 1945; *Steeple Bush* and *A Masque of Mercy*, 1947. The first published only two years after he established his new life, was in large measure the lyric outpouring of the tragic loss he had sustained; he sang of his beloved, and of love itself, the many guises it may take. In a forlorn and lonely two-part poem, "The Wind and the Rain," he described his feelings with heart-breaking sadness and the poem ends:

Rain was the tears adopted by my eyes
That have none left to stay.

The section opens with the celebrated sonnet "The Silken Tent," the poet's tribute to his beloved Elinor, to their incomparable relationship, the culmination of the thought expressed in the early "Bond and Free." Written in a single sentence, the subtlety of metaphor and perfection of form in "The Silken Tent" has led to its interpretation (by Charles R. Anderson) as a sonnet to the sonnet form itself, and it may well have been. In the same manner, in a poem he often read as a companion piece, "Never Again Would Birds' Song Be the Same," a sonnet praising the voice of Eve, Robert Frost sought to illustrate his theory on the "tone of meaning" in speech overheard as the basis of his own poetry. Another in the group of love poems is "Happiness Makes Up in Height What It Lacks in Length," which, again, seems to be a tribute to his marriage to Elinor, to their happiness together, which now seemed but a day. In these poems, Frost, to use his own words, is "skirting the hem of the goddess." Love is implied without being stated. He was never one to exhibit openly the private and passionate emotion love was to him. He had told his students once that he felt that sex can be overt; love is covert.

In this group was perhaps the only poem dealing with sex that he ever wrote, "The Subverted Flower," which tells the story of a girl, highly educated, but too frightened to give way to the wild sweetness of love. Here also was "The Discovery of the Madeiras," a narrative of illicit love, and "The Most of It," the love of the egoist, who "thought he kept the universe alone." The ephemeral quality of happiness is expressed in "Carpe Diem," and "The Quest of the Purple-Fringed" deals with the love of youth for nature. Here was the eloquent lyric "Come In," in which the poet states that he is "out for stars."

The next section of the book contained "The Gift Outright," which Frost read before the Phi Beta Kappa Society of William and Mary College, two days before Pearl Harbor, December 5, 1941, increasing his stature as prophet. Here also was the Horatian satire, "The Lesson for Today," and the intriguing couplet, "The Secret Sits," possibly his way of expressing his acceptance of Fate's insolvable riddle.

A Witness Tree received the Pulitzer prize in the spring of 1943, at the time that Frost was poet in residence at Indiana University and composing in a new form. On April 2nd, he confided to George Whicher that the night before he had finished writing *A Masque of Reason,* the 43rd Chapter of the Book of Job; and he was contemplating a companion piece from the whole Bible, to be called *A Masque of Mercy.* Perhaps neither would see the light of publication, but it satisfied his soul to dabble in religious drama.

In the fall, he accepted the George Ticknor Fellowship at Dartmouth, where he dealt largely with GI's, to whom he gave some of his most cogent talks on current events, particularly the era of scientific discovery which the world was entering. This was the man who had so lately known such wildness of heart that he did not want to go on living. Citing Shakespeare's sonnet with the famous lines, "Love is not love that alters when it alteration finds" and "It is the star to every wand'ring bark, Whose worth's unknown, although his height be taken," Frost pointed out to the boys that science, for all its precision, can only measure height; it can never measure worth, love. Science could never tell them how true anyone's love might be, because science could never know. It was only half the world; human relationships made up the other half.

For the second time in his life, now as in 1918 at Amherst, Frost tried to give students facing a crucial experience a set of values they could hang onto in a world gone berserk. The boys leaving for war benefited from the wisdom of the poet that shone through the fires of his suffering.

The volume *Steeple Bush,* published in 1947, was almost wholly concerned with the times, the poet's reactions to the war, some of his "glimpses" into the future. He dedicated this book to a future generation, his six grandchildren—"Prescott·John·Elinor·Lesley Lee·Robin and Harold"—listing them according to their age. (*A Witness Tree* indicated his gratitude to his intrepid and devoted secretary in its dedication: "To K.M., For Her Part in It").

In *Steeple Bush,* the title is not only a reference to a native New England weed of that name, but to the contrasting religious note the book strikes in the section "A Spire and Belfry," and in the deeply religious, philosophical "Directive," perhaps the most revealing of all the Frost poems dealing with the spirit of man. It is a revelation of the poet's own search, perhaps, to find salvation in the midst of his sorrow; and when he commands, in the last line, "Drink and be whole again beyond confusion," he has discovered more than "a momentary stay against confusion" to keep him above despair, the despondency he knew in those first years after Elinor's death. In the volume is a section "Five Nocturnes," witness, like "Acquainted with the Night," to his sleepless hours, filled with struggle and meditation. The poem "Directive" is no doubt the result of his all-night wrestling with the eternal question of the soul, the inner being of man. Coming, as it did, after the two Masques, which, for all their wit and flashing insight, remain more skeptical than positive in their conclusion, the single poem "Directive" seems to be a distillation of the poet's deep probings in the realm of religion.

It was immediately hailed as a great poem by his rivals as well as his admirers and the critics. He found amusement in the fact that the Eliot school of poets changed their minds about Robert Frost with the advent of this poem. He said with a good deal of irony in 1949, when his *Complete Poems* came out, "This is the poem that converted the other group. The one these fellows have taken to build my reputation on. The boys call it great. They have re-estimated me. This is great and most of the rest, trivia." He could not write trivia if he tried. Some of the short poems in *Steeple*

Bush, like the seldom-quoted quatrain "It Bids Pretty Fair"—one of his intuitive flashes—or "Iota Subscript"—a display of wit in word-play—would indicate that his "trivia" is more profound than many a poet's "great" work.

In the years that followed the publication of his *Complete Poems* in 1949, Robert Frost, far from retiring into the hermitlike poet he could so easily have become on his Ripton farm retreat, emerged more and more as a public figure. Starting in 1950, with his seventy-fifth birthday (March 26) he was projected into national prominence by the unprecedented Senate Resolution, No. 224 of that year: "Whereas, Robert Frost in his books of poetry has given the American people a long series of stories and lyrics which are enjoyed, repeated, and thought about by people of all ages and callings . . . and whereas, These poems have helped to guide America's thoughts with humor and wisdom setting forth to our minds a reliable representation of ourselves and of all men . . . and whereas his work throughout the past century has enhanced for many their understanding of the United States and their love of country . . . and whereas Robert Frost has been accorded a secure place in the history of American letters. Therefore, be it *resolved,* That the Senate of the United States extend him felicitations of the Nation he has served so well."

Medals and honors were showered upon him from all sides, and when he spoke or read his poetry, it was to capacity audiences. He was appointed Consultant in Poetry to the Library of Congress for the year 1958. Characteristically, he exercised his nonconformist attitude in the quasi-political post as much as he had in education, and sought to further his cause by finding ways in which poetry and politics might be successfully blended. His accomplishment in a single year led Quincy Mumford, Librarian of Congress, to appoint Robert Frost, in the spring of 1959, Consultant in the Humanities for three years. He accepted the post with great delight, ending his letter: "It sets me up mightily that my venture into the capital of my country wasn't for nothing."

Yet, for all his career as the official bard of his country, Robert

Frost continued to sing in seclusion, to create poetry when the urge of a song was upon him. The time he was able to spend at Ripton served to refresh him and to renew his creative powers. His old friend George Whicher, in an essay on the poet entitled "Out for Stars," described him on the farm as "a stocky figure, but alert in motion, wearing an old suit and scuffed shoes, freshly laundered soft shirt, open at the throat, his white hair tousled in the wind, his seafarer's blue eyes twinkling." If the cold was out of the ground when he came up from Florida, he and his farmer-care-taker-friend, Stafford Dragon (whom he had set up on one of his marginal farms a mile away through the woods), would plant the vegetable patch. Dragon belonged to a big, ballad-singing clan of Vermonters, descended from a French dragoon, who uncon-sciously furnished color notes for the poet. He had another friend, the railway clerk in the crossroads station, whom he liked to "gos-sip" with of a summer afternoon. The fellow knew the history of every family for miles around, and nearly always had some tale especially attuned to the poet's ear for drama.

(At one of his lectures in 1956, Frost went so far as to say that he considered Gossip the greatest of the three elements in human thought—Religion, Science, and Gossip—into which he had finally been able to divide life. Gossip was "our guessing at each other" in daily chatter, in journalism, in fiction, but most of all in poetry, for poetry was the exaltation of gossip.)

The poems he composed during his late seventies and eighties were for the most part hoarded until there were enough for a new volume, published on the poet's eighty-eighth birthday, March 26, 1962, following his appearance as the country's first inaugural poet. Entitled *In the Clearing*, its individual pieces had a unity of purpose, just as the eleven volumes that preceded his final offering were unified. Here, as in "Directive," Robert Frost was seeking a lasting clarification of his beliefs, an enduring rather than a "mo-mentary stay against confusion." The collection represents the ripe wisdom of these years of living alone, living on long after the death of the central figure in his life. Forty poems, some of them his

pithy couplets, over a span of fifteen years, was hardly a comparable number to his former output, but the poet had become so
much a public figure that any new work was an accomplishment.

The critics approached the 101-page volume with a wary eye,
not wishing to commit themselves. But after the immediate success of the book with the general public, after its title poem, "A
Cabin in the Clearing," and several others, had been quoted and
reread with a thoughtful rather than a wary eye, and with a careful ear, the value of the poems emerged. As in the past, the poet's
aim was song, and he had not missed the mark. "The volume's distinctive quality," said William G. O'Donnell in the *Massachusetts
Review*, ". . . is its bardic tone." Then a dozen or more poems were
cited for their lyricism, the excellence of the blank verse, the music
of the lines, as well as the "affirmative" content of many of the
poems. It is true that the complex witticism which Robert Frost
often read during his later appearances—"Forgive, O Lord, my little jokes on Thee, And I'll forgive Thy great big one on me"—may
be interpreted as skepticism, or as a Dickinsonian irreverence,
implying a closeness to God that allows easy familiarity. The frontispiece of the book, however, a lyrical stanza from "Kitty Hawk,"
seems to be a positive statement of the poet's deeply religious feeling, more akin to the mysticism of Emerson, Thoreau or Emily
Dickinson than to any organized religion or conventional concept
of God.

Here also was the masterful Frost touch, the teasing "In a Glass
of Cider," a poem as youthful and buoyant as any written in his
prime. Here were "Questioning Faces"—a nature poem to stand
with any of his earlier short lyrics—and the significant "Auspex";
"Escapist—Never," and "In Winter in the Woods Alone."

For the story in "Auspex," the poet turned back in time nearly
eighty years, to that memorable incident during the summer in
Santa Cruz when he was coming home from his friend's and an
eagle had almost carried him off. He had no way of telling then
that his parents' refusal to believe his tall tale would be rebuked
in a poem, with the belligerent line, "Not find a barkeep unto

Jove in me?" expressing his resentment in no uncertain terms in the last three lines. He had been a small boy of eight or nine at the time of his encounter, and three quarters of a century later could still feel the indignation, the challenge of being underestimated.

No, there was no falling off of quality in the final volume of the elder statesman-poet, and he showed scarcely any lessening of activity. He made a journey to the Soviet Union, "to assert" himself, as he said, and he succeeded. He had an interview alone with Khrushchev, and exchanged political views with the Premier and with other heads of state in Russia. It may well be that his talks cleared the atmosphere between east and west, providing the sunnier climate needed before any nuclear test ban treaty could be signed. When he returned, in the fall of 1962, he continued his "barding around" at colleges, universities, museums and more, with the vigor of a much younger man. In December, several days before he entered the hospital for major surgery, he spoke to filled auditoriums on two successive days at Dartmouth, the college he had run away from seventy years before.

While convalescing in the hospital, he carried on correspondence of a wide and varied nature. His Christmas card poem was prophetic in tone, but defiant, not defeated. He was on the way to recovery, but suffered a relapse and died in his sleep in the Boston Hospital on the 29th of January, 1963, at 1:59 A.M.

Robert Frost was a songster till the end—and a lover of life, with all its imperfections, its tribulations, its increasing traumas. He was a singer whose aim was song, whose leitmotif was love. He wrote his own epitaph in "A Lesson for Today," when he expressed the wish to have written of him on his stone, "I had a lovers' quarrel with the world"; and one might add that, quarrel or no, he was always faithful to the world he loved.

INDEX